CATS
UP CLOSE

by

Jamie H. Vaught

Champions of Kentucky Basketball

CATS UP CLOSE

by

Jamie H. Vaught

McClanahan
Publishing House

Cover design and book layout by James Asher Graphics

Manufactured in the United States of America

All book order correspondence should be addressed to:

McClanahan Publishing House, Inc.
P. O. Box 100
Kuttawa, KY 42055
(502) 388-9388
1-800-544-6959

CONTENTS

ACKNOWLEDGMENTS

This basketball book, *Cats Up Close*, wouldn't have been possible without the cooperation and assistance of many individuals who contributed in one way or the other. Special thanks go to the University of Kentucky Wildcat personalities — past and present — who took the time to be interviewed for the book. Like my two other books which were published in 1991 and '95, *Cats Up Close* is primarily another entertaining look at UK's hoops program through the eyes of celebrities — players and coaches — who have strong ties with UK. There are many other former players whom I didn't interview or discuss because of time constraints and space limitations. Perhaps they will be interviewed for another book in the future.

Needless to say, the material for the book primarily came from exclusive taped interviews with various individuals, including current UK coach Orlando "Tubby" Smith. In addition, background information and notes from my old newspaper and magazine columns, that I've written in the past 25 years, were helpful. The schools' basketball media guides, including UK, were very useful as well. Also, special thanks go to publisher Larry Donald of *Basketball Times* for allowing the use of some materials which appeared in the magazine. Sports editors Neill Morgan (*The Daily News* in Middlesboro) and Jim Kurk (*The Gleaner* in Henderson) were very helpful.

Many photos, including Wildcat great Dan Issel when he was with ABA's Kentucky Colonels in the early 1970s, were found in the archives of Rogers Photography in Somerset. David Rogers and Bob Flynn, both of Rogers Photography, were instrumental in getting many photos of Issel and other individuals ready for the book. Thanks also go to Harlan photographer Chris Jones, who is the public relations man at UK's Southeast Community College

(SECC). Basketball publicists from various schools — Steve
McClain (University of Florida), Christi Thomas (Campbellsville
University) and Brooks Downing (UK) — were cordial in arrang-
ing interviews and providing photos. Public relations staffs of the
Charlotte Hornets and the Denver Nuggets granted photos as well.
The University of Kentucky Archives were helpful in verifying a
couple of facts which came up in interviews.

I would like to thank Delores Taylor for transcribing the
lengthy interviews. She was very efficient and dependable. Robert
Cox, associate professor of English at SECC, did a good job in
proofreading the manuscripts. My teaching colleagues Joe
Marcum, Tom "Chalk" Stapleton, Astor Simpson, Georgeina Billings,
Joyce Dotson and Ed Frost all contributed in one way or the another. Special thanks go to SECC president Dr. Bruce Ayers for support.
Officials at High Point University in North Carolina, including
Betty Lou Blount, Christine Rollins and Alison Lawrence, were ben-
eficial in providing information about coach Tubby Smith, including the college's alumni magazine.

Finally, I would like to thank my wife Deanna, my mother
Betty, and the rest of my immediate family for their support and
encouragement. And I sincerely hope I didn't leave out anyone else
who helped with this book. If I did, special thanks go to them as
well. Enjoy the book!

Jamie H. Vaught
August 1998

THE HORSE

In 1970, when 6-foot-8 All-American center Dan Issel guided the Kentucky Wildcats to a very impressive 26-2 mark and a final regular season No. 1 national ranking, he finished with 2,138 points, becoming the men's all-time leading scorer in school history.

Amazingly, nearly 30 years later, Issel still holds UK's career scoring mark. The all-time record is even more remarkable when considering the fact that Issel played only three years of varsity competition. Unlike today, the freshmen were not eligible to play for the varsity team. In addition, college basketball didn't have the exciting three-point field goals back then.

While Issel admitted that the scoring record is nice, he said winning games was more meaningful. During his three-year varsity career at Kentucky, Issel and his teammates compiled a rather impressive overall record of 71-12, a winning percentage of nearly 86.

"I was never really concerned with individual records," Issel said in an interview for this book. "Winning the basketball games was what it was all about. But when you look at all of the great players who have played at Kentucky, I'm very proud of that record and one day it is going to be broken. It is amazing to me that almost 30 years later, I still have it."

It appears Issel's scoring record will be safe for a while as many collegiate stars are leaving early for the NBA's green bucks. Former UK stars Rex Chapman, Jamal Mashburn and Ron Mercer left school before their collegiate eligibility expired. Each could have easily become the school's all-time leading scorer. For instance, had Mashburn stayed at UK for his senior year, he more than likely would have broken Issel's mark. Mashburn, who is currently No. 5 on the UK all-time scoring list with 1,843 points, needed only 296 points to set the record.

In the spring of 1988, when Chapman was considering the possibility of leaving UK for the NBA, Issel tried his best to persuade Chapman to stay at Kentucky. Chapman eventually did not take Issel's advice as he began his NBA career with the expansion Charlotte Hornets.

"I did talk to Rex Chapman and I tried to talk Rex out of jumping to the pros after his sophomore year," said Issel, who is currently the Denver Nuggets' general manager. "I told him that if he stayed he would be one of the fan favorites, that he would break my record and be the all-time leading scorer at Kentucky, and how neat I thought it was to have that record.

"I told him even after playing 15 years of professional basketball, my four favorite years of basketball are the four years that I spent at UK. I tried to talk him into staying, but the money is too big now."

While at Batavia High School, near Chicago, as one of the country's top prospects, Issel was not aggressively sought by Kentucky. UK coach Adolph Rupp, who was just recovering from his all-white, top-ranked squad's stunning loss to five black starters of Texas Western in the 1966 NCAA title game, and his staff didn't recruit the blond-haired youngster very hard because they had two other prep centers in mind. In other words, Issel was their third choice.

In the spring of 1966, UK invited the 17-year-old Issel to visit the campus and its beautiful Bluegrass surroundings, including the horse farms. So Issel boarded his first-ever airplane ride to Louisville where assistant coach Joe B. Hall and Wildcat guard Phil Argento met him at the airport. They drove to Lexington where Issel made his official visit.

There Issel got to meet the Baron of the Bluegrass, the 64-year-old Rupp. Before meeting Rupp in his Memorial Coliseum office, Hall gave Issel some pointers about how to carry on a conversation with the legendary coach. "If he doesn't laugh, don't you laugh," Hall told Issel. "And he might say something funny that you don't think is very funny. But if he laughs, then you laugh."

On his initial visit with Rupp, which lasted about 15 or 20 minutes, Issel recalled, "I hadn't followed college basketball real closely. I certainly knew who Adolph Rupp was and the success that he had. It was very intimidating to go into that office and meet with him one on one for the first time."

But something happened during his visit to UK. Issel saw a copy of the school newspaper, *Kentucky Kernel*. The prepster from Batavia noticed his name wasn't mentioned in a recruiting story. Therefore, Issel began to wonder if the Wildcats were really that interested in him. Issel was having second thoughts about the visit even though he enjoyed the horse farms and meeting the team players and coaches.

"They had an article about recruiting. It mentioned about 15 guys in the article and my name wasn't mentioned," Issel said. "(The Wildcats) were interested in a couple of other people at center. One was Joe Bergman. He was supposed to be the top center prospect in the country. He wound up going to Creighton University in Nebraska. The other was George Janky from downtown Chicago and he wound up going to Dayton. After reading that article, Kentucky was at least third on my list and maybe lower."

Since Kentucky seriously looked at a couple of other players, Issel concentrated on his other top collegiate choices — Northwestern and Wisconsin. "I wanted to go to the University of Wisconsin and my parents wanted me to go to Northwestern University," Issel commented. "I kind of went back and forth, and I finally signed a Big 10 letter (of intent) with Wisconsin. But I knew my parents weren't happy with that. In the meantime those other centers that Kentucky was recruiting went elsewhere and they (Wildcat coaches) kind of stepped up their recruiting. They were more interested in me."

So Issel visited UK campus again. Unlike the last trip to Kentucky which was paid for by UK, his dad, Robert, took care of the expenses incurred on the second trip due to recruiting rules. This time they received royal treatment at the Lexington airport where Rupp and his assistants welcomed Issel and his father.

Although Issel had already inked a Big 10 letter of intent with Wisconsin, that didn't stop him from signing with UK. "So as a kind of compromise between Wisconsin and Northwestern, I wound up at UK," Issel explained.

And Issel has not regretted his decision since then.

Ex-Wildcat Dan Issel of the Kentucky Colonels attempts to shoot over Julius "Dr. J" Erving of the New York Nets in an American Basketball Association game held in Louisville in the 1970s. Ironically, both Issel and Erving were inducted to the Naismith Memorial Basketball Hall of Fame in 1993.

Photo by
Rogers Photography

Joe B. Hall — a former Wildcat player who had just returned to UK in 1965 as a thirty-something Rupp assistant — primarily recruited Issel for the Wildcats. He was the first contact Issel had with anyone from UK. Rupp's head recruiter also made an in-house visit to Issel's home in Batavia. And Issel has a very interesting story to tell about Hall's visit. Shortly before Hall visited Issel and his family, he phoned to tell them that he was coming.

"Well, that's fine, but I've only got about a hour because I have a date tonight and I'm going out," Issel told the UK assistant.

"That's fine. A hour will be good."

After a short meeting with the assistant coach, Issel left the house. But Hall stayed and continued his recruiting pitch to Issel's parents. The elder Issel, however, didn't stay around long to listen. He went to bed. "It didn't matter what was going on or who was there," Issel said of his father, who was a painting contractor. "At 10 o'clock he went to bed. My dad was a working man."

Then Issel came back to the house about 11 o'clock that night. There Hall was, still sitting at the kitchen table with Issel's mom. "He recruited my mother more than he recruited me," laughed Issel.

On his recruitment of Issel, Hall added that he stayed in the Chicago area for a week and "visited with the Issels every day. I finally got so much of a family that I was having evening dinner with them. And during the day, I would go to the apartments where he (Issel's father) was decorating and sit on a paint can while he painted."

 In the fall of 1966, when basketball practice began, Issel wasn't the player that UK fans eagerly talked about. They mostly talked about Mike Casey, the other star freshman who was listed as one of the nation's top 10 prep All-Americans. A native Kentuckian, the 6-3 Casey was extremely popular. Several months earlier, he had led Shelby County High School to the Sweet Sixteen crown with a 33-1 mark and captured Kentucky's "Mr. Basketball" honors.

In addition to Issel and Casey, Mike Pratt of Dayton, Ohio, and Terry Mills of Barbourville, Ky., also garnered some attention, playing on a highly-regarded freshman team, coached by Harry Lancaster. The so-called Kittens squad, rated by experts as one of the best in UK history, finished the 1966-67 campaign with an 18-2 mark. For the entire UK basketball program, the freshman team was one of the season's very few highlights as Rupp's varsity team struggled to a shocking 13-13 worksheet. It was to be Rupp's worst squad in his 42 years of coaching at UK.

But that season saw many freshmen facing academic problems. They simply didn't study much. It was so bad that Rupp had to make a personnel move on his staff, hiring an instructor from UK who also had been involved with the basketball program for several years. "(In) my freshman year, we had 12 people on scholarships, and at mid-term three of us were eligible. Three of us had above 2.0 (grade-point-average), " Issel said. "It was me, Bill Busey and Jim Dinwiddie. None of the other freshmen had above a 2.0. So they had a huge problem on their hands. The trainer of the team was supposed to be following the academics. Well, obviously, he wasn't doing a very good job.

"So coach Rupp decided (to make a change). Coach Rupp was a smart man. He decided it would be easier to train an academic man how to tape ankles than it was to teach a trainer how to be an academic man. And Claude (Vaughan) was hired and he became our babysitter, our tutor and got just about everybody eligible and then the next year coach Rupp hired him as the trainer (and academic advisor)."

As for Issel, he had a fine freshman season, averaging about 21 points (behind Casey's 24-point average) and 18 rebounds a game. He also received Freshman Leadership Award presented by Lexington Junior Chamber of Commerce (Jaycees) for his leadership on and off the court.

 About two weeks before he began the 1967-68 season as a promising sophomore, Issel suffered a setback. "Right before the season I'd had a benign tumor removed from the roof of my mouth," Issel said. "So I got off to a pretty slow start and it wasn't until late in my sophomore year that I really started playing like I thought I could play."

His best game took place in the NCAA tournament when he pumped in 36 points and grabbed 13 rebounds, both game-highs, in leading Kentucky to an 107-89 victory over colorful coach Al McGuire and his Marquette Warriors on UK's home floor in Lexington. Before the contest, an angry McGuire, attempting a psychological ploy to fire up his team, insisted the Wildcats not wear their home uniform. It didn't work as the Wildcats went on to win by a comfortable margin. However, the campaign ended on a sour note as Ohio State upset Kentucky 82-81 in Mideast Regional finals, which was also held in Lexington. For the season, UK's so-called three super sophomores — Casey, Issel and Pratt — led the Wildcats to a 22-5 mark and a No. 4 national ranking. They were also the team's top three scorers with Casey leading the pack with a 20-point average. Issel was second at 16.4 points.

While Joe B. Hall loved Issel's "blue-collar" work attitude, the assistant said he was pleasantly surprised with the player's rapid rise in stardom as a sophomore. "The thing I remember most about Dan Issel was the great work ethic and the improvement that he made from his freshman year to his sophomore year," Hall said in 1997. "It was the middle of his sophomore year when he really started demonstrating what a great player he was gonna be.

"I knew he was an awful good prospect. I knew that he would be a very good player, but his dramatic improvement and the work that he did to develop himself was just outstanding. I've never seen a player make as dramatic improvement as Dan Issel made."

In the following season — Issel's junior year — McGuire got his revenge, however, as his rugged Marquette squad eliminated UK from the NCAA tourney in an 81-74 verdict. With the same Issel-Pratt-Casey gang leading the way, Kentucky finished with a 23-5 mark and a No. 7 national ranking.

 Rupp protested when Issel informed the 67-year-old coach in the summer of 1969 that he was getting married. Throughout his coaching career, Rupp had tried to enforce his unwritten policy of not allowing his players get married.

"Do you have to?" said an irritated Rupp, looking at Issel.

"No, sir, I don't have to," Issel responded.

"Well, we haven't had anybody around here get married that didn't have to for a long, long time."

"Well, we don't have to."

"You know when you marry this girl, basketball won't be No. 1 anymore."

"Well, coach Rupp, with this girl basketball hasn't been No. 1 and I still think I have done okay and that's why we are going to get married because she's No. 1," said Issel, thinking he had a good answer for the Baron.

"Well, I don't like it. I am going to tell you right now. I don't like it because basketball won't be first."

Issel's "girl" was the former Cheri Hughes, the UK cheerleader from Lexington and the daughter of Mr. and Mrs. Virgil Hughes. Cheri cheered for the varsity Wildcats during Issel's sophomore and junior seasons.

As a wedding gift, Rupp and his wife, Esther, gave the couple a sterling silver tea set. "It was probably the nicest wedding present that we got," Issel laughed.

 In the fall of 1969, at a time when many rebellious college students protested United States' involvement in the Vietnam War, UK's basketball program faced a potential boycott by the players. Several had vigorously complained about assistant Joe B. Hall's strenuous running program, which ran for several weeks from the first day of classes in August to mid-October. They were very upset and threatened to quit the squad. At an emotional team meeting, they asked Issel, a senior, to address the issue to Rupp as their representative after Hall refused to ease up. It was an uneasy moment for Issel as the team's co-captain.

As Issel entered Rupp's office, he said, "Now, coach, this isn't my idea. I want you to know I'm here as a representative of the team. Some of the guys think the running program is a little too difficult and they want it cut back."

"Do you know you have a chance to become the all-time leading scorer at the University of Kentucky?" Rupp questioned.

"Yes, sir, I have looked at the records and I know with a good year, I can do that."

"You go out and run today and I'll do everything I can to see you get that record."

As soon as Issel heard Rupp's statement, he was on cloud nine and later ran with only five other players — all freshmen — that afternoon. Recalled Issel, "Rupp never addressed that issue, but he knew what carrot to dangle in front of me. He knew at that point what was going to motivate me. I don't know what went on, but the next day everybody was back out at the track running again."

Rupp, needless to say, kept his promise as Issel went on to become the men's all-time leading scorer at UK.

 The pre-season episode wasn't the only controversy that faced the basketball team during the 1969-70 school year. The other incident, which took place in February during Kentucky's two-game road trip in the South, saw two players suspended from the squad. On a Sunday evening in Starkville, Mississippi, assistant Joe B. Hall and trainer/academic advisor Claude Vaughan saw several players in a bar. The players had violated the team's curfew regulations. Consequently, Rupp dismissed two of them — senior Randy Pool and junior Bob McCowan — from the squad for breaking the

Like in his University of
Kentucky days, Dan Issel
wore jersey number "44"
for the Kentucky Colonels
and then for NBA's
Denver Nuggets. Both
UK and Denver have
retired his jersey.

Photo by Rogers Photography

rules again.

Regarding UK's trainer, Issel said it's fairly accurate to say that
Vaughan, who was also an economics instructor at UK, worked like a spy
for Rupp. Furthermore, several players didn't like it. "Claude made sure
that coach Rupp knew everything that was going on," said Issel, who is
now good friends with Vaughan.

"Now, I will have to say this: if you were a good player and you
were earning your scholarship in their estimation, there might be a few
things you could get away with. If they saw you as a player who was just
taking a spot on the roster, who wasn't earning his scholarship, you had
better not get out of line that much or they'd find something wrong with

it. He (Vaughan) became an unbelievable friend to coach Rupp. He was coach Rupp's confidant. He was coach Rupp's chauffeur. Claude and coach Rupp were almost inseparable until coach Rupp passed away (in 1977)." Vaughan, who earned his Ph.D. in economics in 1967 from UK, later taught at Eastern Kentucky University for many years and became the state's budget director in Gov. Brereton Jones' administration.

 Throughout his UK career, Issel had many good moments. He was a three-year starter with his dependable shooting touch, his quickness, his famous head fakes and good work ethics. However, one incident stands out the most.

It happened during his senior year on February 7, 1970 in the sleepy town of Oxford, Mississippi. There Issel established a school single-game record by scoring 53 points against Ole Miss in a 120-85 victory. The previous record was held by ex-Wildcat cager Cliff Hagan, who had 51 points, set in 1954. Also in that contest, Issel became the school's all-time leading scorer, passing Cotton Nash's 1,770 career points.

But Issel almost did not get Hagan's single-game scoring record. With Kentucky leading the game in a very comfortable fashion, Rupp took Issel out shortly after the 6-9 center had broken Nash's career mark. A few moments later, one of the team's managers, who noticed Issel was getting awfully close in breaking Hagan's record of 51 points, got up and informed Rupp about the mark. The coach immediately put Issel back in the game and the rest is history.

Obviously, for Issel, the records were nice. But that memorable evening was made extra special because his father, who had not been able to attend many road games, saw his son's record-breaking performance.

"The best moment I remember is the game at Ole Miss when I broke the single-game record and became the all-time leading scorer at Kentucky and the reason it meant so much to me is my dad," said Issel, who during his senior year scored at least 40 points six times and at least 50 points twice. "My father each year would go on one or two trips so that by the end of my senior year he would have visited every town in the Southeastern Conference. It just happened to work out that he was at Ole Miss. So that's my most unforgettable Kentucky game in a good way." Issel's wife also attended the game.

While they didn't go to many of Kentucky's road games, Issel's parents went to practically every home contest. At a time when many interstate highways were not available or not completed in many parts of the country, they drove 400 miles from Batavia to Lexington. "It was about an eight-hour drive and back then the Interstate 65 wasn't done all the way through Indianapolis (from Chicago)," Issel recalled. "They missed only three home games the whole time I played at UK."

 106-100.

That was the final score of Kentucky's heart-breaking upset loss to the Jacksonville Dolphins in the 1970 NCAA Mideast Regional finals. The top-ranked Wildcats had four of their key players, including Issel, fouled out in a nationally-televised encounter at Columbus, Ohio.

"My most memorable Kentucky game is (this) last game I played when I fouled out with 10 minutes and 16 seconds still left in the game," commented Issel, who scored game-high 28 points. "That's probably the one I remember the most. But that was in a bad way, not a good way."

Issel — who shared the cover of *Sports Illustrated* magazine with three other collegiate stars in its 1970 tournament issue — said he thought the officiating for the game "was okay." However, on his fifth foul, he protested the official's call. "I was just running down the floor, looking back to see who was taking the ball out of bounds. Their point guard (5-10 junior Vaughn Wedeking) came up and set up, and I ran right over the top of him out in the middle of the floor. I didn't think it was a very good call, especially since it was my fifth foul."

The Wildcat loss would mark the end of Rupp's last great team at Kentucky. With the stunning victory, Jacksonville, featuring two 7-footers Artis Gilmore and Pembrook Burrows, advanced to the Final Four where it defeated St. Bonaventure before dropping to UCLA in the title game in an 80-69 verdict.

A two-time All-American selection, Issel said Rupp and the team took the NCAA tourney loss hard. "He was real upset and we were all upset because we were the number one ranked team in the country," commented Issel. "That was the year after Kareem Abdul-Jabbar (then called Lew Alcindor) had left UCLA. Nobody was going to win the NCAA tournament but UCLA while Kareem was there because they not only had Kareem, they had other great players around him.

"But when Kareem left everybody thought it (NCAA tourney) was wide open again and that everybody would have a chance. We were rated

No. 1 and we thought we had a great chance to win the NCAA tournament. Well, it turns out we got beat by Jacksonville. We didn't get to the Final Four and UCLA still won the championship even without Kareem."

The Wildcats also had to play the entire season without the services of their injured star Mike Casey, who suffered a severe broken leg in an auto accident the previous summer. Issel said today that he believes that UK would've gone to the Final Four if Casey hadn't been hurt.

While Issel and his teammates earned three SEC titles and three trips to the NCAA tournament (which only had 23 and then 25 teams in the field from 1968 to '70), he regrets that he didn't have the opportunity to play in the Final Four.

"I would say probably the biggest disappointment that I had in basketball was the fact I never got to the Final Four because we were real close (in 1970) and we had a real good team all three years that I was playing varsity at Kentucky," said Issel, who completed his senior year with an impressive average of 33.9 points and 13.2 rebounds.

By the time he left UK, Issel had established 23 school and SEC records during his varsity career at Kentucky.

 Even though Issel was a college basketball superstar, joining the ranks of other All-Americans Pete Maravich (LSU), Rick Mount (Purdue), Calvin Murphy (Niagara), Bob Lanier (St. Bonaventure) and Charlie Scott (North Carolina), he was intimidated by Rupp, a very strict coach who was domineering in his ways. Issel was never exactly comfortable with the "Man in the Brown Suit."

"I think that's kind of the way coach Rupp wanted it," Issel said. "While you were at the University of Kentucky playing for coach Rupp, he left no doubt who was the coach and who was the player. There are players who need a kick in the seat to be motivated, and there are players who need a pat on the back to be motivated. Coach Rupp's philosophy was to kick everybody in the seat and if they weren't strong enough to take it, he didn't want them on his basketball team. You had to be tough to play for coach Rupp. You couldn't be sensitive or be thin-skinned. That wouldn't work. So he was intimidating until the day I graduated."

Because of Rupp's overbearing personality, several ex-UK players didn't like him. They either loved him or they couldn't stand him, Issel said. "You can find as many players who played for coach Rupp who hated him as there were who loved him. There didn't seem to be too many people right down the middle of the road."

But Issel is thankful that he got to be friends with Rupp after his UK career ended. "I think the reason that I loved coach Rupp was because of our relationship after I played (at UK). I don't think I would feel nearly as grateful and as appreciative to coach Rupp for what he did for me if I hadn't had the opportunity to get to know him after my playing days.

"I was very lucky that I did a couple of things with coach Rupp after I played there (at UK). No. 1, we had a summer basketball camp together and No. 2, after he had coached here (at UK), he became associated with the Kentucky Colonels, the pro team that I played for. So I got to know coach Rupp pretty well and really got to enjoy coach Rupp."

Issel and Rupp sometimes got together for a drink in Louisville when both were involved with the Colonels of the old American Basketball Association. It is no secret that Rupp adored his bourbon whiskey.

"When he was with the Colonels (as vice chairman of the board of directors in mid-1970s), he would come out to our house after a game, not often but once or twice a season, and visit. Claude Vaughan (Rupp's former trainer) would bring him back and forth (from Lexington) so coach Rupp would come to the house. I would mix him up a bourbon." Later, Rupp, who was approaching mid-70s, however, had to stop drinking bourbon for health reasons and Issel fondly recalls his favorite Rupp story.

One night on his visit, Rupp spoke out and said, "Dan, I can't have any bourbon. My doctor is worried about my circulation and my diabetes. He said I have to lay off the hard stuff. Do you have any vodka?"

In his collegiate and pro roundball career, Issel has faced criticism. As a result of Rupp's fatherly advice, Issel said he has been able to handle criticism fairly well.

"He said, 'Anytime you stick your head above the crowd, anytime you are successful, anytime that you are able to accomplish a little something better than ordinary or average, people are going to take shots at you,'" Issel recalled. "I'll never forget that as long as I live."

Issel said the media's negative portrayal of Rupp in recent years is "very unfair." He was a product of the environment during his time, Issel explained.

"If coach Rupp was here today in 1997, I think you would have to say he was a racist," he said. "In 1970, in Lexington, Ky., in the South, his attitude toward the differences in the races wasn't much different than what everybody else, all other white men, thought about at that time. By today's standards, Coach Rupp was probably a racist, but I would say every white person in the South in the 1950s and the 1960s was a racist."

The likable Issel credits his good upbringing and work habits to his blue-collar parents in a Christian environment. He grew up on a large farm in Missouri before his middle-class family moved to Illinois when he was a very young teenager. His dad held two jobs. Besides working as a painting contractor, he worked at the farm in late afternoons. Issel's mom did the typical chores as a housewife.

"We were kind of an average, ordinary family with good morals and good work ethics," said Issel, an excellent student who grew up with a brother and a sister, both younger. "My mom and dad were hard-working people and hopefully some of that rubbed off on me."

Issel said his parents, who are now retired and living in Florida, didn't really encouraged him to play basketball. However, they just wanted their oldest child to have an opportunity to play basketball.

"They always supported me," said Issel. "I remember that when I was in the seventh grade, which was my first year of organized ball, I was awful. I didn't start. I didn't get in the game unless we were way behind or way ahead.

"But my dad and mom were there for every game. My dad would go into work an hour early so he could take off an hour early to come to my junior high games. They were always real supportive. They didn't say you have to do this or you have to go in this direction."

Issel and his brother, Greg (who later played on the freshman team at the University of Missouri), often squared off against each other in pick-up basketball games. "My brother is three years younger than I am. He played basketball in high school and he wouldn't be as good as me," laughed Issel, who has a healthy sense of humor. "He was okay."

Issel — who once lost his three front teeth in a gym class when he was in the sixth grade — is hopeful that his niece (Greg's daughter) will someday play for the UK women's basketball team. As this book was written, his niece was playing at the same high school the brothers had attended. "We've got our fingers crossed that in a couple of years Kentucky might have another Issel playing for them," Issel smiled. "She went to the girls' basketball camp at UK."

Basketball was not the only sport Issel was interested in. Like most kids, he participated in many sports, including baseball and football. While he enjoyed baseball, he struggled to play in that sport. Issel was a faithful Chicago Cubs fan, attending several games at Wrigley Field in Chicago. "Ernie Banks was Mr. Chicago Cubs and he was really my sports hero when I was growing up," remembered Issel.

 When the two professional basketball leagues — National Basketball Association and the three-year-old ABA — got into a bidding war for the top collegiate stars, including Issel, in the spring of 1970, Issel sought Rupp for advice.

The UK coach told Issel to make sure the franchise had strong financial backing. Some pro basketball teams, especially in the less-established ABA, were financially-strapped.

Issel decided to remain in Kentucky and signed a multi-year $1.4 million contract with the Colonels, who were one of the ABA's stronger franchises. Issel's five-year pact, at the time, was reportedly the largest amount ever given to a pro basketball rookie. Kareem Abdul-Jabbar also had signed a reported $1.4 million contract with the Milwaukee Bucks in the previous year. Issel's Wildcat teammate Mike Pratt joined the Colonels for a reported $400,000. University of Tennessee's 6-10 All-SEC center Bobby Croft also signed with Kentucky.

"The Colonels were a very sound team," said Issel, who has a bachelor's degree in business. "They were owned by five men — Wendell Cherry and David Jones who had started Humana (medical care chain), John Y. Brown Jr., of course, who had the Kentucky Fried Chicken, Stuart Jay who is a real successful lawyer in Louisville, and David Grissom who was president of Citizens Fidelity Bank.

"So there was sound financial backing. If coach Rupp hadn't known who the men behind the Colonels were, I don't think he would have given me the advice to sign with an ABA team, but he knew the Colonels were strong."

But Issel said the Colonels and the ABA exaggerated his fat contract for public relations. "They played it up," he recalled. "It wouldn't be as big as they said it was. Of course, that was right when the ABA was getting competitive with the NBA and going after (top) players. They said the five-year deal was for $1.4 million, but there were a lot of investments that had to work out and things like that. My actual salary was $75,000 a year. I loved the fact that I got to stay in Kentucky and play professional basketball. So that was kind of a dream come true going right up the road and playing in Louisville."

All-Americans Rick Mount and Charlie Scott also joined Issel in the ABA as they inked big contracts. Mount signed with the Pacers, while Scott went to Washington Capitols (which shortly became the Virginia Squires).

Despite the horror stories about some ABA teams failing to meet their payroll, Issel said he never worried about being paid during his ABA tenure. "I was always fortunate that I was with some teams (Kentucky and Denver) that had pretty good financial backing. We never had to worry about our payrolls, our check not cashing and clearing, and things like that.

"But there were a lot of shaky ABA teams financially. I know a lot of players in the ABA who did have to worry about their paychecks clearing. In fact, a friend of mine who was with the Virginia Squires told a funny story. He said everybody who played for the Squires went out and bought a real fast car because when they got their paychecks only the first two or three guys to the bank would have their paychecks be good. Everybody bought a fast car so they could get to the bank quick. But I never had to worry about that."

 With Issel and Pratt joining three-time All-ABA guard Louie Dampier as ex-Wildcats on board, the 1970-71 campaign was an exciting time for the Kentucky Colonels and the ABA. Anticipating larger crowds because of Issel's popularity, the aggressive new ownership group decided to hold many of its home games at 16,933-seat Freedom Hall. In the previous three years since the ABA began in 1967, the Colonels usually played all of their home games at smallish 5,733-seat Convention Center in downtown Louisville. In addition, the Colonels, under the new leadership of innovative president and general manager Mike Storen, featured a modern look with new uniforms, new colors (from green to blue) and new logo.

The franchise also signed new three-year contracts with Louisville's WLKY-TV (Channel 32) and powerful WHAS Radio. Lexington's WKYT-TV (Channel 27) also joined the Colonel Television Network, increasing statewide television coverage for the ABA club. The team received more local and regional newspaper coverage than it ever had before.

And the Colonels, occasionally, got national attention. The weekly *Sporting News* magazine had Issel on its cover (January 23, 1971), calling him the "Golden Boy," for a cover story about the upcoming ABA All-Star Game. In the mid-season classic, Issel had a remarkable game. He scored 21 points and snatched 11 rebounds in leading East to a 126-122 victory before a record 14,407 fans in Greensboro, North Carolina. The all-star game, which was nationally televised by CBS network, also featured ex-NBA superstars such as Joe Caldwell of the Carolina Cougars, Rick Barry of the New York Nets and Zelmo Beaty of the Utah Stars.

"Any (national) publicity that the ABA got then was kind of unusual because we played in a lot of small markets," Issel said. "We weren't in New York or Chicago or L.A. You know we were on Long Island (where the New York Nets headquartered), and we were in Greensboro (North Carolina), Louisville and Indianapolis. So we didn't get a lot of publicity. It was real unusual when an ABA player would get on the cover of a national publication or get a story done in the national press."

The publicity-starved ABA didn't have a single nationally-televised contest until its third season (1969-70) when CBS carried its third annual All-Star Game in Indianapolis on a Saturday afternoon. The following season saw CBS televising several ABA games, showcasing the league's new superstars from the NBA and collegiate ranks, including Issel. Unlike today's television broadcasting industry, these were the days when the cable TV didn't even exist.

As a rookie, Issel encountered many interesting moments throughout the 1970-71 campaign. Sometimes the Colonels played in front of very small crowds when they faced some of the league's weaker franchises. Commented Issel, "I remember one night we were playing (the Texas Chapparals) in Dallas, and this is before they moved to San Antonio and became the San Antonio Spurs. During the national anthem, Louie (Dampier) took one side of the arena and I took the other side. We counted the crowd while they were playing the national anthem. And I don't remember the exact total, but it was 200 and something. That's how many people were at the gym."

The team also became embroiled in a controversy when the departing trainer Bill Antonini made some comments, which first made the front page of the old *Louisville Times*. He charged the Colonels were having

Seven-foot-two ABA giant Artis Gilmore of the Kentucky Colonels goes up for two points against the New York Nets. Gilmore, the league's MVP in 1972, was named first team All-ABA five times before playing in the NBA.

Photo by Rogers Photography

racial problems and that coach Frank Ramsey, a former UK All-American, was doing a poor job of coaching.   For several days, the city of Louisville was bombarded with media reports about the racial issue.   Several black players, however, defended Ramsey, denying the trainer's charges.   The Colonels had seven black players with five whites on the squad, according to the team's media guide.

"We had a trainer who made a charge that I was a racist," Ramsey said in a 1994 interview. "That wasn't very pleasant. When that happened, I think it solidified the team. It allowed us to go on and go to the (ABA) finals."

The Colonels, who finished with a 44-40 worksheet in the regular season, advanced to the league's exciting championship series with the Utah Stars before dropping in seven games. In the regular season, Issel captured the league's scoring honors with a 29.8-point average, beating out Rick Barry, who had 29.4 points. For his efforts, Issel also shared the ABA rookie of the year honors with Virginia's Charlie Scott. As far as average home attendance was concerned, the Colonels fared well at the gate, drawing league's second-best 7,500 fans, behind Indiana's 8,200. "We always drew pretty well in Freedom Hall," said Issel.

 In the following season of 1971-72, the Colonels had more help. The team, gunning for its first ABA championship, featured 7-2 high-priced star Artis Gilmore, an intimidating shot blocker from Jacksonville who led the country in rebounding his junior and senior years. To make room for Gilmore, the Colonels moved Issel, who had played center as a 6-9, 235-pound rookie, to forward.

Kentucky, with Issel and Gilmore in the lineup, improved dramatically, posting a remarkable regular season mark of 68-16, a league record. The fifth annual ABA All-Star Game was held in Louisville and a record crowd of nearly 16,000 saw Issel capture the Most Valuable Player award.

But the Colonels, guided by former Los Angeles Lakers mentor Joe Mullaney, didn't win the league crown later in the campaign. They didn't go very far in the post-season playoffs. The New York Nets, who finished the regular season with a 44-40 record, stunned the heavily-favored Colonels in seven games in the opening round.

It would be three more years before Kentucky would win its first ABA championship. It was May 1975 when the Colonels, with coach Hubie Brown at the helm, finally captured the league title in defeating arch-rival Indiana Pacers in five games. Winning the league championship is the highlight of his career, Issel said. The ABA title will always be a special one for Issel. It's the only championship he has won in his long basketball career.

 Even though his team won the championship, Kentucky owner and future governor John Y. Brown Jr. said he was still losing a significant amount of money in operating the Colonels. To recover his losses, Brown decided that he would

sell one of the Colonels stars — Artis Gilmore or Dan Issel.

It was Issel who went to the Baltimore Claws franchise (formerly the Memphis Sounds) in a very controversial move. In the transaction, Brown got 6-10 center Tom Owens and approximately $500,000 for Issel.

Issel said the 1975 trade was the most depressing moment of his pro basketball career. "I was very upset. Very upset," he commented. "We had just built a brand new home in Louisville after four years at the University of Kentucky, and five years with the Colonels. I thought I was going to live in Kentucky for the rest of my life.

"It was not only depressing in having to leave (Louisville), but it was depressing being in Baltimore because I would go to practice, and Cheri would try to go out and find a decent place to live. She couldn't find any place that she liked. We were (staying) in a hotel room with (daughter) Sheridan, a dog, and a parakeet, if I remember correctly. It was easily the most depressing moment."

Issel, however, wasn't the only one miserable. Issel's boss was having problems of his own. The highly-publicized trade got Brown in a big firestorm as he went through a giant public relations disaster. The Kentucky fans were outraged, feeling betrayed. To them, Issel was their hero.

"(Brown) was getting very negative press in Louisville after he had sold me," Issel said. "The people were really upset in Louisville and the worse part is the people in Baltimore never paid John Y. the money for me they said they were going to pay."

So, about a week later, without Issel's knowledge, Brown flew to Baltimore and checked in at the same hotel where Issel and his family were staying. And the phone rang in Issel's room. It was Brown.

"He was the last guy that I expected to be hearing from," Issel said. "He said we need to talk and I said okay.

"Can you come down to my room?" Brown asked.

"You're here?" said a confused Issel.

"Yeah, I'm here in the hotel in Baltimore."

After Issel arrived in Brown's hotel room, they had their conversation.

Brown told Issel, "Here's the deal, if you'll say something that will get the people in Louisville off my back, I'll get you out of Baltimore and get you with a good team."

Replied Issel, "You got a deal. Get me out of here!"

Issel was on his way to the Denver Nuggets, one of ABA's best franchises. With him was a paycheck from the Baltimore Claws, who eventually folded without having played a single regular season game. "I got one paycheck that I didn't have a chance to cash before I left Baltimore," Issel said. "So I went to Denver and I went to the bank. I started a new account with this check I got from the Baltimore Claws. No good. It bounced. And (Denver general manager) Carl Scheer had to make good on that check. But that is not a great way to get off a good relationship with a new bank — to open an account with a check that bounced."

While Denver coasted to ABA-best 60-24 mark during Issel's first year with the Nuggets, the ex-Colonel recalled a bizarre incident involving the financially-troubled Virginia Squires, who were in Denver to meet the Nuggets. "They were in a hotel in Denver. They had been there a time or two before, but hadn't paid their bill. (The hotel) put the teams' bags out on the street and weren't going to let them stay there until they paid their bills. Our owner (and president), Carl Scheer, had to go down to the hotel and write a check for everything that the Squires owed them or they weren't going to let them come in and spend the night."

As for the 1975-76 season, Issel, who averaged 23 points and 11 rebounds, earned All-ABA honors for the fifth time, as the Nuggets went to the championship series before losing to high-flying superstar Julius "Dr. J" Erving and the New York Nets. About a month later, ABA sent four teams — Denver, Indiana, New York and San Antonio — to the NBA in a merger. Issel's former team, Kentucky Colonels, meanwhile, declined to join the NBA, saying the entry price of approximately $3 million was too high.

So it marked the unfortunate death of the Colonels and ABA. With the merger, ABA's popular innovations — the red, white and blue basketball, and the three-point field goal — disappeared. The NBA rejected these so-called gimmicks, but it later embraced the three-point basket in 1979.

Many of ABA's star players continued to thrive in the older league. The newest NBA standouts included Issel, Gilmore, Erving, David Thompson, George McGinnis, Rick Barry, George Gervin, Billy Knight, to name a few. In his first year of NBA action, Issel finished as one of the league's top 10 scoring leaders, averaging 22 points. He also appeared in the NBA All-Star Game. By the way, a former ABA player captured the MVP honors in the All-Star classic. His name? Future Hall of Famer Julius Erving.

Issel would remain in Denver as a member of the NBA establishment for the rest of his playing career until 1985 when he retired at the age of 36. Toward the end of his last pro season as a player, Issel went through a so-called "farewell tour," receiving many gifts from several NBA clubs, including an exotic trip to Hawaii. The Nuggets also retired his famed "44" jersey number.

In his 15-year pro career, Issel scored 27,482 points, which is good for No. 7 on the all-time ABA/NBA scoring list going into the 1998-99 campaign. Kareem Abdul-Jabbar is the all-time leader with 38,387 points.

Issel "was one of those people that they said was not big enough to play center at 6-9," said Frank Ramsey, who coached the Colonels in Issel's rookie year. "Dan had a tremendous attitude about practice and working. They said he was too slow and couldn't jump, but by golly look what he's done. He is now in the basketball Hall of Fame. He had a tremendous career at Denver after the ABA (merged with the NBA). Dan is one fine individual."

Interestingly, one of Issel's other pro coaches was Larry Brown. Yes, the same nomadic Larry Brown, who has coached several teams on the professional and collegiate levels. At Denver, Brown, who is now the head coach for the Philadelphia 76ers, coached Issel for nearly four years in the late 1970s.

 While Issel was in the ABA, he knew a little girl who would someday become a well-known sportscaster. She was the oldest child of Mike Storen, who worked for the Kentucky Colonels as their top executive.

That little girl is Hannah Storm, the former CNN sports anchor who is now working with NBC. Before she went big time with CNN in 1989, Storm had changed her name while she worked as a radio sportscaster in Texas. She didn't want people to think she had the TV job because of her father's strong background in sports. Her dad also served as ABA commissioner for one season after a three-year stint with the Colonels.

Issel said Storm didn't play or practice on the court with the players very much when she was small. She wasn't a tomboy, Issel explained. "I didn't see her much at practice," said the former Wildcat. "She would be at the games and (I would see her) when we went to the Storens for parties and things. I wasn't real close with her, but I definitely remember her when she was growing up."

Many years later, they both met again in the 1994 NBA playoffs. While Issel coached the surprising Nuggets in the playoffs as they upset Seattle (which posted the league's best record with 63-19) in the opening round, Storm covered the post-season games as a reporter for NBC. They shared stories about their early days in Louisville. "We have talked about this because Hannah has interviewed me several times," Issel said. "She was in the playoff series when we played Seattle and Utah. I told her that the last time I saw her she was a little skinny girl about 10 years old." Interestingly, Issel later returned to television broadcasting ranks for the second time in 1997 as a sportscaster, joining NBC as a color analyst on its NBA telecasts.

 When Rupp died in 1977, Issel wasn't able to attend the coach's funeral in Lexington. Issel, at the time, was still playing for the Nuggets. He learned of Rupp's death via a telephone call from Claude Vaughan.

"That was a sad day," Issel commented. "I loved coach Rupp. He always did exactly what he told me he was going to do. A lot that I had and have, I think I owe to coach Rupp, not only from the basketball angle and what he taught me about the game of basketball, but about being a human being — the work ethic and honesty. I learned an awful, awful lot from coach Rupp."

 As far as his working relationships with the news media are concerned, Issel is one of the more cooperative former or current players you will find in the NBA ranks. Unlike some of the NBA's ego-centered stars today, well-mannered Issel is a refreshing change for sportswriters or broadcasters. He is usually a pleasant interview.

But everyone has their bad moments. That includes Issel. He once became very upset when one of two Denver major newspapers ran a story about Issel's NBA salary. "There was one that I remember that was inaccurate and it had to do with how much money I was making," Issel said. "It was after I got to Denver and the fellow wrote an article which said I was the next-to-the-lowest-paid center in the NBA. It was inaccurate and I told him it was inaccurate. I told him I wasn't going to tell him what I was making, but he was low on his (salary) projections. It not only made me look bad, but it made my representatives look bad and things like that.

"So he said he would write another story. Well, he wrote another story, but he still didn't get the facts right. The second story just said how upset I was about the first story. He was a beat writer (who regularly covered the Nuggets). I didn't talk to him for the rest of the season. That was the only article that I remember really getting upset about."

 After his retirement as NBA player, Issel became involved in the horse breeding business. He and his family moved to Versailles, Ky., where he operated his 160-acre Courtland Farm. Raising horses was always one of Issel's favorite hobbies.

Still, he soon found out that he couldn't leave the basketball scene. Even though Issel had followed the Wildcats closely by attending most of their home games, sitting several rows from the UK bench, he wanted to get more involved. Therefore, he tried his hand in broadcasting, doing some work for the UK basketball radio network. He even did backup work as a color commentator for the SEC's network package.

On a wintry December day in 1987, as Issel was preparing his commentary work for the UK radio broadcast in the Kentucky-Louisville matchup at Rupp Arena, he received one of the biggest surprises of his life. His jersey was officially retired by UK. As a substitute for Ralph Hacker, who was broadcasting a college football game for ESPN, Issel served as a color analyst that afternoon, working with play-by-play announcer Cawood Ledford.

As Issel will tell you, it was an exciting day for him and the Wildcat fans. In the nationally-televised encounter, Cedric Jenkins, a 6-9 senior reserve from Dawson, Ga., led top-ranked UK to a thrilling 76-75 victory over Louisville on his last-second tip-in.

For his radio/TV stint, Issel received praise from many folks, including Joe Dean, who had recently retired from his SEC's television broadcasting job to take the LSU athletic directorship. Dean liked Issel's work, saying he was impressive for a newcomer and might have a good future as an announcer.

In 1988, the thoroughbred industry took a severe economic beating, so Issel, with his promising TV broadcasting future, moved back to Denver and served as the Nuggets' color commentator for four years.

Nicknamed "the Horse" for his durability and his passion for horses during his playing days in Denver, Issel said that he is practically out of the horse breeding business. "It was something I did from the time I graduated from Kentucky," he said. "I bought my first horse and I've always had at least one or two. At one time I had 25 or 30. So it's gone up and down (over the years), but it's something I really enjoy. I don't know if I will ever be back to that extent but I think I will probably always have a horse or two."

 During his three-year stay in Kentucky in the late 1980s, Issel also became involved in state politics. In the summer of 1986, he was chosen the state chairman of Brereton Jones' campaign for lieutenant governor, traveling throughout the state. Like Issel, Jones operated a farm in Woodford County. They were both fellow horse breeders. "I knew Brereton, but we weren't close friends before he ran for lieutenant governor," Issel said.

Before Jones announced his candidacy for the state's No. 2 office, he asked for Issel's help in the upcoming campaign during a hour-long meeting which was arranged by a mutual friend. Jones told Issel that he would like for him "to go around (the state) because I can't draw a crowd. But you will be able to draw a crowd. After you've talked about basketball for a little bit, then I want to tell them what I think, what I believe, and why I am running for lieutenant governor. So go home and talk to Cheri because it is going to involve some traveling and some time, but I'd like your help."

In a conversation with his wife, Issel said of Jones, "I really like this guy. I believe in him. I believe in what he stands for."

So Issel went back and informed Jones of his decision, saying, "Now, Brereton, I know that you are going to be elected lieutenant governor of Kentucky and then you are going to be elected governor of Kentucky. I'm going to do this and this is what I want in return. The governor of Kentucky in every (Kentucky) Derby gets to go over to the infield and stand in that cupola and watch the Derby. When you are elected governor, I want to go over to that cupola with you and watch the Derby."

About six years later, Issel attended the Derby with Gov. Jones, who had been elected to the state's top post in 1991. Said Issel, "About 45 minutes before they ran the Derby, one of the security guys came and tapped me on the shoulder. He said, 'You and Mrs. Issel come with me.' We went across the track, went up the cupola and watched the Kentucky Derby."

Gov. Jones obviously remembered his promise to Issel. "That shows what kind of a man Brereton Jones is because he kept his word," said the Wildcat great. "That had not been discussed for six years."

 When the NCAA investigated Kentucky's roundball program for possible rules violations in late 1980s, Issel and his horse farm got entangled in UK's fight with the NCAA. In one of NCAA's many charges against UK, it was reported that one of coach Eddie Sutton's assistants, James Dickey, had taken a prospect to the farm in Woodford County during a 1987 visit. In a chance meeting, the recruit also met with Issel at the farm in violation of NCAA regulations since the former star was considered a representative of UK.

Issel, who briefly talked to the recruit without realizing he had broken a rule, said that was a honest mistake on his part. "I'd never do anything knowingly to hurt UK," he told the Louisville *Courier-Journal*. Issel also pointed out that many prospects had seen the farm without meeting him.

Meanwhile, in the entire UK-NCAA controversy, the most serious of 18 charges against Kentucky involved then-freshman standout Eric Manuel in an academic fraud (for allegedly cheating on a college entrance test) and assistant coach Dwane Casey (for allegedly sending $1,000 to a recruit in an express package), according to NCAA. As a result, NCAA penalized Kentucky by banning the Wildcats from post-season tournament action in 1990 and 1991. Also, UK was prohibited from appearing on live television during the 1989-90 season. For all of its mess, the controversy earned Kentucky's infamous *Sports Illustrated's* May 29, 1989 cover, titled "Kentucky's Shame."

 After a four-year stint (1988 to 1992) in Denver where he served as a television analyst for the Nuggets, Issel prepared to leave Colorado to become the secretary of the Kentucky Tourism Cabinet in the Gov. Jones administration. One day he received a intriguing phone call from a Denver Nugget official. It was general manager (and Kentucky native) Bernie Bickerstaff on the line.

He wanted to know if Issel, 43 at the time, would like to coach the Nuggets, the once-proud franchise which had sunk new lows with horri-

Hair-flying Dan Issel in his
Denver Nugget uniform.

Denver Nuggets Public Relations

ble records of 20-62 and 24-58 in the previous two years. Issel didn't
know what to think. He didn't know if he was that interested or not.
Bickerstaff, who was also looking at other coaching candidates, told him
that was fine, but wanted him to consider the possibility of coaching the
NBA team. After three or four days, Issel informed Bickerstaff he would
like to be considered for the position.

Three weeks later, Issel was introduced as Denver's new coach on
May 20, 1992. "I was really surprised (to get the job) because I didn't have
any coaching experience," he said. "I had never coached at any level
before. There are only 29 of those in the whole country to be a NBA coach

and to get that (position) with no experience, I was really surprised. I certainly thought I could do it. I had been around (basketball for a long time)."

As a Rupp disciple, Issel appropriately wore a brown suit in honor of legendary UK coach in the first regular season game as the Nuggets' coach. "It was against the San Antonio Spurs and we won in double overtime. That was the first game I coached," Issel said. For the record, a near-sellout crowd of 17,022 witnessed Issel's successful coaching debut in a season-opening thriller as the Nuggets prevailed 125-121 in Denver. Issel said his players "didn't really understand the significance (of wearing a brown suit). Most of them had probably never even heard of coach Rupp before."

In Issel's first coaching season, the youthful Nuggets went on to finish the season with a 36-46 mark, a 12-game improvement over the previous 1991-92 club.

And Issel's troops did even better in the following season of 1993-94. The Nuggets posted a winning record (42-40) and advanced to the playoffs where they stunned the NBA world by beating a tough Seattle club in becoming the first No. 8 seed (in the conference) to beat a No. 1 seed since the league's 16-team playoff format was first initiated in 1984.

With the series deadlocked at 2-2, Issel said of the fifth and deciding game in Seattle, "All of the pressure was on Seattle. We didn't know what we were doing. We weren't even supposed to be there. They, on the other hand, were about to get beat by the worst team that made the playoffs. In the fifth game that went to overtime, they played just tight as a drum and we played loose and somehow we pulled it off."

Issel said it certainly was his best moment as a coach. "It was a great feeling. I can't remember many bigger games even as a player. I think you could say that was the best moment in the NBA."

Denver then faced the Utah Jazz in the Western Conference semifinals where it lost 4-3 in the series. But the hungry Nuggets, down with an 0-3 deficit, almost pulled another upset as the series went the full route.

In Issel's first two years as Denver mentor, Mahmoud Abdul-Rauf (formerly Chris Jackson) served as the team's leading scorer both times. Abdul-Rauf, who changed his name because of his Islamic faith, was a former All-American at LSU under then-coach Dale Brown.

 Issel's brief coaching career came to a surprising end in the middle of the 1994-95 season when he resigned. Although the Nuggets were 18-16 despite the loss of 6-8 star forward LaPhonso Ellis with a season-ending knee injury, Issel informed Bickerstaff that he wasn't happy and wanted to quit coaching.

On his resignation, Issel said the biggest reason he stepped down was because some of his players "had become selfish and winning the game wasn't the most important thing (to them). It just wasn't fun to see a bunch of hard-working guys, who had accomplished a lot, all of a sudden be concerned about themselves and not the team first." Also another factor in Issel's departure reportedly was his "strained" relationship with the team's general manager Bernie Bickerstaff, who is from Benham in Harlan County, Kentucky.

As far as coaching the technical aspects of the game, like the X's and O's, Issel felt he proved that he "knew a little bit what I was doing." But he pointed out there were a couple of things he would have done differently if another coaching opportunity arose.

"How I handled the media was not good. How I handled the pressure was not good," he said. "So I learned some things that I would do differently the next time."

At the press conference when Issel announced his resignation, he told reporters that he wouldn't coach again. However, he apparently had a change of heart. In this book interview, he said he would coach again only in the right situation.

"I don't have to coach again," Issel explained. "You know there is no burning desire in me to coach again. But if the right situation came along, I would probably do it. If it doesn't, then I don't feel like I will have missed anything."

Assistant coach Gene Littles — who was Issel's teammate on the Kentucky Colonels' ABA championship team in 1975 — and Bickerstaff coached Denver the rest of the season.

 In the NBA, there have been several ugly incidents in recent years. For instance, Latrell Sprewell twice attacked coach P.J. Carlesimo at a Golden State practice. At Phoenix, forward Robert Horry (ex-Alabama star) once threw a towel in the face of his coach, Danny Ainge. Anthony Mason angri-

ly yelled at Charlotte mentor, Dave Cowens. Dennis Rodman, of his rainbow-colored hair fame, kicked a cameraman on the courtside. (Rodman's strange behavior, by the way, cost him an 11-game suspension and a rather-low $25,000 fine by the NBA.) During the 1997 NBA Finals, the league also fined Rodman $50,000 his derogatory comments about the Mormons.

Issel said many of the NBA players need to improve their attitude by showing more respect for the game. "Not only is there little respect for the coach, I really don't think there's much respect for the game," he said. "I don't think a lot of these young players, who are getting paid millions of dollars to play a sport that they love, take the time to realize what price former players paid to give them the opportunity (to play). You know we shouldn't indict everybody because not all young players are like that. But there are many. I'd like for them to show more respect to the coaches, but I'd like to see them show more respect to the game.

"Nothing that Dennis Rodman would do would surprise me, but I'm glad that the NBA finally took a strong, strong stand, instead of just slapping him on the wrist. I think if they would have done that for some of other things (incidents) before, this problem never would have come to this point."

As a former NBA player and coach, Issel has a perspective about whether or not the professional players are making too much money. He is especially concerned with the fact collegiate stars are earning big bucks when they first arrive on the NBA scene as rookies. "I really have a problem with these rookies coming into the league being the highest paid players on their team, having never played a game in the NBA," he said. "I think that's bad for the sport."

However, as far as the veteran players, especially the superstars, are concerned, they deserve big contracts, according to Issel. "I don't think the players make too much money," he said. "It's a form of entertainment, like the actors make $20 million a movie, musicians make a couple of million a concert. You don't hear people say they make too much money. In the movies, the biggest stars make the most money. That is the way it ought to be in the NBA. Michael Jordan ought to make the most money. Then the second-best player, whoever you think, ought to make the second (largest) amount."

 Interestingly, ever since Rupp's successor, Joe B. Hall, announced his retirement from coaching in 1985, Issel has been mentioned as candidate for the prestigious UK coaching post every time there is a vacancy. When Eddie Sutton left Kentucky in 1989, Issel's name popped up. In 1997, when Rick Pitino departed the Wildcats for the Boston Celtics, Issel's name was mentioned as well. And while he didn't have any coaching experience, Issel somehow made the list of coaching candidates in 1985 and 1989.

Issel, after spending two and a half years as the Nuggets head coach, was especially interested in the UK job in 1997 when Pitino resigned after eight years at Kentucky. But Kentucky athletic director C.M. Newton had someone else in mind. Georgia mentor Orlando "Tubby" Smith, a former Pitino assistant at Kentucky, got the plum job.

"I think that coaching basketball at the University of Kentucky might be the best job in the world," said Issel, who remains a very popular figure in the commonwealth, serving as a leading spokesman for a well-known Kentucky insurance company.

Issel had previously said he wouldn't mind working in the NBA front office someday as an executive. He got his wish in late March of 1998, signing a three-year pact with the woeful Denver Nuggets to be the franchise's general manager. "I think that if I had my pick of anything — whether it be college administration, college coaching, professional coaching or professional management — I would pick professional management," he said prior to being named to the GM post. "If I had a chance to be a general manager or president of an NBA franchise, that would be my number one choice (for a future job)."

When Issel took his new post, the Nuggets were on the verge of becoming the worst team in NBA history. Denver, however, avoided that distinction as it barely finished with 11 wins in 82 games. The 1972-73 Philadelphia 76ers hold the league's worst mark with 9-73. And Issel began Denver's rebuilding project with his first major move by firing the rookie head coach and his former teammate of three years, Bill Hanzlik, saying the organization needed to move in a different direction.

Before taking the front office job, Issel had worked as the Nuggets TV commentator and operated a printing business in Denver. By the way, Nuggets star LaPhonso Ellis, one of Issel's friends, also has a share in the printing company.

Adolph Rupp, who was the nation's winningest college basketball coach for many years until 1997 when North Carolina's Dean Smith took over the top spot, speaks to a Memorial Coliseum crowd during a special ceremony honoring the Baron in the mid-1970s. Former UK star Dan Issel said the news media have incorrectly or unfairly labeled Rupp as a racist.

Photo by Rogers Photography

What do Adolph Rupp, Cliff Hagan, Frank Ramsey, Dan Issel and Cawood Ledford have in common?

They are UK's only representatives named to the Basketball Hall of Fame in Springfield, Mass. As for Issel, he was inducted in 1993, joining former ABA rival Julius Erving, Bill Walton, Calvin Murphy, Walt Bellamy, Dick McGuire, Ann Meyers and Uljana Semjonova (whose name has been spelled or misspelled different ways in various publications). As a historical footnote, Issel and Erving became the first Hall of Fame players who started their careers in the ABA and played in the same league until its merger with the NBA in 1976.

"It's a great honor," Issel said, "when you look at all the people over the years that have played college basketball and have played professional basketball, to be among the few who are elected to that great post."

Issel, who was coaching the Nuggets at the time, was very surprised when an official from the Hall of Fame office congratulated him on the phone for his election to the Hall of Fame. Earlier, Issel had thought he didn't make it because he had heard and understood that TV sportscaster Bill Walton, a former NBA and UCLA star, had gone to New York City supposedly for the Hall of Fame's press conference. "I was really surprised because in my mind I had not been elected that year because of what Walton was doing," Issel said. As it turned out, Walton reportedly was in New York for his duties with NBC and stayed an extra day or two in the city for the news conference after learning he was picked for the Hall of Fame.

 When Kentucky had a basketball game on national TV, Issel and his family usually cleared their schedule so they could enjoy the game. However, since they live in Colorado, they often had to miss some of UK's locally- or regionally-televised games. As for UK games not shown on national TV, they couldn't get the stations from the UK Television network, which includes affiliates from Lexington or Louisville, and the SEC network.

Fortunately, that is not the case anymore. As a Christmas present for her husband, Cheri purchased a small television satellite dish. "I just signed up for the college basketball program (offered through the satellite dish) and now I can get almost every game that Kentucky plays," Issel smiled. "(In 1996) my son, Scott, and I went to the Meadowlands for the Final Four and saw them win the national championship. So we follow Kentucky very closely." The Issels also have a daughter, Sheridan.

What about his wife, a former Wildcat cheerleader? Did she go to the 1996 Final Four in East Rutherford, N. J., where Kentucky defeated Syracuse 76-67 in the title game? "No," Issel grinned. "She stayed (home). We only had two tickets so Scott went. But I promised her that next time Kentucky's in the Final Four she will get to go."

In the following season of 1996-97, Kentucky did make another memorable journey to the Final Four in Indianapolis, where Arizona edged UK 84-79 in the title game. Issel, however, said he and his wife didn't attend that event.

What about the 1998 Final Four when UK stunned the nation with its second national title in three years? Issel did go to San Antonio, Texas, for the highly-publicized hoopla, but Cheri didn't make it. That's because she was busy with a planned wedding shower in Lexington. However, the ex-yell leader still found the time to watch the victorious Wildcats on TV at her parents' home.

Issel said that Cheri reminds him of his unfulfilled promise. She undoubtedly would love to cheer at the Final Four, a once-a-lifetime opportunity she never had in college, and yell "Go Big Blue!" And it's safe to say that Issel and his wife will try to be there the next time Kentucky makes its coveted Final Four journey.

COURT(EOUS) WILDCAT

Rick Robey and Dean Smith will always be linked by one infamous incident from the late 1970s.   When Smith, college basketball's winningest coach with 879 victories, announced his retirement in the fall of 1997, he was front page news across the country. That meant Robey, a former UK All-American, garnered some publicity because of that unfortunate episode.

While the sportswriters praised Smith's phenomenal achievements, some liked to mention the heated Robey-Smith shouting match which took place during the 1977 Kentucky-North Carolina's NCAA East Regional finals. In *The Sporting News* magazine, contributing writer Dave Kindred, a former Louisville *Courier-Journal* sports editor, led off his column about the legendary coach by recounting that incident, which saw Smith rebuke Robey. In Kentucky, Jerry Tipton of the *Lexington Herald-Leader* also pointed out the episode. Noted author John Feinstein, in his 1997 book *A March To Madness*, wrote of the furor as well.

What they discussed was that clean-spoken Smith, who had the reputation of not using profanity, supposedly had called Robey a dirty player after a bumping foul late in the game with North Carolina winning. The 6-10 Robey said Smith cursed him, but Smith said that wasn't so. They later sort of made up and everything was fine, but it's not easily forgotten.

On the disappointing 79-72 setback to the Tar Heels, Robey

recalled from his Louisville area office, North Carolina "four cornered in on us when they got a lead (with 15 minutes remaining). We weren't able to overcome that because they hit their free throws." For the foul-plagued game, North Carolina made 33 out of 36 free throws, while the Wildcats hit 16 of 18 from the line. Three UK players — Robey, Larry Johnson and Truman Claytor — fouled out with Robey getting 15 points in 23 minutes.

The loss forced Robey, then a junior, to wait another year before savoring the school's fifth national championship in the 1977-78 campaign.

During UK's championship season, Robey, a likable fellow who had now become an experienced senior, was considered the squad's leading spokesman along with fellow All-American teammate Jack Givens. A product of New Orleans, Robey was very articulate. The media loved to interview him. When he talked, people listened.

The Wildcat fans also appreciated the center's aggressive style of play. They liked his hustle. Former *Lexington Herald* sports columnist D. G. FitzMaurice called Robey the Pete Rose of college basketball. Others compared him with NBA star Dave Cowens. Coach Joe B. Hall and his assistants admired Robey because of his never-ending dedication and hustle.

As history will note, it was Robey's aggressiveness that played a very significant role in Kentucky's successful run for the NCAA crown. While everyone remembers Givens' stunning 41-point exhibition in senior-dominated UK's 94-88 victory over a young Duke squad in the nationally-televised title game, Robey had a near-flawless performance. In 32 minutes of action, Robey scored 20 points, making eight of 11 field goals, and was the only Wildcat player to hit double figures besides Givens. In addition, he grabbed a team-high 11 rebounds and committed only two turnovers.

With the impressive victory, which was held in St. Louis, Kentucky's so-called "Season Without Celebration" came to an end. The serious-minded Wildcats, the pre-season favorite to win the national crown, had finally celebrated. Robey and the rest of his teammates were on cloud nine. Despite UK's business-like atmosphere, Robey said the entire ordeal was worth it. Added senior forward James Lee, "A lot of the media said we weren't having any fun, but I thought we had a blast. We had a good time. We were focused on what we had to do, but we had a good time within our surroundings."

The newly-crowned national champions, who finished with a sparkling 30-2 mark, sure felt like celebrating, especially on their return flight to Lexington in the wee hours. Some of them, including 22-year-old Robey, wanted to drink beer. But Hall and his staff didn't approve it even if some of the players were already beyond their drinking age limit.

Said Robey, "I can remember flying home, and James Lee and I were sitting in the back on a private flight on Delta Airlines. We said, 'By golly, we are going to drink a beer and celebrate.' So I went ahead and ordered a beer."

But one of UK's assistant coaches — it was either Dick Parsons or Leonard Hamilton, said Robey — saw what they were doing. "You all are not allowed to drink," the assistant told the players.

Robey replied, "I no longer play for Kentucky. You know I am (over) 21 years old and I can have a beer if I want a beer."

Hall shortly came over to find out what the disagreement was all about. "(Hall) was still trying to be that protective father of you," smiled Robey.

Robey didn't say if they drank any more beer on the plane after that minor incident, but you can bet they probably had a few drinks after arriving in Lexington when Hall was out of their sight.

 Another highlight of Robey's Wildcat career was the Senior Day festivities at Rupp Arena on March 4, 1978 when the Wildcats faced the Runnin' Rebels of Nevada-Las Vegas. Before a national television audience, the Cats, in a spectacular show filled with many thunderous slam dunks, dominated the contest, winning 92-70. Red-hot Robey led all UK scorers with 26 points.

"That was one day that all of us seniors had a great game and I remember getting the player of the game (Most Valuable Player award)," Robey said. "It couldn't have worked out better for the four of us. All of us had exceptional games and that kind of boosted us right into the NCAA (tournament)."

 Robey said he never really felt like he was under pressure to win or produce at Kentucky. "We didn't have time to think about it," he commented. "It didn't bother me."

The ex-Wildcat said if he had truly known about the pressure at UK, especially in the NCAA Final Four, when he was playing he would've nearly folded. He finally realized the pressure the college players had to face when he played with NBA's Boston Celtics. In 1986, when Boston traveled to Dallas to play the Mavericks, Robey attended the NCAA championship game between Louisville and Duke. And he simply found out what the NCAA tournament hoopla was all about .

"I walked through the hotels and felt all the tension and excitement," Robey said of NCAA tourney's festive atmosphere. "Then I went (to the game) and I sat down. If I would have known how much tension and excitement was in the air, I'd have never been able to go out and play.

"So that is why a lot of people come up and say, 'How could you play in front of all of those people.' As a player you are not exposed to all that. You just go out. It's like the show must go on. You weren't exposed to what was going on around you. You'd go to practice, go to school and play the game."

During UK's championship run, Hall did a good job of protecting the team from unnecessary off-the-court distractions, according to Robey. "Joe Hall did a good job of doing that," said Robey. "(In) my senior year, we knew it was our last go around. I mean if we didn't do it (winning the championship) that year, our career probably would be somewhat a failure because in my junior year we should have won it all."

 Before Robey attended UK, the school's basketball program went through some very difficult times. Unlike its glorious past, UK suffered during the 1973-74 campaign. It was a horrible season. The Wildcats, under the guidance of second-year coach Joe B. Hall, struggled to a 13-13 mark. While Kentucky had outstanding juniors in Kevin Grevey, Bob Guyette, Jimmy Dan Conner and Mike Flynn, along with 5-10 senior guard Ronnie Lyons, it couldn't play together very well. Although the Wildcats had a small team, there were signs of jealousy on the squad. The players frequently blamed others for mistakes. As a result, UK missed its first NCAA trip since 1967 when Rupp also had a 13-13 team.

However, Hall wasn't ready to wave a white flag. He wasn't ready to quit coaching. Determined to show that his basketball program would prosper again, Hall aggressively sought big players in the high school ranks. His team needed size desperately. Hall signed five prospects, including three 6-10 prepsters, completing one of the school's best recruiting years. One of the players was Robey, a prep All-American from state champion Brother Martin High in New Orleans. Joining Robey were 6-10 Mike Phillips, 6-10 Danny Hall, 6-4 Jack Givens and 6-5 James Lee.

Robey said Kentucky's shockingly poor performance in the 1973-74 season didn't concern him. "The 13-13 record didn't bother me," he commented. "It probably motivated me (to sign with UK). If I had come in and they had a 31-1 season the year before, it would be hard to improve on that. So, after a 13-13 season which was a little bad, all we could do was to get better and better, and it worked out great for me.

"I think the main reason I felt like Kentucky was the right place for me because they had a great group of (incoming) seniors in Flynn, Conner, Grevey, Guyette, G.J. Smith and Jerry Hale, and they had already signed Jack Givens, James Lee, Mike Phillips and Danny Hall. They had one scholarship left and I decided, with the tradition of Kentucky basketball, it would be a great place to play."

Kentucky, of course, wasn't the only big-name school which courted Robey. Schools like Notre Dame, North Carolina, Kansas, UCLA, LSU, Florida all wanted Robey's services. But it was UK, Notre Dame and Florida that made Robey's short list . They were his top three choices. Why Florida, a football-crazed school? Why would he look at the Gators, who at the time had earned only one trip to a post-season roundball tournament in their entire school history (NIT in 1969)? "The main reason I considered Florida was because of my dad," explained Robey, whose father had graduated from the Gainesville school.

With Kentucky signing two other big men, was Robey worried that he might not get to play much as a Wildcat? "Well, the way I looked at it I was either going to sit on the bench a lot or I was going to become a good player," Robey said. "I could have gone to Florida and knew I was going to start and play a lot of minutes. Or I could have gone to LSU or Tulane and be the star on the team right off the bat.

"But I felt like, heck, I might as well go to a school where I was going to get pushed every day, have good players to play against (in practice) and hopefully develop my skills and make me that much better of a player. You know I was lucky enough to be able to start that year (freshman season) at center."

During his high school days, Robey had several head coaches who visited him at his home in New Orleans. Of the coaches who visited, Notre

UK star Rick Robey (53) is shown here snatching a rebound against Auburn. He was one of the team's popular players in the 1970s.

Photo by Rogers Photography

Dame's Digger Phelps was probably the most interesting one, according to Robey. While Phelps was known for his flamboyant coaching style on the floor, Robey said, "He was down to earth. Digger was more relaxed (than others) at home."

On LSU's colorful Dale Brown, who ended his 24-year head coaching career with the Tigers in 1997, "I didn't really care for Dale," Robey said. "He was one (of those people who told you) how to be a winner, how to do this and how do that. It didn't impress me."

On Kentucky's Hall, Robey commented, "I liked coach Hall. You could tell he was a disciplinarian. He was more like a drill sergeant type fellow. He was set in certain ways but I liked that. (If) I got him on my back every day, I felt I could maybe develop into something (in being a good player). The players that I got to meet on my visit (on the UK campus) respected him a whole lot. You know he just seemed like the type of coach that I would enjoy playing for and it turned out to be the right decision.

"Joe did come down (to New Orleans) one time to visit. Jim Hatfield, who was assistant coach, spent many evenings down there. In fact, he probably watched 85 percent of my high school games that season. So Hatfield is the one who played a major role in me coming to Kentucky." (By the way, it was Hatfield who later served as the head coach at Mississippi State for three years. In the early 1980s, he returned to Kentucky for his second stint under Hall.)

Meanwhile, New Orleans was not Robey's permanent home. In fact, it was one of Robey's many stops during his younger days. He was a well-traveled youngster. Because of his father's federal government job, his family had to move frequently. In addition to Louisiana, he lived in states such as Alaska, Tennessee and Florida. His dad, Fred, served in the Defense Investigative Service, a federal agency which works with the U.S. Marine Corps or U.S. Navy.

"My dad played a major role in my career," said Robey. The elder Robey provided much needed support to his son. He frequently managed to find some time off from work so he could visit and watch his son play at UK. Fred Robey, who is now retired, and his wife (Rick's stepmother) moved to Louisville in 1996 where they make their home. "It's good to have them back in Kentucky," said Rick Robey, whose real mother died of cancer when he was 11 years old. The younger Robey also has one younger sister and two older sisters.

At UK, Robey had a banner rookie year in 1974-75. While he started 27 of the team's 31 games, he earned All-SEC freshman team honors and helped the Wildcats go all the way to the NCAA championship game in San Diego. That squad, which would finish at 26-5 after dropping to UCLA in the title game, had an unusual makeup as it was led primarily by a group of six seniors and five freshmen. Because of that, there was some concern about the team's chemistry. Even though some folks had viewed the freshman class as the program's savior after the senior players had struggled in the previous season as juniors with a .500 worksheet, Robey said both groups got along very well.

The relationship "was real good," Robey commented. "Those (senior) guys were probably some of the better friends that I had. You know Grevey went on to play with the (Washington) Bullets. When I went to pros, he and I were buddies. In the summer time, Kevin would come back and we would rent a house — Grevey, Jerry Hale and myself. So we stayed close friends.

"They were a group of seniors that came in with all the hype of being the next great Kentucky team. You know the year before they struggled. I think they realized that a real good freshman group came in and if we were able to nurture all of that together, we could really have a great team. It ended up being a season that probably wasn't expected."

In 1971-72, when those seniors were rookies, the UK freshman squad, sometimes called the Kittens, posted a shining 22-0 mark under the leadership of Joe B. Hall, who was serving as coach Adolph Rupp's top assistant on the varsity team. *Basketball News* named the Kittens as the nation's No. 1 freshman team that season.

The highlight of Robey's freshman season came during the NCAA tournament. No, it wasn't the championship game against UCLA and its retiring coach, John Wooden. It was the Mideast Regional finals in Dayton, Ohio, the site of Kentucky's earth-shattering 92-90 upset of top-ranked and unbeaten Indiana. At the time, it was arguably the greatest Kentucky victory in its storied basketball history. With the win, the hungry Wildcats had avenged their regular season loss to Indiana and its thirty-something coach by the name of Bobby Knight. In December, Indiana had dominated Kentucky 98-74 in Bloomington. "(That) was a real embarrassment and I think that's when they even had the conflict at midcourt where Bobby Knight hit Joe Hall in the back, in the head or something," Robey remembered.

In the second UK-Indiana matchup, Robey said the Wildcats, playing in their very rare role as the underdogs, were definitely relaxed. "There was no pressure on us because we weren't picked to win," he said. "They had beaten us earlier in the year by 20 some points and there was no way we were supposed to win that game. So we kind of went in loose. We let it all hang out and we were able to beat them by two. It was fun."

Hall, who has reached the Final Four three times in his coaching career at UK, said in a 1990 interview that the victory over Indiana "was probably the most exciting game I've ever been a part of, even the national finals."

Five Wildcats scored in double figures with Flynn — a native of Jeffersonville, Ind. — taking the honors with team-high 22 points. Conner and Grevey each had 17 points. For Indiana, 6-11 sophomore center Kent Benson — who was once heavily recruited by UK — poured in 33 points and grabbed 23 rebounds, both game-highs. All-American junior Scott May, making his first start since he had broken his arm, was ineffective, scoring two points and committing three turnovers in seven minutes of action. Coach Knight had inserted May, who wasn't quite ready to play, in the starting lineup to rejuvenate the Hoosier squad. But IU coach's strategy backfired.

"I think it hurt Indiana by having Scott May (in the game)," Robey recalled. "They were a little bit different team than we saw earlier, but we played a great game. Our guards, Jimmy Dan Conner and Mike Flynn, had great games and we were able to beat them. It was probably one of the greatest games in Kentucky history, other than maybe the Duke game (in 1992)."

The ecstatic Wildcats, riding high after their surprising win over the Hoosiers, managed to recover and regroup in time for the 1975 Final Four, joining other participants Syracuse, Louisville and UCLA. "It's a dream come true," said Robey of his first Final Four appearance.

And the folks in the state of Kentucky were buzzing about the possibility of Kentucky and Louisville meeting each other for the first time in the championship game since 1959 when unranked U of L defeated UK in the NCAA tourney. However, the so-called "Dream Game" didn't materialize. In national semifinals, Kentucky did beat Syracuse 95-79, but Louisville dropped to UCLA 75-74 in overtime. Robey said he had hoped to play U of L in the finals. "I'd have loved it," he said. "In fact, Louisville should have won the game in the semifinals. I think they were up by a couple of points (actually one) when one of their players, who was a 90 percent free throw shooter, missed a free throw, and they got beat right in the last minute of the game."

The Kentucky-Louisville series finally became a reality in a regular season game in 1983 after U of L had won the first "Dream Game" in the NCAA Mideast Regionals in Knoxville, Tenn., in the previous season. Robey said he would have enjoyed the rivalry. However, he understood UK's strong stance against the series which became more evident in later years.

"They were talking about doing it," Robey said, "but I think really Kentucky looked at that as 'Why should we play Louisville? We are already the No. 1 team in the state. Why should we jeopardize losing any of our fan support and all that?' Now a player coming from New Orleans, I didn't know what Kentucky Basketball was. I knew they had great programs, but players probably weren't as involved in the rivalry.

"I would have loved to play the local school (U of L). I think it is something everybody looks forward to every year, football and basketball."

Instead of playing the Cardinals, UK ended up facing coach John Wooden and his UCLA Bruins for the national crown. Wooden's impending retirement was too much for Kentucky to overcome as the emotional Bruins, using only six players, won 92-85. The UCLA victory gave Wooden his 10th NCAA title in 12 years. A couple of days earlier, shortly after UCLA had beaten Louisville, Wooden had surprised reporters by saying that he was retiring after the championship game. While Robey, who fouled out in the title game, agreed that Wooden's sudden retirement played a significant part in UCLA's title victory, he pointed out the officials made several questionable calls. He added, "That is just part of the game. You can't use that as an excuse why we lost."

Kentucky's heartbreaking setback, meanwhile, ended the collegiate careers of All-American forward Kevin Grevey — who gunned in a game-high 34 points against UCLA — and his senior teammates. And the highly-regarded freshman clan of Robey, Phillips, Givens and Lee would become experienced sophomores in the fall of 1975 when they would be expected to carry a heavy load.

The 1975-76 season, as history will show, was a rocky one for Robey and the Wildcats, who were playing their last year at Memorial Coliseum. Kentucky, missing the crucial senior leadership from the previous season, struggled most of the campaign, hovering around the .500 mark. But in mid-February, when the sophomores began to understand their team roles, UK

got hot and won 10 straight games, including four post-season games in capturing the National Invitation Tournament championship.

Robey, after starting nine of UK's first 12 games, had to sit out most of the season because of a serious knee injury. Not surprisingly, he said that was the unhappiest moment of his Kentucky tenure. "I was discouraged my sophomore year when I got hurt," Robey commented. "I had really started off playing well and then I had that knee problem. Because of this injury, it was the only time I was ever discouraged or ever thought that my career could have ended.

"I just kept telling myself once I get well, I still have two more years to play. They (UK staff) took me down to a clinic in Memphis, Tenn., to see the doctor that did (ex-pro football star) Joe Namath's knees. Because some doctors in the Lexington area wanted to do surgery on it and my dad was really against doing that, we went down there. They ended up putting me in a cast for 14 weeks to totally immobilize my leg and that knee never gave me any more trouble. My other knee ended up being the one that caused me the problems professionally."

 After Robey's sophomore year, North Carolina coach Dean Smith — who many years later surpassed Adolph Rupp as NCAA's all-time winningest coach in 1997 — invited the Wildcat star to play for the 1976 U.S. Olympic team. Smith needed someone to play at center. Robey was the logical choice since he had gained some valuable international basketball experience as the only freshman member of the U.S. Pan American team in 1975.

The Wildcat standout wasn't interested. He gave Smith an excuse in which later Robey regretted. "I probably should have played in the Olympics," said Robey, who is one of the very few (if not only) players to have played on championship teams in high school (state), NCAA, NIT and NBA. "I didn't like Dean Smith so I used my tonsils and hand surgery for an excuse not to play in the Olympics. That's probably the only disappointing thing (in my career). They asked me to play and I turned them down. He called because I had played (in Pan American Games). I already had international experience by playing on that team."

Without Robey, Smith and the Olympic squad went on to capture the coveted gold medal in Montreal, beating Yugoslavia in the medal game. Members of the U.S. squad included Mitch Kupchak of North Carolina, Quinn Buckner (Indiana), Walter Davis (North Carolina), Phil Ford (North

Carolina), Scott May (Indiana), Adrian Dantley (Notre Dame) and Ernie Grunfeld (Tennessee), to name a few.

 Robey's junior year marked the beginning of the new Rupp Arena era. The Wildcats, coming off a surprising NIT championship season, were moving from a fading 11,500-seat gym to a new spacious palace with 23,000 seats in the downtown. Another new development in the UK camp was *The Cats' Pause*, an independent magazine which had just hit the newsstands and was undergoing some growing pains under the leadership of Hazard newsman Oscar Combs.

Meanwhile, on the hardwood floor, Robey was eager to play after missing most of his sophomore year. The Wildcats — led by a foursome clan of juniors Robey, Givens, Lee and Mike Phillips, and senior playmaker Larry Johnson — began their 1976-77 season on a very optimistic note with six consecutive wins, including the first game ever played at Rupp Arena, before losing to Utah in UKIT finals. The fans began discussing Kentucky's NCAA title hopes. Highly-ranked UK lost only two more games in the remainder of the regular season — both times to a tough Ray Mears-coached Tennessee squad (71-67 in overtime and 81-79).

When the regular season concluded, Kentucky and Tennessee both ended up in a first-place tie in the SEC. Both schools posted a 16-2 conference record. Since UT defeated Kentucky twice, it was awarded the league's automatic bid to the 32-team NCAA tourney and the Wildcats received an at-large bid.

In NCAA East Regional's opening round, Kentucky stopped Princeton coach Pete Carril and his Ivy League team 72-58. After beating VMI 93-78, the Wildcats faced North Carolina and its four-corner trademark offense in the regional finals. But the Tar Heels, led by future NBA All-Star Walter Davis' team-high 21 points, ended Kentucky's remarkable season with a seven-point victory. UK finished with a 26-4 mark. "My junior year's team was probably just as good as our senior year's team," said Robey.

 The Wildcats were not very successful against arch-rival Tennessee during Robey's four-year tenure at Kentucky. At the time the Vols featured two superstars — Ernie Grunfeld and Bernard King — and went to the NCAA tournament a couple

of times (1976 and '77).   At one point, UT even defeated Kentucky five straight times, including a 1976 controversy which saw Tennessee illegally switching its free throw shooter in an overtime thriller in Lexington. Overall, Robey managed to come out a winner only three times in eight tries against the Vols with two taking place during UK's NCAA championship season.

Regarding the heated Kentucky-Tennessee rivalry, which has subdued considerably in recent years, Robey said, "I can remember the Ernie and Bernie show of Bernard King and Ernie Grunfeld who were down there. They were probably the two greatest players of all time for Tennessee. I mean those were two guys who carried mediocre players along with them. We always had a tough time with them. I can remember Grunfeld came to Memorial Coliseum and scored 51 points (actually 43) one night on us. (The series) was always one of our big games every year."

Former Tennessee coach Ray Mears, the seventh winningest coach in SEC history with a 278-112 mark, recalled several interesting stories in the UK-UT rivalry.   Unlike other coaches, the flamboyant Mears — who once charged that UK played "karate" defense in mid-1970s — was fairly successful against the Wildcats, posting a 15-15 record against coaches Adolph Rupp and Joe B. Hall.

"The Kentucky-Tennessee rivalry is a lot of things," Mears told Middlesboro's *The Daily News*. "The main thing is that we probably wanted to beat Kentucky better than anyone else in the league. Or players felt that way. We were mentally prepared.

"The most interesting moments we had with Joe Hall — we almost got him fired — were during the time we beat Kentucky five straight times ...... It's an interesting story. Bernard King was a freshman when we got beat up (in Lexington) by three points (actually six). We were walking off the floor and somebody pitched a lighted cigarette and it hit (King) in the face. He got mad and started to go up after this guy. Stu Aberdeen, my assistant, tackled King and we got him under control and took him into the locker room.

"Somebody from a Lexington newspaper was going to say something when Bernard King said, 'I want to tell you something. As long as I'm playing for the University of Tennessee, you're never going to beat us.' From that point on, that's five ballgames, and we won them all. He lived up to his word. Bernard King had a lot to do with those wins.

"I give Joe Hall a lot of credit (for his career success) even though

I beat him seven times and he beat me three. That's a pretty good percentage, but Joe Hall won a national title, finished second place in the country, and won the NIT."

As for King, who was UT's first black All-American, he advanced to the NBA, leaving UT after his junior year. The New York (now New Jersey) Nets selected the 6-7 forward as its top pick in the 1977 NBA draft.

Before moving to the 24,535-seat Thompson-Boling Arena in 1987, UT played its home games at Stokley Athletics Center. The 12,700-seat gym, which was the home of the Vols from 1967 to 1988, is "a little old place and when you come out of this tunnel, rotten oranges were being thrown at you," Robey recalled. "It was a tough gym to play in because of the noise level. You know now they are in that big arena which probably is a totally different atmosphere, very similar to us leaving Memorial Coliseum and going to Rupp Arena.   It's two different types of gyms."

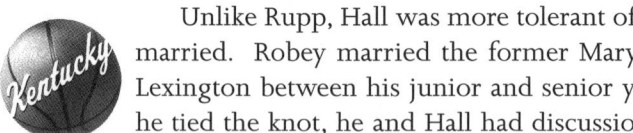

Did he ever break a team rule while at UK? Robey was asked.

"You put me on the spot there," he laughed, looking at the author. "Well, I'm sure I may have snuck out on a date here or there and broken a rule or two, but I wasn't one of the bad actors. The game meant so much to me that the rules really were pretty lenient as far as when you had to be there and when you didn't. You know (the phrase) like 'boys will always be boys,' and I probably was a boy every now and then."

Unlike Rupp, Hall was more tolerant of his players getting married. Robey married the former Mary Diane McCord of Lexington between his junior and senior years at UK. Before he tied the knot, he and Hall had discussions.

"Are you sure this is what you want to do?" Hall wondered.   The coach was frank with Robey and wanted to make sure that player knew what he was getting into.

On his meeting with Hall, Robey said, "I just let him know that I was getting married and that I was going to have to be living off campus. You know I had to rent an apartment."

But, after his UK career, they eventually divorced. "That marriage didn't work out," said Robey, who has since remarried. "I think a lot of it was just because we were young. Neither one of us knew where we were going with our lives. And the next year (in 1978) I was getting ready to go into the NBA. It wasn't something that really suited both of us."

Robey said they remained good friends. "I see her every now and then in Lexington and she's remarried, doing good. I'm remarried doing good. So it all worked out." Robey and his wife, Bonnie, who is from Ohio, have a son.

 While most UK fans agreed Joe B. Hall was a good coach, some felt that he should've done more with the talent he had at Kentucky. That attitude bothers Robey, who felt Hall should have had more respect in what he has accomplished by taking over a pressure-packed post previously held by legendary Adolph Rupp. Afterall, Hall compiled an overall coaching record of 297-100 in his 13 years at Kentucky, winning eight SEC regular season titles. Besides capturing two national championships (NCAA and NIT) and making two other NCAA Final Four appearances, Hall is also ranked fifth among the all-time victory leaders at SEC schools.

"It is frustrating to me because if you really look at his record he had a great career and anybody who takes over after a legend like Adolph Rupp or a John Wooden (deserves more respect). Look how the coaches have struggled at UCLA (since Wooden retired)," Robey said. "I don't think people have really given Joe Hall the credit he deserves and I feel like coach Hall realized the game had passed him and he retired at the right time. I'm a Joe Hall supporter."

 Many folks liked to compare Robey to then-NBA star Dave Cowens because of their similar aggressive playing style. And he didn't mind the comparison. In fact, he enjoyed it and his childhood hero was none other than the 6-9 center Cowens, who is originally from Newport, Ky.

Robey said people compared him with Cowens probably because of "my rugged style of play and giving the 110 percent effort in going after loose balls and playing that physical type of game. As a kid, he was my idol. I would go out on the playgrounds and try to be the next Dave Cowens."

And later when Robey was playing as a promising rookie for the Indiana Pacers, he had a chance conversation with player-coach Cowens of the Boston Celtics after an early-season matchup. "I can remember, after the game, walking off the floor when Dave came up to me and said, 'Rick, I want to tell you something. You will be a Celtic within the next six weeks.'"

Cowens' prediction turned out to be true. Robey, who was NBA's third pick overall in the 1978 Draft, was sent packing to Boston. The struggling Celtics — who had fired coach Tom Sanders after a poor 2-12 start and named Cowens as their new mentor — finished the campaign with a 29-53 mark. At the time, it was Boston's worst season since 1950. Robey completed his rookie season with a 10.4-point average in 79 games with the Pacers and the Celtics.

However, it was a different story in the following season of 1979-80. The tradition-rich Celtics started to win again, just like the old times. With new coach Bill Fitch and rookie forward by the name of Larry Bird, Boston bounced back in a surprising fashion, recording a stunning 32-game improvement over the previous season. The Celtics, who finished first in the Atlantic Division with a 61-21 mark, saw their NBA title hopes fade away as Philadelphia knocked out the Celtics 4-1 in the Eastern Conference finals. Statistically, it would turned out to be Robey's best season in his eight-year NBA career, averaging 11.5 points.

That season marked the beginning of NBA's famous Larry and Magic show. The exciting show of superstars Larry Bird and Magic Johnson invigorated the sagging NBA and they were rivals for 12 years before retiring in the early 1990s. Said Robey, "The NBA was struggling in (TV) ratings in the early 1980s. I feel like he and Larry Bird were the two guys that turned the NBA around." (In 1996, Magic returned to the Los Angeles Lakers for a brief 36-game stint before quitting for the second time. He had previously retired from his playing career because he tested positive for the virus that causes AIDS.)

 Robey, a key member of Boston's NBA championship team in 1981 as a backup center to Robert Parish, spent nearly five years with the Celtics. He said those were his happiest years in the NBA. "I feel like I played for probably the best franchise that you could play for in professional sports as far as basketball is concerned with the Celtics," Robey said. "The tradition is the same there as it is here in Kentucky for college. So I was lucky."

He also made close friends, including Bird, who was from the small rural town of French Lick in southern Indiana. Now the head coach of the Indiana Pacers, Bird was also Robey's roommate on road trips for four years.

Robey has a favorite NBA story about Bird when the latter was a rookie. One evening during the exhibition season in the fall of 1979, both Robey and Bird decided to grab a bite, dining in a nice restaurant while on a road trip in New York. They were very hungry and ordered the same menu — a juicy steak dinner. Of course, before leaving the establishment, they ended up paying the meal ticket which turned out to be more than reasonable. The conservation, as Robey recalled, went something like this:

"Larry, you know, we got to leave a tip on this and it's $50 plus the tip," Robey told his teammate after finishing their meal.

"Fifty dollars! Hell, I ain't paying!" said the shocked rookie. "We should get the dishes and everything for that amount."

Looking back, Robey explained Bird "wasn't used to it" because he hailed from a rural environment. He was an ordinary country boy with simple taste. Still, "he was a real pleasure to be a close friend."

Because of their friendship, Robey got a closeup view of a rising superstar. He saw how Bird handled his fame and the demanding fans. The former Wildcat standout said many folks misunderstood Bird for his actions or attitude. "I think sometimes people say, 'Oh, Bird isn't very friendly to people,' " Robey commented, "but you got to realize someone of his magnitude or a Michael Jordan or a Magic Johnson, you never have any time to yourself. There are certain times of the day when you are eating dinner or you are trying to get something done, you might not be as friendly as you ought to be.

"Anybody who ever says Larry Bird is not a very nice person, I always say, 'Well, you ought to get to know him because he is really a good person.' So it is hard for everybody to like him. You know you aren't going to please everybody. If you try to please everybody, you are never going to make it. My wife gets on me. She said, 'You can't tell everybody yes.' Sometimes you have to say no because you try to do everything you can. You have to think about your family and your own time."

Ironically, it was Bird who once embarrassed star Dan Issel of Denver when both played in the NBA. According to *Parting Shots*, a 1985 book written by Issel (with Buddy Martin), Bird was somewhat rude and didn't acknowledge the young fan Issel had brought along after a game so that she could ask the popular Celtic superstar for his autograph. Issel said in the book that he was doing it as a favor for her father.

During his NBA career, Robey got to meet his former college teammates. Kevin Grevey, who played in the NBA for 10 years, including the first eight for the Washington Bullets, was one of them. Sometimes they hang around and talk about the good old times. They occasionally get together at Grevey's popular restaurant in the Washington, D.C., area. "Kevin and I used to get together and most of the time it was after the game," Robey said. "He would take me out to his restaurant. Kevin was such a down-to-earth guy. He and I got along real well."

Red Auerbach, who proudly smokes his trademark cigar, is truly an NBA legend. The former Boston head coach is the one who pioneered one of pro basketball's greatest dynasties, directing the Celtics to nine NBA titles in the 1950s and 1960s. With a 938-479 mark, he was once the league's winningest coach of all time for many years until Lenny Wilkens topped the record during the 1994-95 season. In 1997, when former UK coach Rick Pitino took over the Celtics as coach and president, Auerbach moved up in the front office and was named the vice-chairman of the board. He had previously served as the club's president.

When Robey was at Boston, he had many discussions with Auerbach, who played an active role in the front office. "Red was involved with the team when I was there," said the ex-Wildcat. "When I renegotiated my second contract, my dad and I went into his office, sat down and came to an agreement on an amount, and it was done. That's the type of person Red was. I had one more year on my contract and Boston wanted to talk to me about an extension.

"(The contract discussion) wasn't real difficult. I used (agent) Larry Fleisher to negotiate my first contract, but really on the second contract it just came down to what your market value was and to what similar players were making. They have standard contracts that you sign and you just fill in the blanks. So Red Auerbach was a fun person to be around.

"Red was good (to trust) and Red has pulled off some of the greatest trades of all time. I still say my trade (in 1983) to Phoenix for Dennis Johnson was probably one of the best trades for Boston in its history." Johnson, a two-time All-NBA performer at Phoenix and Seattle, later helped Boston win two NBA championships in the 1980s.

Joe B. Hall served as the head coach at Kentucky for 13 years, winning nearly 300 games. Hall guided the Wildcats like a military sergeant, according to Rick Robey, who liked his coach's disciplinary approach.

Photo by Rogers Photography

 For Robey, the summer of 1983, meanwhile, was not a very happy time. Heading for the deserts of Arizona, he didn't want to leave Boston. He loved the Celtics and had made many friends. Larry Bird wasn't too happy about the trade either. He said losing Robey was like losing a brother.

Robey's three years at Phoenix would be the worst of his basketball career. "When I got to Phoenix, I had a lot of injuries and a lot of problems with my knees and my Achilles' tendon," said Robey, who sometimes struggled with his weight. "So I caught a lot of heat out there. It wouldn't be the most enjoyable three years of my life and plus I just had my total hip replacement (in December of 1995). That was due to my days at Phoenix."

His stay at Phoenix led to a reunion of two former Wildcats. Robey, who made Lexington his summer home during his NBA career, and Phoenix guard Kyle Macy got to spend some time together. That made playing for the Suns more bearable.

"It was nice to see Kyle, but I'd have much rather probably started in the cold weather of Boston," he said. "It was always nice to get back with one of your old teammates and be able to play. (But) the Phoenix trade for me was a very difficult trade. I was disappointed in the trade because I had close friends — Bird, Quinn Buckner, Parish, (Kevin) McHale, all those guys I had played with. We had a good group of guys."

With ex-NBA star playmaker K.C. Jones taking over the Celtics as the new head coach, Robey understood why the team made the deal with Phoenix. "I could understand K.C. Jones' (situation). K.C. and I were real close. I think if I'd stayed there and K.C. didn't play me, I'd have been upset. And if he did play me, he might have caught some heat. So the trade was probably the right thing for the Celtics."

About a couple of months after 1985-86 campaign ended, the Phoenix Suns decided not pick up the final year of Robey's contract. Although he later rejected a lucrative offer to play in Italy, Robey's playing days were over. He retired from NBA at a relatively young age of 30.

 Now a Louisville-based real estate agent and a publisher of popular sports calendars, Robey still follows UK basketball religiously. In 1989, he even attended the news conference on the UK campus when Kentucky hired New York Knicks coach Rick Pitino. Robey has some revealing thoughts on various subjects.

On Kentucky's punishment by the NCAA in 1989: "I felt bad. The sad part about it is normally when a school gets penalized, it is for things that were done before the kids who are there. I know you have to have some governmental thing like the NCAA overseeing the colleges, but I feel like some of their policies are a little bit too stringent. You know it has caused some problems, but Rick Pitino has come in and totally revived Kentucky Basketball."

On differences between former UK coaches Rick Pitino and Joe B. Hall: "They are two types of coaches. Rick Pitino is a very excitable-type coach. I think he is more of a coach of this day and age. He knows how to communicate with the kids of today and you know Pitino would have been a fun coach to play for. I'd had an 18-foot jump shot (Robey laughed). I think Joe Hall was good for his day and I think Rick Pitino is good for today.

"I don't know if I was a huge Rick Pitino fan when he first got here, but I have become a huge Rick Pitino fan. If my son had the opportunity to play for someone, I think Rick would be the type I would like to see him play for. He would instill the right things in a young kid."

On NBA players' multi-million dollar contracts: "Well, it is us, the fans, who are paying for it. We are paying to go to see them. We are paying extra for the milk and food we buy. I think it has gotten outrageous. I mean I was the third player picked in the NBA Draft in 1978 and I had the largest contract signed up until that time for $1.1 million (in a five-year contract). Ten years later, the third player picked in the draft signed for $64 million. Think about it. That's a lot over a 10-year period. It's got to stop somewhere. I mean that is just too much money. Something's wrong."

GOOSE

In the spring of 1997 in sunny Orlando, Fla., where ex-Wildcat star Jack Givens was residing and working as the color analyst for the Magic Television Network and Sunshine Cable Network, he admitted that he was hoping that then-UK coach Rick Pitino would take a similar post for the NBA's Orlando Magic.

"I would have loved to have seen him come here," Givens said. "He's a great basketball coach. That would've been great to have Pitino here. I know the Magic would have liked to have had him."

Pitino declined Orlando's overtures and eventually accepted a reported 10-year, $68 million offer from Boston to coach the Celtics. Givens doesn't "blame him for taking the offer the Celtics gave him. A lot of people (Wildcat fans) are disappointed that he left Kentucky, but I think everybody understands. Hey, you've gotta jump on a situation like that, particularly with a team like the Boston Celtics. They have great tradition. They have the support. They are going to be good again soon. He has his work cut out for him. No question about that. But they are going to be a very good basketball team and it is going to come a lot quicker because he is there."

The Magic later hired a big-name coach in then 66-year-old Chuck Daly when they signed him to a three-year pact worth $15 million. Daly

— who was working as a commentator with Turner Sports before taking the Magic job — once guided the Detroit Pistons to two NBA titles, and directed the gold medal-winning Dream Team in the 1992 Olympics.

 Nicknamed "Goose," Givens is best known for his outstanding 41-point performance in Kentucky's national championship victory over Duke in 1978. His output came within three points of tying an NCAA record for most points scored in a championship game. (Bill Walton of UCLA holds the all-time championship game record for 44 points, set in 1973 against Memphis State. Bill Goodrich, also of UCLA, is second with 42 points against Michigan in 1965.)

For Givens, a two-time All-American forward, it was his last game as a Wildcat. He was a senior. His UK career-high 41 points placed him on the front cover of *Sports Illustrated*. The weekly magazine appropriately titled its cover "The Goose Was Golden." Looking back, the 6-4 Givens — who usually scored in the 18-22 point range during his senior year — said UK coach Joe B. Hall didn't devise a special game plan for him in the title game.

"I was surprised because you don't expect to score that many points in a game like that," Givens said. "I think I was very relaxed even though it was a very pressurized game. I think the 41 points was an indication of that and we didn't discuss any strategies that were geared to me. We didn't do that for any player in any game."

Losing Duke coach Bill Foster told the sportswriters that Givens "scored from everywhere. He beat us every conceivable way. He made everything he threw up. I don't think anybody scored that many points on us all year. He just had a fantastic game."

Since UK earlier had defeated coach Eddie Sutton's quick Arkansas club 64-59 behind Givens' game-highs 23 points and nine rebounds in the national semifinals, the Wildcats felt more secured about their title clash with the youthful Blue Devils, according to Givens. Because of that, he was able to play relaxed basketball.

"Having beaten what I thought was the best team (Arkansas) other than ourselves in the country, I just felt we were better than Duke," he said. "We were prepared. We were on top of our game. I didn't think there was a whole lot Duke could do to beat us. I was as comfortable going into that game with our team as I was in any game because once we got to the final game, I knew we were going to win that one. I just felt very confident that we were going to win."

After the 94-88 victory over Duke at St. Louis' aging Checkerdome ended a tension-filled campaign burden with extraordinary high expectations, the Wildcat players and coaches celebrated.

"Well, the thing that leaves the biggest impression on me, the feeling or the moment, was when the final horn sounded and just looking up at the scoreboard, knowing we were on top and we had won it all," Givens recalled. "(It's) the feeling of relief — thousands of pounds on our shoulders had been lifted when James Lee dunked the ball through to end the game and when the final horn sounded. I think that's the feeling of saying, 'Hey, it's over. We did it. So let's go home.' It was a pressure-packed year and we were expected to win. Nothing short of winning (the championship) would've been enough."

 When Givens was 17 years old, attending Lexington's Bryan Station High School, he seriously considered UK's longtime rival Tennessee. UT coach Ray Mears wanted him badly. Very badly. Had the coach signed Givens, he would have had a super squad composed of future All-Americans in Givens, Bernard King and Ernie Grunfeld.

"They recruited me very aggressively," Givens said of UT. "The only basketball camp I ever went to was at the University of Tennessee and I was very familiar with the people there — Ray Mears, who was coaching at the time, and Stu Aberdeen, who was one of the assistants. I would have probably gone there had I not gone to Kentucky. We (UT) could've had a very good basketball team because they were good in their own right."

Tennessee's ball-control offense didn't hinder Givens from considering the Vols as one of his top collegiate choices. "It didn't bother me at all," he said. "I knew about the program. I had seen a basketball game there and I knew the style they played. That wasn't a problem. I didn't think a whole lot about it."

However, in April of 1974, Givens, the newly-chosen Kentucky's "Mr. Basketball," signed with UK. A prep All-American and twice All-State, Givens guided Bryan Station to a 76-17 mark in three years. "I felt Kentucky was the best school for me," he recalled. "They were the best basketball school around and it was an added bonus that they were right there in Lexington. I didn't really want to go far away to play basketball. I was

Kentucky's Jack Givens (21) drives to the basket as a Kansas defender approaches in UK's 90-63 victory at Rupp Arena in 1976. Wildcat Tim Stephens looks on in the background.

Photo by Rogers Photography

close to my family and I wanted them to have an opportunity to see me play.

"Also at that time I really had never flown on an airplane so I just didn't feel comfortable going far away and having to fly. Of course, since that time, I obviously have flown a lot, but one of the main reasons (I picked UK) was I wanted to stay close to home." With Givens spending his college years in Lexington, it allowed him to remain close with his mother, and nine brothers and sisters. His father died when he was in junior high.

 Before Givens inked with Kentucky, the school didn't have many blacks on its roundball team in the early 1970s. Like most southern schools, though, UK was slowly changing its image as an all-white basketball squad. While coach Joe B. Hall only had one black — Reggie Warford — on his first

team at UK, he recruited more blacks, signing Merion Haskins and Larry Johnson. By the fall of 1974, when the preseason practice began, the Wildcats had five blacks, including freshmen Givens and James Lee, a signee from Lexington's Henry Clay High.

Even though UK was practically next door to his Lexington home, Givens didn't follow Wildcat basketball when he was growing up. That's because "they didn't have any black players. It was difficult for me to look at the players they had there and try to picture myself as one of those guys," Givens explained. "It was easier for me to look around the country, particularly in pro sports, and see some of the guys like Dr. J (Julius Erving) and Kareem Abdul-Jabbar at that time. I looked at (the superstars), but I really didn't have a hero at the time.

"I didn't follow sports very much when I was growing up and only started concentrating on basketball when I was in high school at Bryan Station. So I really didn't have anyone that I watched. As I started watching more and see a little bit more UK basketball, the guy that I really kind of liked was Dan Issel. I had seen him play. Dan was a great basketball player.

"But Tom Parker probably was the guy I looked at. He was a left-handed player, just like me. He shot a lot of jump shots, a lot of corner shots. (He was) the same kind of player I was. So he really was the only University of Kentucky player that I watched at all. But it was difficult for me to look at UK and say, 'Hey, I want to be like these guys,' because they were so different than me."

The 6-7 Parker, as you will recall, starred at Kentucky in the early 1970s as a two-time All-SEC choice. In Adolph Rupp's last season at UK, Parker received the SEC Player of the Year award from the Associated Press.

In choosing the Wildcats, Givens said Hall's aggressive attitude of making the blacks feel more welcome at UK played a key role in his decision. "Only until coach Hall got there did I even consider UK as a possible choice because of the reputation that Adolph Rupp had. He was not really an advocate of black basketball players," he said. "So that was another reason I really didn't consider Kentucky as an option. Once coach Hall got there, he went out of his way to recruit black athletes. I think the whole attitude was starting to change at that time."

The usually low-key Givens said he is very pleased that he is a member of a select group at Kentucky. He is among the first five black basketball players to graduate from UK, joining Warford, Haskins, Johnson and

Lee. "That is a source of pride," Givens said. "I know changes had to be made. We all took a big step in going to the University of Kentucky because there were some other schools that we could have very easily gone to that had a track record and history with minority players. We took a chance in going there because we didn't know what it was like and we heard it from both sides — black and white — (about whether) we should or shouldn't go there because of that situation. So I'm very proud to have been a part of the change."

And shortly after Kentucky had chosen Orlando "Tubby" Smith as the first African-American to head its men's basketball program, Givens was obviously moved that UK had hired a rising superstar coach who happened to be a black. "Well, I think it's wonderful," he said. "I think it's long past due not only at the University of Kentucky, but a lot of places. In a lot of fields (jobs), you (should) take the best person for the job regardless of what color he is and it's too bad that has to be an issue — the skin color in any walk of life. So, I'm very, very proud. I think we took a big step."

Since many folks unfairly, including some writers who have never met Rupp, like to portray the Baron of the Bluegrass as a racist, Givens said he would have liked to sit down and have a nice talk with Rupp. Although he had met the ailing Rupp briefly a couple of times during Givens' early UK days, he didn't really know the man. Because of that, Givens didn't want to make a judgment. What he knew about Rupp was what he had heard from other sources about the legendary coach. What he had heard about Rupp wasn't very flattering, though.

"I never did have a chance to talk to him, get to know him," Givens said. "Sometimes I wish I had the chance. I would've taken advantage of opportunities to sit and talk to him and hear his side of everything. But, by the time I got there, he was not in real good health. So he didn't come to the coliseum very often. He didn't come to his office (at Memorial Coliseum) very often. I just didn't have a chance to meet him but a couple of times."

On Dec. 10, 1977, only minutes after eventual national champion Kentucky defeated host Kansas, Rupp's alma mater, 73-66, the "Man in the Brown Suit" died of cancer of the spine. Rupp was 76.

Since his father had died, Givens didn't have a true male role model at home during his high school days. But there was one person whom he admired and respected: Bobby Barlow, the head basketball coach at Bryan Station. Currently retired from coaching, Barlow is involved in the construction business.

"Bobby was a good man, a good Christian man," Givens commented. "He was a caring man. He cared about his players more than just as athletes and as basketball players. So I respected coach Barlow. He probably had as big an influence on me as any coach I've ever had. Of course, during those years, you're very impressionable. My father wasn't at home. So he (Barlow) was in some ways a father figure or a male authority figure which I didn't have. I think he had as much impression on me as any coach I ever had. I still see him a lot when I'm in Lexington. If I had a problem today, I feel I could call and talk to him about it."

After Givens went to UK, another male figure played a prominent role in his life — Joe B. Hall. Like Givens is with Barlow today, he is comfortable discussing problems with the former Kentucky mentor if he needs to see someone.

"I feel that way about coach Hall as well," Givens said. "Particularly now that he is out of coaching, I think the relationship I have with coach Hall is probably better now than it was then because he is not a coach and he doesn't have to be the coach. He's just a friend now. He's a totally different person having gotten out of the situation where he has to win games and the pressure that goes along with that."

Other than his 41-point outburst in Kentucky's national title victory, Givens said his most exciting moment at UK came during his freshman year. That was in March of 1975 when Kentucky upset No. 1 Indiana 92-90 in Dayton, Ohio, to advance to the Final Four. And the post-game celebration was especially sweet for Givens, who had eight points and six rebounds in 29 minutes of action as a reserve. Riding the team bus on the memorable Dayton-to-Lexington trek on I-75, he saw hundreds of Wildcat fans cheering them on once it crossed a bridge on the Ohio River near Cincinnati.

"That was without a doubt one of the best moments I've ever had in sports," Givens said. "I think that was, maybe to some extent, even better than winning it all (in 1978) because that was the first real experience

I had had at winning on that level.

"Once we got to the state line, we were escorted (by Kentucky State Police) all the way to Lexington from northern Kentucky, seeing the people as we rode down on I-75. On every overpass there were people with signs and in the fields along the road. (There were) cars behind us and the people cleared the road and let us just roll right on through.

"You know it doesn't rank obviously with winning the national championship because that's what you play for, but the experience and the excitement of the fans (were wonderful). While we were good, we really were not expected to make it to the Final Four. We weren't expected to beat Indiana in that game because they had beaten us pretty badly earlier that year. So we kind of overachieved. We did a little bit more than everybody thought."

Added Knoxville broadcaster Denny Trease, who covered the Wildcats in the 1970s as the TV play-by-play man, "There was just so much emotion in that game. And the Cats were so ready to play and, of course, earlier that year there was the whole thing with Bobby Knight and the little slap (he did on coach Hall's head in UK's 98-74 loss). It just seemed like the Cats were not going to lose that game. They just refused to lose it."

 When Adolph Rupp was coaching, some of his players couldn't stand him. And you almost could say the same thing about Joe B. Hall. While Givens usually — not always — had a good player-coach relationship with Hall, several players had a rocky or up-and-down relationship with Rupp's successor. That's because much of Hall's rigid coaching style came from Rupp, according to Givens.

"Coach Hall learned from Adolph Rupp, and from what I understand, Rupp was very dominating, domineering type coach who wanted things done his way and only his way," Givens said. "If you didn't do it his way, you know, you heard about it. I think coach Hall was the same way, and for some players that's okay and for some it's not. I think it's the responsibility of the coach to change his style to get the most out of a player and in that day and age, the coaches didn't change. It was their way or no way at all. So I think that's the reason why a lot of players, including myself, had a tenuous relationship with coach Hall at times."

During Givens' freshman year, his teammates advised him not to take every word Hall said at face value. Givens said he learned that Hall

Tennessee's colorful Ray Mears, shown in a UK-UT contest in the mid-1970s, was one of the Southeastern Conference's toughest coaches. Jack Givens said he would've gone to Tennessee had Kentucky not shown any interest in him.

Photo by Rogers Photography

could be very firm and that he was even tougher on a star player.

"He was that way with Kevin Grevey, who was the star of that team," Givens commented. "I think, for the other guys, if they see coach Hall getting on the star player and kind of keeping his thumb on that player, they know he's gonna expect that (effort) from them. It was just coach Hall's way.

"He was that way with me after my freshman year. I was a very sensitive player, but I learned just to kind of let it go in one ear and out the other. If you take everything he says 100 percent to heart, you're not going to make it.

"I think that really hurt a lot of players who played for coach Hall. He was pretty hard on some guys and probably harder than he needed to be. I think that really hurt a lot of guys and kept them from being as good as they possibly could have been."

Since Hall retired his post from UK, he became involved in television broadcasting. Besides working at a Lexington bank as a senior vice-president (from which he later retired in 1997), Hall served as a basketball color analyst for the ABC network in the late 1980s. He also did TV work with the UK basketball network. With his television job, he got to travel and observe many practices by different teams. Partly because of that, Hall changed his attitude toward various methods used by other coaches. In other words, he became more tolerant of various coaching philosophies.

"He has accepted the fact that there are other ways to get it done, not just his way," Givens said of Hall. "I've talked to coach Hall a lot of times since he got out of coaching and particularly when he went into broadcasting. He was in broadcasting, going to other practices and seeing how other coaches do things and how successful they have been doing things their way. It was a revelation to him that there were other ways to do it and other ways to relate to players, which is good. That's especially true now with the way guys are."

 There are many stories about Hall. Some are funny. Some are hilarious. Givens has a favorite story about his coach. He said it happened during the 1978 Final Four when tournament favorite Kentucky was feeling pressured and tense as it prepared to face Arkansas in the national semifinals. Here's the story as told by Givens:

"We were sitting in the locker room and nobody was saying anything. I mean it was very quiet — you could hear a pin drop. We were just so tight. We were wondering what the coaches were going to do and what they were going to say when they came into the locker room. Coach Hall and the coaches came in and just kind of looked around and didn't say anything. There was a big garbage can in the room with a big trash bag in it. We were waiting to hear what he was going to say. And he just went over to that garbage can and he climbed inside, stooped down in it, pulled the bag up over his head and just sat there.

"Now that's very uncharacteristic for coach Hall. We just thought he had flipped out. But he just did that. He got up out of the garbage can. He looked around the room and said, 'Go out and play basketball.' And that's what we did. It kind of relieved the pressure and it gave us something to laugh at. It took all the tension out of the air. We went out and played basketball. We got the job done. I've said time and time again, that's the best coaching job he's ever done. He did what had to be done at that time and he could've come in and discussed a lot of strategy. He could've talked to us about the teams we were playing. He could've done all of that and not gotten across to us what he did by doing that (garbage can act)."

During his UK career, especially the championship season when he was a senior, Givens followed the team rules. He respected them. Considered one of the basketball program's top goodwill ambassadors, he didn't want to embarrass his coach or the school. However, he sometimes broke curfew established by Hall. For Givens and his teammate James Lee, missing curfew wasn't considered a serious violation of the team rules since both players were from Lexington.

"We had curfew and a lot of times I would go to my mother's house and just stay home when I was supposed to be in (the Wildcat Lodge)," Givens recalled. "James would do the same thing. We would go home and just get away from everything. The coaches understood. You know we had the right to do that at that point because we didn't get in any trouble. We weren't doing anything wrong. We were just getting away from it. I would do stuff like that — break curfew at times.

"As far as any other team rules, I don't think I did anything really all that serious that I can remember. Of course, those are kind of things you try to forget. We were pretty structured. We were fairly in tune with what the rules were and what we had to do and what was expected of us. We knew anything that we did against what we were supposed to be doing was going to be a news-making item. We respected the program and we didn't want to do anything to hurt the program. I think we were pretty consistent with what we were supposed to do and didn't step out of line too often."

Givens finished his UK career as the school's second-leading all-time scorer with 2,038 points, ranking behind No. 1 Dan Issel. Since then, Givens has dropped to the No. 3 spot on the list as former UK All-American Kenny Walker scored 2,080 points in the mid-1980s under the coaching regimes of Hall and Eddie Sutton.

At UK's graduation exercises, Givens received the prestigious Sullivan Medallion from then-university president Dr. Otis Singletary. It is the highest award given to a student by the university. "I was just amazed," said Givens, who received a bachelor's degree in business. "I was just surprised, totally honored because it kind of took me out of the realm of basketball and placed me into the group with all the other seniors that year. I know my playing basketball had a lot to do with me winning that award, but I think the fact I was able to do some other things (helped). I graduated with fairly decent grades. I did a lot of things off the basketball court as far as community-related things. That's everything the Sullivan Medallion stands for.

"That goes beyond my (winning the) MVP of the NCAA tournament. It goes beyond winning the national championship. It goes beyond being an All-American. It goes beyond being the SEC Athlete of the Year. That award goes beyond all of that because it kind of takes you away from basketball, and gives you credit and recognition for things other than what you did on the basketball court."

All four seniors from UK's 1978 NCAA championship team had opportunities to perform in the NBA. They were drafted in either the first, second or third round. As expected, Givens, along with Robey, were selected in the first round. The Indiana Pacers picked Robey as the third pick overall, while the Atlanta Hawks chose Givens as the league's 16th pick. Seattle selected Lee in the second round. Phillips was chosen in the third round by New Jersey.

At Atlanta, coach Hubie Brown — who moved over to the Hawks after the Kentucky Colonels folded as the result of the 1976 NBA/ABA merger — placed Givens at guard because of his 6-4 size even though he played at forward in college. That made his adjustment in the NBA tougher. And he stayed in the league for only two years.

"I never did really get all that comfortable playing professional basketball," Givens said. "I enjoyed it, but not as much as I probably should have. I think back on it a lot. (I had) my opportunity to play professional basketball and I wish I had of taken more advantage of it. I didn't love it, which is what you have to do. You have to really enjoy it to be successful. I wasn't as successful as I would've liked to be.

"It was a tough adjustment being on the road, traveling and taking the initiative to do all the things that needed to be done. (While) playing at the University of Kentucky, everything is done for you. Your meals are prepared for you, your wake-up call, you know everything is so structured. When you go out on your own, you have to take care of all these things yourself. It takes a little while to really know there are other ways to do things to be successful. I mean you don't have to eat the same meal every-day before a game. You don't have to sleep the same way and you don't have to practice the same way.

"(After) being in a very structured program like the university, it takes some time to learn that. I wish I'd had another opportunity to play in the NBA because I think it would've made a difference, knowing a little bit more (about self-discipline) as I got older a few years after I played."

Like today's grueling NBA schedule, Givens went through a 82-game slate and he didn't care for that. He said traveling was the bad part and life as a NBA player can be lonely. He was away from his family in Lexington for the first time. "A lot of people think it's a great lifestyle, but it's very difficult to travel," Givens said. "(You) get up at 5 o'clock in the morning, travel to a city, play a game that night, get up early the next morning and move on to another city. It is very difficult. It is lonely. It takes some getting used to and I don't know if you really ever get used to it.

"You have to learn to make good decisions. You have to learn to budget your time. You have to learn to take care of yourself — make sure you eat right, sleep right and not stay up all night and not party. (You don't) do a lot of things that could very easily make you fall into that lifestyle."

In his two years with the Hawks, Givens averaged nearly seven points a game before he was selected by the new Dallas Mavericks in the 1980 NBA expansion draft. In the preseason camp at Dallas, according to Givens, he played well. However, coach Dick Motta and the Mavericks' officials thought otherwise. In their opinion, he wasn't good enough to make the team. So Givens had the biggest surprise of his basketball career. He was cut by the expansion team.

"It was a shock," Givens recalled, "because I had never been cut before. It was a very numb feeling. I didn't know what to think. I was embarrassed and I didn't understand why. I thought I had played fairly well with Dallas. I'd always been wanted and very welcomed on the teams I had played for (previously).

The Mavericks really didn't explain to Givens why he was cut. "They just said, 'We decided to go in another direction,' " Givens recalled. "You know, what does that mean? Can I stay and do something differently? But you don't get a chance (to do it again). It was just a strange feeling for me. It took a long time for me to recover from that because you just don't know why and what happened. It was just kind of a tough situation for me to deal with."

While Givens and Rick Robey played in the NBA, two of their teammates at Kentucky — Mike Phillips and James Lee — didn't make it. Phillips, however, had a successful pro basketball career in Spain for several years.

But Givens didn't quit his playing career. While pursuing his business opportunities, he continued to play pro basketball. He played overseas. His destination? Japan. Earlier, he became interested in the country when the Wildcats visited Japan on a seven-game tour in June of 1978.

"I was there for about two and a half years," Givens said of his post-NBA stint in Japan. "I was in a small town in the northern part of Japan called Akita. The team was owned by the Isuzu automobile company. All the teams over there are owned by various companies."

Givens wasn't the only ex-Wildcat to play in Japan. Fred Cowan and Larry Johnson also participated in the same league. "We played against each other," he said. "The main competition at the time was Larry Johnson's team. (They were) the best team over there. Fred Cowan's team was pretty good. Our team, before I got there, wasn't very good. So we got better when I was there."

Asked if he made more money in Japan than he did in the NBA? "No," Givens replied, "I sure didn't. They were just beginning to have American players come over. So the money wasn't as good as the NBA. It has gotten a lot better (since), so has the NBA for that matter. But there were some other business opportunities that opened up which I took advantage of. I went there with an opportunity to play ball and to do some other things I was interested in doing at the time."

 Givens is not particularly proud of Kentucky's highly-publicized problems with the NCAA in the late 1980s when the school was slapped with a severe three-year probation. He believes UK learned its lesson the hard way.

"You hear a lot of stories about infractions and (about) what did happen and what didn't happen," he said. "There had been other places that had done more (rules violations) and had been guilty of bigger crimes than the University of Kentucky. So it could be that the penalties were a little bit harsh.

"But I think at the time there were some things going on at the program that, as an ex-player there, I was not really proud of and I didn't want (any part of) it. I'm sorry it took going on a probation and those kind of sanctions to get the program straightened out. If it straightened out the program which it did, I don't feel bad about it.

"I mean I'm glad the program is back where it is today. I'm glad (Rick) Pitino was there because it needed someone strong. Someone with credibility to do what he's been able to do with the program. And it's good to know that after being down and going through some hard times, you can get back on top.

"So I was a little disappointed (with the NCAA sanctions), but I'm glad it happened if it served a purpose and I think it did."

In the early 1980s during a long break from Japan's basketball season, Givens would return to Kentucky. He became involved in radio and TV broadcasting. He did some high school basketball games in the Lexington area, including the state tournament. He also provided commentary on the Wildcat games for the UK television network.

Givens credited some folks at Lexington's WVLK Radio for helping him get started in the broadcasting field. "Guys like Ralph Hacker who gave me a job as a radio broadcaster back before I got into TV," he said. "Ralph and I worked together a lot doing games. Ralph gave me a lot of advice — a lot of little things that helped me out a lot. Dick Gabriel in Lexington (also helped). Dick's been around a long time. He and I worked radio and TV together early in my career. He gave me a lot of little lessons that make you a better broadcaster. I look at those days and look at those people. (They) were very instrumental in getting me started in broadcasting and got me interested in it." Hacker, who began broadcasting Wildcat games in 1971, is currently the play-by-play announcer on the UK Radio Network. Gabriel, meanwhile, is the sports director for Lexington's WKYT-TV (Channel 27).

As more people took notice of Givens' natural roundball knowledge on television, he received job offers to broadcast basketball games on regional or national basis. He has held positions as a color commentator with ESPN, Jefferson-Pilot Productions, USA Network, NBC Sports, Host Communications and Turner Sports.

In the late 1980s, Givens nearly landed a job with the Atlanta Hawks as a member of their broadcasting team. "I was trying to get into the NBA as a broadcaster," Givens said, "and had really pretty much secured a job with the Atlanta Hawks at the time but it kind of fell apart at the last minute."

However, nearly at the same time, the Orlando Magic, an expansion team, was searching for people to fill in on their TV and radio broadcasting teams. Givens, living in Lexington, called around and found out the name of the person who he needed to talk to about the Magic job: Pat Williams, the president and general manager of the Orlando club.

"I called Pat Williams on the phone and told him what I was interested in doing and I wanted to broadcast the games on TV," Givens said. "Pat asked me to send a tape of some of my work, which I did."

Williams, who is now Orlando's senior executive vice president, liked Givens' style and interviewed the Wildcat great. After he was told that he would be notified in two weeks whether he got the job or not, Givens nevertheless felt good about his chances. Instead of two weeks, the Magic quickly made the decision. Givens got the job in August of 1989. "It was a blessing to be able to have that job," Givens said. "I was needing something different than what I was doing in Lexington at the time. It has worked out very well. I have been here since."

Meanwhile, Williams, a long-time NBA executive, is well known for his promotional and marketing wizard and has written several books. Williams and his wife also have captured national attention as they have 18 children, including 14 adopted from several countries. "I have met most of them at least one time or another," Givens said of the children, adding that it would take a whole year to learn all about them.

Williams "does a lot of good things in the community," Givens said of his boss. "He's done a lot of wonderful things for this club and I don't think this team definitely would have been where it is today if he hadn't been a part of the team."

 One of the NBA's marquee players is Shaquille O'Neal of the Los Angeles Lakers. When O'Neal left LSU after his junior

season in 1992, he signed a reported seven-year, $42 million contract with Orlando and played four years with the Florida club. Givens, who became friends — not close — with O'Neal, was disappointed when the star went to the Lakers as a free agent in the summer of 1996. That meant Orlando probably wouldn't be able to avenge its Eastern Conference Finals loss — a four-game sweep — to the eventual champion Chicago Bulls, and duplicate its 60-22 mark of 1995-96, the third best in the league.

"I was surprised and disappointed," Givens said of Shaq's leaving the Magic. "Shaq is a great basketball player and obviously makes your team good. He is one of those franchise players that comes along just every so often. I was surprised he left because they were saying all along if the Magic matched the money (offer sheet) then you know he was going to stay. The Magic matched and would've done more than what their final offer was, but he evidently wanted to go to Los Angeles and we lost a great player.

"Another bad thing about losing Shaq is that he was a good guy in addition to being a great basketball player. It sent the team into a tailspin because you just don't recover from losing a guy like that. It was just unfortunate that we had to lose him." In their tumultuous first year without Shaq, which saw a players' revolt that forced the team to dismiss coach Brian Hill, the Magic compiled a 45-37 mark.

Givens was asked about Shaq's mansion-like house in Orlando. The former UK cager — who has visited the home — just smiled and said, "He's got a fairly large house. It has about 9,000 square feet or something like that."

 The 1996 NBA Draft saw a record 17 college underclassmen who were selected in the first round, including a couple of high school stars. Members of that elite group were Allen Iverson (from Georgetown), Marcus Camby (Massachusetts), Antoine Walker (Kentucky), Stephon Marbury (Georgia Tech), Shareef Abdur-Rahim (California), to name a few. In the 1997 draft, six early-entry prospects were taken among the first 10 spots. The 1998 draft saw eight underclassmen picked among the first 10 selections. While it may help or hinder NBA, Givens doesn't like the idea of college players leaving early for professional ranks. He believes they should wait and finish college.

"I would like for guys to stay in college," he said. "I think it is bet-

Kentucky's 1974 "Mr. Basketball,"
Jack Givens (21), goes up for a
field goal against Vanderbilt in SEC
action at Rupp Arena.

Photo by Rogers Photography

ter for the college game. The quality of the games in college has decreased because the experience of the players is not there as you have guys after their second and third year leaving to go to the NBA. I think it really hurts the college game.

"It hurts the pro game as well because you're getting guys in the league who are not as fundamentally sound. The quality of the NBA is down because you have expansion teams and you get more marginal players in there. And you're getting guys coming out of college who are not quite ready. If they stay around long enough, they're going to be ready. They are going to get better."

Givens said he wished there was some way to stop the influx of underclassmen to the NBA. But the league or the NCAA can't halt them for legal reasons. Over 30 years ago, both organizations had agreed that the

players couldn't turn pro until they finished four years of collegiate eligibility. In the early 1970s, the courts knocked down NCAA's agreement with
the NBA, saying the college players can go to professional ranks through
hardship cases. Eventually, the college players, regardless of their financial
situation, jumped to the NBA as they wished, just like a regular student
who decides to leave early to work for a large corporation. Unlike the mid-
1990s, the 1970s and '80s did not have a very large number of underclassmen heading for NBA (and the now-defunct ABA in early 1970s).

"You can't take away a guy's ability to earn money," Givens said of
the court rulings allowing the early-entry players. "Any time you go to
college, you put yourself in a position to make money. So who says you
have to go for four years in order to make money, earn the maximum
you're going to be able to make. There's nothing those guys can do staying in school that's going to enable them to make as much money as
they're going to make in the NBA. A degree is not going to change that so
(NCAA and NBA) really can't say you have to stay in school because it
would open all kinds of legal problems and that's not a call the league can
make."

Several former UK players, including Givens, attended the
1996 Final Four in New Jersey where Kentucky had captured
the NCAA title for the first time since 1978. Not surprisingly, Givens was very proud of his alma mater. "I was very
happy to have been there," said Givens, who happened to be at the right
place at the right time when the Orlando Magic had a date with the New
York Knicks. "Over the course of the years since I won it, I know how difficult it is to win. A lot of things have to happen for you to have a chance
to win. I mean being good is not necessarily all it takes. So it was a great
feeling for me to be there and see them win the game. I think that was a
team that wouldn't have been totally satisfied with anything less than winning (the championship) because they were a very good team. They had
been ranked No. 1 most of the season and they had done everything they
had to do to get there."

After the national title victory over Syracuse, Givens could have
gone to the UK dressing room, and congratulated the team. But he chose
not to do it. For one simple reason. He didn't want to take some of the
spotlight away from the deserving players and coaches.

"I didn't think it was appropriate and it was their night," explained

Givens. "It was their time. They needed to be able to experience that. I know I wouldn't have minded had some guys come to the locker room afterwards from the last time that Kentucky had won it. I didn't want to steal any of that (limelight). That was their moment and they needed to bask in that and enjoy it. So I left the game and went back to the hotel. I saw some guys at the hotel afterwards, but I pretty much removed myself from all of that (publicity)."

Well, you can say, for certain, that Givens was a much happier person than in 1984 when he attended the Final Four in Seattle. The confident UK, which boasted a massive frontline of 7-1 Sam Bowie, 6-11 Melvin Turpin and 6-8 Kenny Walker, got knocked out by Georgetown in a dismal shooting performance. The ice-cold Wildcats shot only nine percent in the second half as they dropped 53-40 to the Hoyas.

 Givens and his wife, the former Linda Thompson, whom he married in 1985, make their home in Windermere, Fla., near Orlando. They have one son (Jeremy) and one daughter (Jaimie Lynn). Mrs. Givens is a native of Paris, Ky., and once worked with the U.S. Secret Service.

"She's a stay-home mom now," Givens said of his wife. "She takes care of the kids. I love my family and my wife and my life as it is now."

Givens is very content with his life in Orlando. However, he knows he may not stay there forever. He wouldn't mind going back to Kentucky someday where he still has many immediate relatives, including his mother, living in the Bluegrass.

"The Lord hasn't told me where He wants me yet," said Givens, who in 1998 was an unsuccessful candidate for the assistant coaching job on Rick Pitino's Boston staff. "Right now, I'm happy being here. If the situation comes that I need to make another life change or I'm lead to a different place, then we'll make that decision at the time and make that move. I know from when I got the job here that being happy doesn't necessarily mean you have to be in a particular place because Orlando would have been the last place I would have thought I would end up. But I ended up here and I'm very happy that I did. So if it comes that I have to make another move, then I'm open for that just simply because of the experience I've had here."

BILLY THE KID

Billy Donovan as a coach?

No way, thought his former basketball coach Rick Pitino in the late 1980s. Pitino had never envisioned Donovan as a coach. He had serious reservations about his pupil's potential ability to coach. Pitino had coached the youngster at Providence and later in the NBA with the New York Knicks. He believed Donovan was too nice a person to enter the brutal profession of coaching in the college ranks.

Nevertheless, Pitino decided to gamble. Pitino asked Donovan to join him as a lowly graduate assistant on his staff at probation-ridden Kentucky in 1989 when he became the head coach of the Wildcats. That was after Donovan had informed Pitino of his interest in coaching and he has been the assistant at UK or the head coach elsewhere ever since.

"I just think that he felt like my personality wasn't one which a coach should have," said Donovan of Pitino. "I think coach Pitino always perceived me as being a good guy, you know, not very confrontational. I don't think coach Pitino ever had anticipated me getting after guys, pushing guys and motivating guys. Coach Pitino always saw me in a player's light.

"On the floor, I thought I was vocal (as a player), but I wasn't probably over vocal. I didn't talk a whole lot. I probably tried to lead by example. (Pitino) probably realized to be a coach you needed to be a lot more vocal. I think I was always capable of that, but when I was playing that just wasn't my personality. So he kind of discouraged me a little bit from it and I told him I wanted to do it. Maybe he said that to see how badly I wanted to coach."

 According to Donovan, now the head coach at Florida, Pitino's offer to come to Kentucky wasn't really surprising since he is well-known for his loyalty to his players and assistants. They had discussed Donovan's future. Since he wasn't very happy with his job at an investment banking firm on Wall Street in New York, he decided to take the UK position. "I just didn't want to (work on Wall Street) and that's when I contacted coach Pitino and told him I had a strong desire to get into coaching," Donovan said. "He spoke to me about the Kentucky situation."

Pitino, however, warned him that the graduate assistant job didn't really pay anything and required a lot of hard work and long hours. Donovan said no problem. "I wasn't making very much money in 1989," Donovan recalled from his office at Florida's Stephen C. O'Connell Center. "(The salary) was like the equivalent of a scholarship. I don't know what it was. It wasn't very much I can tell you that, but I can also tell you that coach Pitino wasn't going to let me starve either. So coach took care of me. He made sure I was taken care of.

"I didn't really think I was going to make a living in coaching and coach Pitino was very honest with me. He said to me, 'You work hard and people in this program move on, coaches move on, I will move you up. But you need to learn and you need to understand what coaching entails.' That is basically what he did. Anytime anybody moved, he moved me up the ladder all the way through (as associate coach at UK before becoming the head coach at Marshall)."

As far as everyday living expenses in Lexington are concerned, it was really his wife, Christine, a New York native, who provided most of the financial support when he started out coaching. The couple married in the summer of 1989, shortly after he took the UK post.

"From a financial standpoint, my wife really was probably providing for us," said Donovan. "She was a school teacher and we lived in an apartment. The apartment on a monthly basis cost more than I was making in a month, so she took care of us."

Besides his coaching duties, helping Pitino and his other assistants, Donovan took some classes. He enrolled in courses such as business management and sports administration. "I took some classes, but it really became very difficult just with the hours I was putting in (coaching)," he said.

Donovan's first season at Kentucky was probably the toughest of his UK tenure. Besides learning to coach in his new graduate assistant job, he had to adjust his new life off the court. Lexington was the first southern city he had lived in. Like Pitino, he was from New York. He also had become a husband. He had many things to adjust. The team also didn't have many scholarship players to work with. Several standouts like LeRon Ellis, Chris Mills and Sean Sutton had departed Kentucky because of a recruiting scandal which left the school in chaos. Folks were writing off the 1989-90 season. The tradition-rich Wildcats could not play in front of television cameras on a live basis. They could not participate in a post-season tournament. With only eight scholarship players on the team, none taller than 6-7, most people had predicted the Wildcats would be lucky to win seven or eight games. They believed, at best, Kentucky would finish with a horrible 8-20 mark. That's how Donovan began his coaching career with a dark cloud hovering over UK's tarnished basketball program.

But Pitino, with his never-ending optimism and enthusiasm, and his staff could see the light at the end of tunnel. They had high hopes for the program. They worked, worked and worked. Endlessly. Most of the players who stayed, including John Pelphrey, Deron Feldhaus, Richie Farmer, Sean Woods and Reggie Hanson, were happy to wear a Wildcat uniform even though their games wouldn't be nationally televised. Lack of national TV exposure didn't seem bother them, Donovan said.

"I don't think they really got caught up in that," he said. "They were just happy to have an opportunity to play. They could care less if the games were on TV or not because I think to those kids being Kentucky kids playing in their home state was like playing on national TV, and putting on a Kentucky jersey was what was important to them."

And Pitino worked his Italian magic, motivating the Wildcats to a stunning 14-14 mark (including 10-8 in SEC action) in his first season at the Wildcat helm. The fans fell in love with the scrapping Wildcats and their aggressive fast-breaking offense, including three-point field goal shooting. Win or lose, the Big Blue faithful had a blast. Senior guard Derrick Miller, with a league-high average of 3.5 three-point field goals a game, led Kentucky with 19.2-point average. For his remarkable efforts in reviving the program, Pitino, whose club led the nation in three-point shooting, was named the national coach of the year by the *Basketball Times*.

In addition to Donovan, Pitino's first coaching staff at UK included Ralph Willard, Tubby Smith, Herb Sendek and Ray "Rock" Oliver. They all worked overtime. Before they held staff meetings at 7 a.m., they frequently played pickup basketball at Memorial Coliseum, especially from October to late December. And Donovan will never forget Smith's reaction when he had to play basketball very early in the morning. That's one of Donovan's favorite stories about Smith, now the UK head coach.

"We'd play ball at 5:30 in the morning and Tubby's wife (Donna) said that he would sleep in his shorts and t-shirt," Donovan said. "And when the alarm clock went off he would just put his sneakers on and go play. So Tubby didn't get very much sleep and probably wasn't used to that type of environment. There are probably a lot of funny stories about Tubby but I can't remember all of them, Tubby was a good, kind of fun-loving guy.

"And I think that Tubby was probably in shock a little bit when he first came to Kentucky with the amount of work that we did and put in. I wasn't surprised because I went through it when I was at Providence (as a player under Pitino)."

Since Donovan was already used to his energetic boss' work ethics, it wasn't real tough for him to get up early in the morning and play. "To me, it wasn't too bad," Donovan said of his early wake-up call.

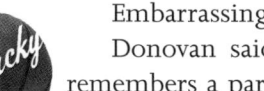
Embarrassing moments.
Donovan said he has had a good share of them. He remembers a particular one when he was working as a graduate assistant.

Before UK played Ole Miss at Rupp Arena, Donovan was given an assignment: a scouting report on Mississippi. It was a task Donovan had not done before, but he agreed to do it to gain some valuable experience. Ralph Willard usually handled the scouting of UK's opponents, but he had to scout another team. Tubby Smith and Herb Sendek were out recruiting on the road. So Donovan traveled to Starkville and watched Mississippi (and All-SEC performer Gerald Glass) play arch-rival Mississippi State.

"I scouted the game and spent an enormous time breaking down the film, doing the scouting report and all of this stuff," Donovan recalled. "(The scouting report) was the first one I did. I wanted to do a good job."

According to Donovan, when he went over his scouting report with his boss and other assistants, Pitino asked several questions. The head coach was especially interested in Ole Miss' Glass, a 6-6, 240-pound forward who later completed the season as the league's second-leading scorer (24.1 points) behind LSU sophomore Chris Jackson (now Mahmoud Abdul-Rauf).

"How do you think we need to play him?" Pitino asked Donovan.

"Well, he's their guy. He's their go-to guy. You got to stop him," Donovan replied.

"Well, what about trapping him every time he gets the ball?"

"Yeah, I think that would be a good idea. Let's take him out of the game."

"That would be great. Is there anybody else on their team that can hurt us shooting the basketball, if we trap?" questioned the boss.

"Well, no, not really. He's (Glass) their main guy. There's no one else that's really a great three-point shooter," responded Donovan.

As it turned out, the scouting report was worthless. In the opening minutes of the Kentucky-Ole Miss game, the Rebels repeatedly attempted to pass the ball to Glass, their star player, but he was trapped in a 2-3 zone defense almost every time. So they went to 6-7 freshman forward Joe Harvell and he took over, pumping in three-pointers to give Ole Miss a comfortable 12-point lead in the early first half.

Donovan said a furious Pitino gave him "that look off the bench, you know, saying who scouted this game?" Kentucky, however, bounced back and won the game 98-79. Ole Miss' Harvell gunned in a game-high 25 points, including six of nine three-pointers, in the setback. While Glass was limited to 11 field goal attempts, he managed to score 23 points, including eight free throws.

"Going back and looking at the stat sheet, Joe Harvell wasn't even making one three-point shot per game (before the UK-Mississippi matchup)," Donovan pointed out. "He made like six in the game so it was one of those things where we kind of burned our scouting reports. We

Florida coach Billy Donovan began his head coaching career at Marshall University in Huntington, West Virginia, in 1994, when he became the nation's youngest mentor at the age of 28.

University of Florida Sports Information / photo by Jason Howey

ended up winning the game, thank God. But that was something that always sticks out in my mind."

 Before he came to Kentucky, Donovan knew UK had a great basketball tradition. But he absolutely had no idea how big the UK program was. "You heard about Kentucky basketball on TV," he said. Donovan finally realized the magnitude of the team's popularity in the summer of 1990 when he and his wife were moving boxes and furniture to a house. And when they unpacked their things, he heard something on the radio. It sounded like a Wildcat basketball game, he thought. Since this was summer, Donovan was somewhat confused about the game. He wasn't sure what was going on, but he heard the name of Kyle Macy and the familiar voice of Cawood Ledford.

As he found out later, a local radio station was replaying an entire Kentucky/Indiana game that took place many years ago. "That's incredible," Donovan said. "The whole game was on radio....I had no idea that type of fanfare and enthusiasm was there throughout the state for the program."

 In Pitino's fourth year at Kentucky, or a year after that famous (or infamous, for that matter) Kentucky-Duke overtime thriller, the Wildcats made their first journey to the Final Four since coach Joe B. Hall's Cats did it in 1984. It would be Pitino's second trip to the Final Four.

In 1987, 34-year-old Pitino had guided his Providence team, with its long-range shooting attack, to the Final Four where the surprising Friars dropped to Syracuse 77-63 in a matchup of Big East rivals in New Orleans. No. 6-seed Providence had stunned everyone in the NCAA Southeast Regional when it upset coach Wimp Sanderson and his No. 2-seed Alabama team (103-82) and No. 1-seed Georgetown (88-73). Also, it was Providence's first appearance in the NCAA tournament since 1978. (In that same tournament, No. 9-seed Ohio State knocked off Eddie Sutton's No. 8-seed Kentucky club, led by freshman guard Rex Chapman, in the first round by a score of 91-77.)

In 1993, Pitino's Kentucky club, guided by All-American junior Jamal Mashburn and All-SEC junior guard Travis Ford, defeated Rider College, Utah, Wake Forest and Florida State in the Southeast Regionals before advancing to the Final Four. In the national semifinals, Michigan dashed Kentucky's title hopes by winning 81-78 in overtime.

Donovan was with Pitino both times in the Final Four — as a player and an assistant. During Providence's magical ride to the Final Four, the 6-0 Donovan led the team in scoring and assists as a senior guard. The first-team All-Big East standout averaged 20.6 points and 7.1 assists as the Friars finished with a 25-9 mark, including a 4-1 mark in the NCAA tournament. In the Southeast Regional, Donovan's outstanding play earned him the Most Outstanding Player award. One of Donovan's teammates included 6-4 guard Delray Brooks, a transfer from Indiana, who averaged 14.4 points, the second best on the squad. (Brooks later served as assistant coach at Kentucky for four years.)

On Providence's Cinderella ride to the Final Four, Donovan said, "We were star struck a little bit, probably very much in awe, just the whole media hype. Coach Pitino was very, very young. He was probably 33 years old at the time (actually 34). We had never been there. We had never been to the NCAA tournament at Providence College in 10 years."

When Pitino was at Kentucky during its NCAA probationary period, he told Donovan that the next trip to the Final Four would be much nicer. "He said when we get back to the Final Four, we're going to enjoy it a little bit more than we did when we were at Providence," Donovan said.

Pitino didn't really change his coaching methods or daily routine for the 1993 Final Four even after experiencing the Final Four hoopla in 1987, according to Donovan. Both of his teams were well-prepared. If he did change, it wasn't very noticeable. "I think coach is one of those people who believes that he has to over prepare. He is going to leave no stone unturned. (He is going to) put his team in the best possible position to win by preparation," said the Gator mentor. "I don't think anything really changed."

 There is one lasting feat that Pitino will always be remembered for during his eight years at Kentucky. He was very successful in the SEC tournament, compiling a 17-1 mark for a winning percentage of 94.4. He won the SEC tournament five times out of six appearances.

Before he left Lexington, Donovan assisted Pitino in three of UK's SEC tournament appearances and he came out a winner all three times. But there was one special moment in Donovan's life that took place during the 1994 SEC tournament in Memphis. Several hours after Kentucky rolled past Mississippi State 95-76 in the first round behind Tony Delk's 29 points, the Wildcat associate coach became a proud father for the second time.

With his wife in Lexington, didn't he see the baby born? Yes, with the help of a loyal Wildcat supporter Brown Badgett who was attending the SEC tournament. Since there were no commercial flights available to Lexington from Memphis in the wee hours, Donovan — who earlier that week had been chosen as the new head coach at Marshall — rode Badgett's private airplane to Lexington.

"I got a phone call about 5:30 in the morning, Memphis time, at the hotel that my wife was going into labor and that the baby was going to be born in several hours," Donovan recalled. "I made a few phone calls and someone kind of directed me to Brown. I called Brown at like 5:45 in the morning and I said 'Brown, I'm sorry to bother you.' He said, 'Hey, no problem,' and I said my wife is having a baby and I need to get back.....He said I was more than welcome to use it (airplane)."

Badgett contacted his pilot right away and Donovan was on his way to Kentucky. He stayed at the hospital for a couple of hours as his wife gave birth to their daughter, Hasbrouck, who weighed seven pounds and 15 ounces. Donovan then flew back to Memphis and was on the Kentucky sidelines against top-ranked Arkansas in the semifinals. The No. 10 Wildcats, hitting an SEC tournament-record and season-high 16 three-pointers, stopped Arkansas 90-78 before a crowd of 20,431 at The Pyramid.

"I don't know if coach Pitino ever anticipated me coming back or not," Donovan said. "But you know when I did, he appreciated it. I felt an obligation there. I was doing the scouting report and had scouted Arkansas. I felt like I needed to be there. And I was fortunate enough to be there (in Lexington) to see the birth and would like to have hung around there for another few hours, but I was there for two hours and I needed to get back."

Pitino knew Donovan and his wife were expecting a baby. Before departing Lexington for the SEC tourney, Pitino had told Donovan that he didn't have to travel with the team so that he could stay with his wife. The assistant said no and flew to the tournament with the Wildcats. Pitino informed him that he could go back to Kentucky if needed. Said Donovan, "Coach kind of said to me, 'Listen, whenever you need to get back there, you get back there.' He was really good about it."

For the Donovans, who now have three children, March 12, 1994 will always be more than a good day. After all, their baby was born and the Wildcats whipped top-ranked Arkansas.

And Kentucky went on to capture the tournament, beating eventual Final Four-bound Florida 73-60.

 In 1996, after spending five apprenticeship years as Pitino aide at UK and two years as Marshall's head coach, Donovan entered the major leagues of college basketball as the head man. He became the head coach of the Florida Gators at the relatively young age of 30, making him one of the country's youngest head basketball coaches.

However, Florida's hiring of Donovan, who compiled a two-year record of 35-20 at Marshall, raised some eyebrows in the Gator community. The fans as well as the local media had speculated that an established coach would be hired to replace veteran Lon Kruger, who had taken the

Gators to their first Final Four appearance in 1994. Kruger left Florida to take a similar post at Illinois.

Instead, in a surprising move viewed by some as risky, the Gators got Donovan, a hard-working promising coach who preached up-tempo Pitino-style offense. Florida athletic director Jeremy Foley compared the hiring with the one Massachusetts made in 1988 when it named 29-year-old and future NBA coach John Calipari as the head coach. Pitino and Kentucky athletic director C.M. Newton offered assurances to Foley that the school made the right decision in hiring Donovan.

"Jeremy Foley called me after Lon Kruger resigned to go to Illinois, and said he was going to look for the next Coach K from Duke (Mike Krzyzewski). A young coach on the rise, " said *Gainesville Sun* publisher John W. Fitzwater, who is originally from Somerset, Ky. "He had a short list and from day one Billy was on that list.

"Of course there were comments about the age when he (Donovan) got here but Florida fans were ready for an up-tempo style. There is such confidence in Foley by Florida fans. No one was disappointed. They felt if Foley thought it would be a good fit, it would be a good fit.

"Lon Kruger was very popular and took UF to the Final Four, but his style of play was not exciting for the fans. The up-tempo Pitino style is what they wanted."

Donovan, who reportedly signed a five-year contract at $375,000 a year, also brought four of his Marshall assistants to Florida, including former UK standout John Pelphrey, Anthony Grant, Donnie Jones and Matt Brown. Pelphrey and Brown are native eastern Kentuckians, while Jones played basketball at Pikeville College in Kentucky.

However, Donovan almost didn't come to Florida. Pitino initially had discouraged Donovan from taking the Gator post because the former UK boss felt Florida's roundball program was overrated and was in need of rebuilding. Pitino relented after being told that Florida was serious about its commitment to rebuild the hoops program.

"He thought that the perception of this program was that it was in very good shape because not long ago they went to the Final Four and coach Pitino really felt the talent level wasn't where it needed to be to really compete and win," Donovan said. "It was going to take a couple of years to get that level back up. Coach just told me I really needed to be careful. I think that we both realized that the athletic director (Foley) was in tune with where the program was at and how long it was going to take to get it back. I think once I understood that and once coach Pitino understood that, I think he felt very good about the situation."

In his interview with Foley and other school officials, Donovan got some answers and felt good about his chances for the Gator position. "I felt everything went well," Donovan said. "I felt Jeremy Foley was looking to go in a different direction and he was not necessarily looking to hire a big-name guy up there. He was looking to hire someone who was young, energetic and was going to work hard and try to build something and stay around for a while. So that's what he was looking for and for whatever reasons I kind of fell into all these categories."

Before Florida hired Donovan, the school reportedly considered head coaches such as Perry Clark of Tulane, Rick Majerus of Utah, Herb Sendek of Miami, Ohio (who is now at North Carolina State), and ex-UK assistant James Dickey of Texas Tech, among others. Duke assistant Tommy Amaker, a former Blue Devil standout, reportedly was also considered by the Gators before he took the head coaching job at Seton Hall.

In Donovan's first year (1996-97) as the head coach at Florida, the Gators posted a 13-17 worksheet, including four setbacks when they had a chance to win or tie at the buzzer, but fell short. Sometimes playing with six available scholarship players, Florida, however, showed that it could run, score, press and shoot with confidence — the Billyball style.

As the head coach, Donovan's first SEC win came against No. 22 Arkansas, beating the Razorbacks in a 75-62 verdict before a regional television audience and a friendly crowd of 5,335 in Gainesville. It was also the school's first-ever victory over Arkansas, which joined the SEC in 1991.

Pitino also watched that game on TV. Naturally, he was pleased to see his former pupil doing well with the Gators. "It was great watching the (Arkansas) game....I saw kids playing their hearts out and doing everything they could to win a ballgame," Pitino said. "I see tremendous improvement in some of the walk-on players and the other guys. When the talent catches up with the system, it's going to be great for Gator fans."

On his first Gator squad, which was picked last in the SEC East in preseason rankings, Donovan said, "Our players certainly overachieved. We asked an awful lot from a group of guys who really didn't have much experience. For the most part they responded. They competed, played hard and were a good group to work with. The things I expected and demanded out

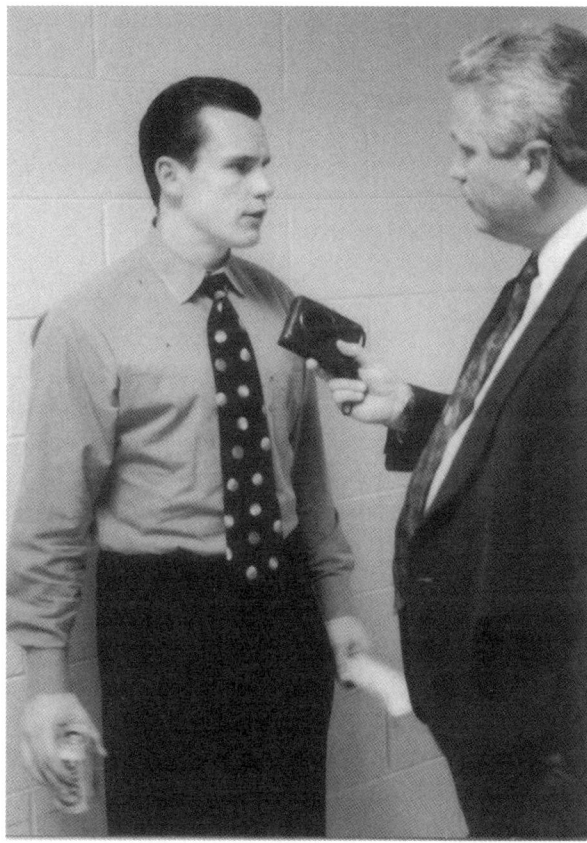

Billy Donovan talks with a reporter after Florida's disappointing loss to the Tennessee Volunteers, in Knoxville, during the 1997-98 campaign.

Photo by Jamie H. Vaught

of this group set the foundation for what we expect every time my players step out on the floor — in practice or in a game.

"I think anytime you try to build a program, it takes a little bit of time and energy. And you want it to happen a lot quicker, maybe. But hopefully through recruiting and through our style of play, we will get better and better. The first year was very challenging. It was also very rewarding because we played with a group of guys that really never played before and they poured out their hearts and souls. It was really good to see them, not necessarily the success as far as wins and losses, but at least they have an opportunity to play and have something to remember their careers by. So, you know, I was pleased with their effort."

 Donovan's second year at the UF helm saw improvement as the Gators posted a 14-15 mark with a trip to the National Invitation Tournament. But Donovan's troops would've done much better had flashy star Jason Williams stayed out of trouble. In mid-February, the coach dismissed Williams from the squad for violating team and university athletic policies. From that point on, the Gators struggled as they dropped six of the last seven games of the season, including a 71-69 setback to Georgetown of the Big East Conference in the NIT.

The highlight of Florida's 1997-98 campaign came during a ABC-TV broadcast of UK-Florida matchup at Rupp Arena when it upset then 7th-ranked Kentucky 86-78. Williams, a 6-1 junior, and Kenyan Weaks, a 6-4 sophomore, each pumped in 24 points, snapping the Gators' 10-game losing streak to Kentucky in the series.

As the Florida mentor, it was arguably the biggest win Donovan has had. In the post-game press conference, the coach attempted to downplay the significance of obtaining his first victory over his former employer, saying the win was a big one for the players and the Gator program.

Assistant coach John Pelphrey was asked if the victory over Kentucky was the biggest one of his coaching career, he politely said no. "I don't think so," said Pelphrey, a Paintsville, Ky., native. "When I was at Marshall, we won a Southern Conference championship and I would say that a championship overrides one victory. It was certainly a very, very good win for our basketball team and certainly I'm very elated after every win. It was good to get a SEC win on the road. That has not happened too often yet for us, and we were very, very excited about it."

The morning after that huge victory, Donovan received a congratulatory call at his Florida home. It was from Pitino. A proud Pitino told Donovan that he had done a fabulous job. As far as Donovan was concerned, it was definitely nice hearing from his former master.

Going into the last week of the regular season action, Florida, playing without Williams, was a long shot for the NCAA tournament. It had a 13-11 record, including 6-8 in the SEC with two road games at Tennessee and Vanderbilt. Still, Donovan was hopeful. He refused to give up. He figured if the Gators could pull a couple of victories plus a decent showing in the SEC tournament, they had a chance to go to the Big Dance.

Going into the Tennessee game in Knoxville, the Gators had a 14-game winning streak against the Vols in the series. Florida, however, came up short this time in an emotionally-charged SEC contest, losing 79-75 before a hostile crowd of 19,110.

It sure didn't look like a basketball game. The fight-marred game looked more like football or hockey as both squads committed a total of 50 fouls. And the first half saw several players erupted in a melee in front of Donovan and the Florida bench. After reviewing Sunshine Network TV monitors on press row, the officials ejected three players — Florida's Dan Williams and Obiora Nnaji, and Tennessee's Tony Harris — from the game.

While UT coach Jerry Green refused to comment about the fight, Donovan had something to say. "We were setting a pick and roll and Tony Harris intentionally lifted his elbow, " Donovan explained. "I commented about it to the officials early. Harris elbowed Dan Williams and our guy retaliated. I thought the officials could have handled it better earlier in the game. Williams shouldn't have responded the way he did. When the elbows are above the shoulder, it's a flagrant foul. I don't know if it was a cheap shot or an accident. If the officials call the fouls early, we don't have that situation. You have to blow the whistle." The setback was a severe blow to the Gators, who saw their NCAA tournament hopes fade away. That meant Florida would have to capture the SEC tournament in Atlanta to receive an automatic NCAA tourney bid. As expected, it didn't happen; Kentucky won the conference tourney for the sixth time in seven years.

Instead, Donovan and the Gators had to settle for NIT. And Donovan got to face John Thompson, the Georgetown coach, on the court for the first time since 1987 when he sparked Providence to an upset over Georgetown in the NCAA tournament. This time Thompson, however, had the upper hand as the Hoyas won the exciting matchup, televised by ESPN, in Gainesville.

Several days later, Florida extended Donovan's contract by one year to 2002-03. The ex-Wildcat aide earns a yearly pay of about $400,000, including a base salary of over $115,000, making him either the fourth or fifth highest-paid hoops coach in the SEC, according to published reports.

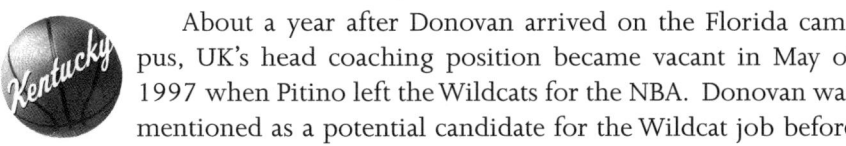

About a year after Donovan arrived on the Florida campus, UK's head coaching position became vacant in May of 1997 when Pitino left the Wildcats for the NBA. Donovan was mentioned as a potential candidate for the Wildcat job before Tubby Smith of Georgia accepted Kentucky's offer. While most folks believed that Kentucky wouldn't hire Donovan because of his lack of head coaching experience at the major college level, it boosted Donovan's standing in the coaching profession and among the Gator faithful. Nevertheless, Donovan's boss, Jeremy Foley, was smiling because a year earlier he had received some heat for hiring a very young person to coach at a major school like Florida.

"The thing I liked about it was a year ago people questioned me hiring a guy that's too young and now everybody's talking about him going to Kentucky," Foley said in *Gator Bait*, a publication covering Florida athletics. He also added the national publicity connecting Donovan with Kentucky's job opening would help Gators' recruiting efforts.

It wouldn't be too long before Donovan made his name as a super recruiter. For the 1997-98 recruiting season, several national publications ranked Florida among the top five in the country. UF signees included 5-10 guard Ted Dupay, 6-4 LaDarius Halton, 6-8 Udonis Haslem, 6-8 Mike Miller and 6-9 Sylbrin Robinson. Both Haslem and Robinson came from Miami Senior High School, the same high school once attended by former UK players Allen Edwards and Gimel Martinez.

"Billy (Donovan) is also known as one of the hardest working coaches anywhere," said John Fitzwater, the Gainesville newspaper publisher. "His recruiting is already a gold mine."

 Florida is well known for its strong fan support in football. Like Wildcat basketball in Kentucky, the Gator football is a popular year-round conversation in coffee shops throughout the Sunshine State. Consequently, Gator basketball is not taken as seriously. To make matters all the more difficult, the football Gators, guided by coach Steve Spurrier, captured the national championship after the 1996 season during Donovan's first year.

Do all the attention and support that go to the Gator football program bother Donovan? "No, not really," he said. "I think that there should be a lot of fan support in football. They've played in two back-to-back national championship games. And they won a national championship. So I think there should be a great enthusiasm for football. I know if we can get back to a Final Four here in Florida, there would be a great deal of enthusiasm for basketball. But we're not at that level right now. So it is going to take some time and I understand that."

 You can safely say that Donovan was born with basketball in his blood. While there is no question that his never-say-die desire and dedication to basketball contributed much of his success as a player and coach in the 1980s and '90s, his childhood environment in the Long Island area in New York gave him an opportunity to learn and play the roundball sport.

He had a very good tutor: his dad. William Donovan, a former Boston College player, coached local teams in the Catholic Youth Organization League. "He coached me from fifth grade to eighth grade," said Billy Donovan, who added that his father was probably the most influential person in his life.

When he was a teenager, his parents placed a concrete floor in the backyard so he could play basketball. They even added lights. "They put a slab of cement down," said Donovan, "put a court up for me in the backyard and put a flood light out there where I could play. That was probably a mistake because they were generally calling me to come in because they had a rule that anything past 10 o'clock would be a little too late to play ball. We had kind of a curfew out there. So generally what we ended up doing after that was we would go down to the high school gym and try to slip through a window and go down and play."

He once scared his mother, Joan, in the middle of the night when she found his bed empty at 2:00 a.m. "I guess one night my mother got up and checked on us and realized I wasn't there," said Donovan, who also has two sisters. "She woke my sister up and said 'Do you know where Billy's at?' And she replied, 'I think he's down at the gym playing ball.' Sure enough my mother came down there and she was scared to death. I'm sure she was happy she found me in the gym and not somewhere else.

"You know, they weren't too happy (about my sneaking out). But they also understood that I really enjoyed playing. A lot of guys I grew up with back then did enjoy playing and it wasn't abnormal for us to do that." Eventually Donovan was given a key to the gym so he could play. He was what you would call a true gym rat.

While at St. Agnes Cathedral, Donovan led his squad to the Long Island Catholic High School championship during his senior year. He also earned first-team All-Long Island honors his last two seasons.

His parents still live in Rockville Centre. "They live in the same house that I was born and raised in," Donovan commented. His folks also have a house in south Florida where they often vacationed even before their son had become the head coach at Florida.

Before he arrived at Providence College in Rhode Island, Donovan wasn't a highly-touted prep player. While many small colleges offered scholarships, Donovan had high hopes of playing for a major college. That made his father nervous.

"Going into my senior year, the majority of the schools that recruited me were (NCAA) Division II schools and I was offered a scholarship from a lot of Division II schools," Donovan said. "My dad told me that he thought I should sign with one of those schools early and I would get my education paid for to play ball. But I had higher expectations for myself and I wanted to try to play at the highest level.

"My dad got a little concerned because he probably felt that if I didn't take one of these offers and if I waited too long, I may not have anything. But the high school team I played on played pretty well. We had a pretty good year and then Providence started to get involved later. Temple got involved as well as Holy Cross and Seton Hall."

So Donovan ended up signing with Providence of the relatively new Big East Conference. He decided to play for the struggling Friar program because of their coach. The mentor's name was Joe Mullaney, who formerly coached the Los Angeles Lakers and the Kentucky Colonels in the pro ranks. Mullaney was coaching Providence in his second stint at the school.

"The main reason I went to Providence was because of Joe Mullaney," Donovan explained. "I had a very good relationship with him. I liked him a lot as a person. I think after having a chance to play for him for two years, it probably wasn't the right style of play for me. But I still have a tremendous amount of respect for coach Mullaney."

Under Mullaney's guidance, Providence's conservative offense featured a half-court game. That wasn't Donovan's type of game and he sat on the bench. The Friars, however, struggled and Mullaney eventually retired after Donovan's sophomore year.

"I think he was getting toward the end of his career," Donovan said of Mullaney's struggles. "We, as a basketball team, were not very talented. Since coach Mullaney was in the NBA, he kind of adopted a lot of the NBA mentality. We didn't really practice long or hard. It was one of those things, if you were like the 11th or 12th guy on the team which I was, that you were expected to kind of keep yourself in shape on your own. I didn't do a very good job of that and I put a lot of weight on. That was probably the reason why I didn't play."

 By the time Mullaney left Providence, Donovan, a part-time player who was 20 pounds overweight, had decided to transfer. He wasn't satisfied. But his cloudy outlook began to clear when the school hired Rick Pitino away from NBA's New York Knicks where he had been serving as an assistant coach for embattled Hubie Brown. Pitino was ready to get out of New York where the Knicks struggled with a 24-58 mark, and he loved the challenge of rebuilding Providence's once-proud roundball program.

"I talked to him about possibly transferring," Donovan said of his first meeting with Pitino. "He sat me down and told me there was no need to transfer, that I needed to get myself in great shape and I needed to improve. He gave me a list of things I needed to do to get better.

"I think after I spoke with coach Pitino I decided not to transfer. The thing that really excited me was he told me he would give me a fair chance to play and that's all I ever wanted. I felt like in my first year I never really had an opportunity to play whether that was my fault (or not). It probably was. I was very impressed (with Pitino) and he promised me nothing. The only thing he did say was it would be the best experience of my life and you know I stayed and it worked out well."

There was something else that caught the attention of Donovan and his teammates in one of their first team meetings with Pitino, who earlier had warned the players to be on time. According to Donovan, it was a meeting that he will never forget. Pitino became infuriated when a player walked into the meeting which had begun five minutes earlier.

"Why are you late?" asked Pitino.

"Well, you know, I had something to do. I ran into a friend and I got kind of tied up," the player said sheepishly.

"Okay, that's good. You can show up tomorrow morning since you are five minutes late and run five miles at 5:30 a.m."

Said Donovan of team practices and meetings conducted by Pitino, "We were expected to be on time and he kind of set the ground rules right away. I don't think any of the guys on our team had a problem with that because I think he was very, very fair. There was a sense of accountability that you were being held accountable for being on time and playing hard and doing those things. Although it was very, very demanding and he was a disciplinarian, that was the best thing that we had for two years."

In Pitino's first year (1985-86) at Providence, the Friars posted a 17-14 mark, a significant improvement over the previous squad which went 11-20. A rejuvenated Donovan averaged 15.1 points and earned third-team All-Big East honors as Providence landed a berth in the NIT. The Friars did even better in the following season. They went all the way to the national semifinals, becoming perhaps the least-talented club to make the Final Four.

Pitino started calling him "Billy the Kid." Why? "I really think it's because I look young," explained Donovan. "He coined that phrase along with being the quickest gun in the east when I was a player. I think coach was doing that as far as trying to build my self-esteem as a player and getting me to think I was maybe invincible as a player. Coach Pitino still calls me that and you know a lot of the guys call me that, too."

Does the nickname bother Donovan? "No, not all," he said. "I look at it as a compliment from coach Pitino."

 Donovan — who received his bachelor's degree with a major in liberal arts and a minor in business — then went on to join the NBA ranks in 1987-88. However, he almost didn't make it. A third-round draft pick of the Utah Jazz, he was cut after playing several preseason games during the exhibition season. Then, for a brief period, Donovan found some playing time with the Wyoming team of the Continental Basketball Association until the NBA came calling. He signed a one-year contract with the New York Knicks as a free agent and joined Pitino once again. Pitino had just left Providence to take the head coaching position at New York.

It was a dream come true for Donovan, who once scored his NBA-career high of 14 points. His New York teammates included stars Patrick Ewing and ex-UK standout Kenny Walker. He finished his only NBA season with an average of 2.4 points in 44 games as Pitino guided the 38-44 Knicks to the playoffs for the first time since 1984.

After the Knicks released Donovan, he continued to play basketball. He was picked up by Utah, the same team which had drafted him in the previous year. However, the former Friar was released before the 1988-89 regular season began and he hooked up with CBA's Rapid City squad in South Dakota. He wanted to try one more time before quitting for good. He wanted an opportunity to play in the NBA again.

A Rick Pitino protege who preaches
up-tempo style of basketball, UF's Billy
Donovan shouts instructions on the floor
as assistant John Pelphrey, sitting on the
bench, watches.

University of Florida Sports
Information / photo by Jason Howey

Things didn't work out. Donovan didn't feel good about his playing career. So he made one of the most critical decisions of his life. He
officially retired as a basketball player in February of 1989.

Donovan went back to New York and landed a job as a stock bro-
ker with an investment banking firm. He took the position to "see what it
was like to get involved down on Wall Street. I did it for a few months and
didn't like it very much. I was with a great group, but I just didn't like it."
Pitino, after learning Donovan's interest in coaching, brought him back in
basketball in the summer of 1989.   As members of UK coaching staff,
Pitino and Donovan were reunited for the third time.

 Some folks call Donovan a Pitino clone. They are both
New Yorkers with dark hair. They love a full-court running
game. They practice Catholicism. They worked together for
eight years, including Donovan's playing days. They began

their head coaching careers at a very young age. So, naturally, people like to compare Donovan with Pitino.

"I think there is always going to be those type of comparisons," Donovan said. "You know I'd be the first one to tell you I'm not Rick Pitino. We both share a tremendous amount of love and compassion for the game of basketball, but to me I think coach Pitino is the best coach out there at any level. That's just my personal opinion and I really have that respect for him because I had a chance to see him do it with me as a player. I had a chance to see him do it when I was assistant coach for the Kentucky program that was down and out.

"So I'm going to get those comparisons because the style of play is the same, philosophies are very similar, but we are different and I've got to be myself. (The comparison) is obviously nice because I know what coach Pitino represents and what he stands for. Anytime I hear that comparison, to me it's always a compliment. But I'd be the first one to say that I'm obviously not in his class, in his league. I'm working and striving to have the success that he's had as a coach and certainly we're trying to make some strides here at Florida to do that."

 As the head coach at Marshall and then Florida, Donovan hasn't won a single game against Pitino. The pupil is 0-4 against the master, including Marshall's embarrassing 116-75 Rupp Arena setback to Kentucky in 1994 in his first game against Pitino. It looks as if the record will remain the same for awhile since Pitino bolted Kentucky for the NBA. Donovan said he missed the competition against Pitino's aggressive Kentucky squads.

"I would've loved to have had the opportunity to play against coach Pitino's teams again because he's the best out there," he said. "I think anytime you have a chance to go against the best, it brings out the best in you. I never really looked at it when Kentucky played Florida, or when I was at Marshall and we played Kentucky. I never really looked at it as myself against coach Pitino. I kind of went out there and tried to do my best job coaching as he did."

On Pitino's leaving Kentucky and college basketball, Donovan said, "I think probably every coach in the SEC was happy to see him go just because he's been so successful. But in my mind I think it's a major loss for college basketball when you lose a guy like Rick Pitino because of the success he's had and what he has done at that program and the way his teams played. You know there is tremendous respect there."

In UK's farewell ceremony honoring Pitino which was held in the summer of 1997, Donovan (along with John Pelphrey) participated in a special video presentation. The taping, seen by some 300 people who paid $150 each to attend the dinner, was made on the Florida campus since the duo couldn't attend the affair. They talked of their respect for Pitino, among other things.

While Donovan said he's happy at Florida, he admitted that he wouldn't mind being the head coach at Kentucky some day. For instance, he would be only 40 years old in 2005 if the Wildcats needed someone to take over their basketball program.

"I would look at something like that," Donovan commented. "To me, Kentucky is a place that's really special. The fans are special. I don't know if there's a more followed basketball program in the country than the University of Kentucky. So it's always something you've got to look at.

"But one thing I do want to say is I am very happy here. I like it here a lot. We're going to try to build something here, but at the same time Kentucky is a place where I developed a lot of good friends. (Lexington) was a great city to live in and you know I just really feel fortunate I had a chance to spend five years there."

DERON
AND HIS DAD

When Mason County High School product Deron Feldhaus came to UK in 1987, he wasn't the first player in the family to don a Wildcat jersey. His dad, who was also his high school coach, had played for Kentucky as well. A key reserve player, Allen Feldhaus played for legendary Adolph Rupp in the early 1960s.

Deron said his father didn't try to persuade him to go to Kentucky. The elder Feldhaus didn't have to. "He knew that's the only place (to play basketball)," smiled Deron, who also participated in high school golf and baseball. "It was always my dream to play at Kentucky. I knew where I wanted to go."

But for awhile it looked as if Deron would have to play college basketball some place else. For most of his high school career, then-Kentucky coach Eddie Sutton and his staff expressed little, if any, interest in Feldhaus. Vanderbilt, then coached by ex-UK cager C.M. Newton, was the player's likely destination in college. "Coach Newton wrote and recruited me hard and I really liked that program," Feldhaus said of the Commodores.

After his junior season, the 6-7 Feldhaus toured with the Kentucky Junior All-Stars, playing in Los Angeles and Las Vegas, and caught UK's attention with his aggressive play and nice shooting touch. The Wildcats changed their mind and signed Feldhaus during the early signing period in November.

At Mason County, Deron led the Royals to the state tournament twice (1985 and '87). In his senior year, he averaged 23.6 points and 10.3 rebounds in leading Mason County to a remarkable 31-3 record and to the quarterfinals of the Sweet Sixteen at Rupp Arena where it dropped to Louisville Ballard and promising sophomore Allan Houston on a last-second basket.

A two-time All-Stater, the younger Feldhaus said his best performance as a prepster came during the 1985 state tournament in Lexington when he was a promising sophomore. In the opening round, "We upset Lexington Catholic," recalled Feldhaus, "and we were not supposed to beat them. I think I had like 20-something points. That gave me a lot of confidence the rest of my career. I know the next game in the state tournament I had 20 some points (against Louisville Doss in a one-point overtime loss). But that first game was the turning point of my career and it gave me a lot of confidence."

 Since Deron had already signed with Kentucky, many opposing fans attempted to rattle him with all kinds of names or catcalls when Mason County traveled on the road, according to his father. As a future Wildcat, the senior was under heavy scrutiny as they watched him make every move on the floor.

"People would sit behind our bench on purpose to taunt us and things like that," said the elder Feldhaus. "Deron went through a hard time being daddy's boy and all this stuff and the publicity he was getting because he signed with the university. That's something youngsters need to think about when signing early, especially if you sign with the University of Kentucky because there's a lot of pressure every night when you go to those foreign gyms. But, my goodness, he (Deron) was so mentally tough that I think it really made him a better person and a better basketball player. He could just hang in there and laugh about it. And we had a big time.

"We learned to laugh and go on, and the first thing you know before the game was over, we would win and then the people would be for us. It was really funny how you could turn them around if you handled it right and didn't do what they wanted us to do — that was to get all upset, talk back to them, look up at them, and wink and things like that. (Eventually) they would change their attitude."

The younger Feldhaus said his senior year was probably more difficult than he had anticipated. "Every game was a challenge for me," Deron recalled. "A lot of fans, you know, gave me a hard time. I remember winning the regional tournament and that was probably the best feeling I've had and it was a great experience. And finally to be able to go to the state tournament was a great feeling, too."

 At Kentucky, Feldhaus didn't play right away. Since he was a rookie on a veteran squad loaded with talented players, including fifth-year senior star Winston Bennett and sophomore sensation Rex Chapman, coach Eddie Sutton decided to redshirt Feldhaus along with other freshman John Pelphrey for the 1987-88 season. Feldhaus supported the coach's decision to redshirt.

"There were a lot of great players," Feldhaus said. "You had Rob Lock, Rex Chapman, Winston Bennett and so on. I really wouldn't have gotten any playing time. So I thought it was a great decision to be redshirted. It gave me one extra year. The way it turned out it really helped my career."

Sitting on the bench, Feldhaus saw UK post a 27-6 mark, including an SEC tournament championship and two NCAA tournament victories. (Kentucky's record was later changed to 25-5 because of NCAA sanctions in 1989.)

Besides Feldhaus and Pelphrey, the other Wildcat freshmen included Reggie Hanson (a Prop 48 victim who sat out the previous season), Johnathon Davis, LeRon Ellis, Eric Manuel and Sean Sutton. Many publications rated UK's highly-touted rookie crop as one of the best in the country.

 As a second-year freshman, Feldhaus didn't see a lot of action. He played enough to learn the ropes, however. He managed to participate in all of UK's 32 games, including a couple of games as a starter, in the 1988-89 season. He posted averages of 3.7 points and 3.3 rebounds.

It was a nightmarish campaign that all UK fans would like to forget. The Wildcats, under a dark cloud of NCAA's bothersome investigation for rules violations, suffered their losingest season ever in school history when they compiled a shocking 13-19 worksheet. Kentucky was even knocked out in the very first game of the SEC tournament in Knoxville, losing to Vanderbilt 77-63. "It was a long year," Feldhaus explained, "and you think 'Why did this happen to me?' It was a very difficult year."

In May of 1989, NCAA penalized UK, hitting the school with several sanctions. Many folks, including Feldhaus, thought the penalties were very harsh. "I was shocked by the severeness," Feldhaus said. "But I knew with all the allegations that we were going to sit out the NCAA tournament."

With his son on the squad, the elder Feldhaus had mixed emotions about whether or not the NCAA was fair in its punishment of UK. "I really think maybe it came down to where something had to be done and I think it was a blessing in disguise," said Allen. "It had to be something shaky going on somewhere or this would not have happened. (But) I don't think anybody will ever know really the full truth about it."

Even with all the problems Kentucky had, the younger Feldhaus said he seriously had no thoughts of quitting or transferring to another school. "I never had that moment," Deron said. "People asked me that question after we went on probation. It never really crossed my mind. I wanted to play at Kentucky and I didn't want to leave very much after being known as a loser. We had a season with a losing record and plus if I left being redshirted the year before (1987-88 season), whatever school I transferred to, I would have had to sit out one year and there was no use in doing that. So I wanted to stay at Kentucky and do the best I could and hopefully become a winner."

When charismatic New Yorker Rick Pitino took over the troubled Wildcat program, Deron wasn't in the best shape of his life. He was about 15 pounds overweight. Pitino warned him that he needed to lose some unwanted pounds. Otherwise, he would not play. He would be a benchwarmer just like the previous year.

"When he first came to Kentucky, he was very hard on us and always yelling, cursing," said Feldhaus. "You know at the time with him coming in there, it was different than what I was used to. It really did motivate us. I would never have achieved what I did at Kentucky without him pushing the way he did.

"Coach Pitino's got so much energy. I've never met a person with so much energy and how he can motivate you. But that's why he's a successful coach because he has that energy."

With Pitino's never-ending encouragement, Feldhaus lost weight and began to improve in practice. He became a hard-nosed contributor to the team. He found a lot of playing time, starting 27 of UK's 28 matchups at power forward, and averaged 14.4 points as UK miraculously finished with .500 mark.

"I got into shape with the new style of basketball," Feldhaus commented. "I was having fun getting to play and I gained confidence. Confidence was the big key to my game. We were having fun. (The) 14-14 season was probably one of the most fun seasons I had because we were not supposed to do that well.

"It really did surprise me that we did that well, but after the season got started, I saw how we came together as a team and that (running) style play was giving other teams problems. We would go in the games thinking we had a chance."

One of the season's highlights was Kentucky's 100-95 victory over a star-studded LSU squad before a new record crowd of 24,301 at Rupp Arena. The ninth-rated Tigers featured a pair of seven footers — Shaq O'Neal and Stanley Roberts — and sophomore guard Chris Jackson, all future NBA players. While Jackson scored a game-high 41 points in a losing cause, UK's stunning victory caught the eye of many roundball observers.

"I still have that game on video," said Feldhaus, who had 24 points and 10 rebounds against LSU's massive frontline. "I've watched that game many, many times. It was one of my better games. I think it (the win) really did give us a lot of respect as a team and they knew that coach Pitino could really coach and was going to be in Kentucky in the future years. The program was going to turn around fast."

Earlier in the season, Feldhaus also had an outstanding game against North Carolina. In a non-conference matchup held in Louisville, he pumped in a career-high 27 points in a 121-110 setback to the Tar Heels. In the high-scoring affair, both teams gunned in 31 out of 68 three-point field goals, including a then-NCAA mark of 21 three-pointers by Kentucky.

 There was some talk in UK basketball circles before the 1990-91 season that Feldhaus was willing to give up a scholarship and become a walk-on so Pitino can sign a big man for the 1991-92 campaign. The coach had used every scholarship

Deron Feldhaus (12)
battles against Oliver
Miller of Arkansas, with
Lee Mayberry (11)
looking on, in the
Razorbacks' 105-88
victory over eighth-
ranked Kentucky at Rupp
Arena in 1992.
Feldhaus scored 22
points in the game.

Photo by Cathy Clarke,
The Gleaner, Henderson, Ky.

available, but was seeking a big guy to bolster his team's frontline. One of
the big prospects UK looked at included 6-10 power forward Chris Webber
of Detroit Country Day High in Michigan. Webber later became an All-
American at Michigan and NBA star.

"We were short of scholarships and we needed a big man,"
Feldhaus said. "We really had no depth inside and I think this guy was
interested in coming to Kentucky. Coach had come to me and asked if I
would have a problem with giving up my scholarship. I said no. You know
I would do anything to help the team, and I knew a big-name player inside
is what our team needed. But the way it worked out the player didn't
come. Without getting him we still were successful. But I would have given
up my scholarship or anything to help the team."

Still ineligible for post-season tournament action, Kentucky managed to crack the 20-victory column in Pitino's second season at UK. Playing primarily with a youthful starting lineup of one senior (6-8 center Reggie Hanson), two juniors (6-2 guard Sean Woods and 6-7 forward John Pelphrey), a sophomore (6-5 guard Jeff Brassow) and a freshman (6-9 forward Jamal Mashburn), the 1990-91 Wildcats compiled a 22-6 mark, including a SEC-best 14-4 mark.

Unlike his sophomore season when he was a starter, Feldhaus saw most of his playing time as a top reserve. In his new "sixth-man" role, he struggled in the early part of the season. According to Feldhaus, his problems were due to a lack of confidence, not his new role. He was very comfortable with his new job. In 28 games, Feldhaus — who also served as tri-captain of the team (with Pelphrey and Hanson) — averaged 10.8 points. His best game of the year came against LSU when he came off the bench to score 27 points, tying his previous career best, in Kentucky's 93-80 victory at Rupp Arena. He also received the inaugural "Reggie Hanson Sacrifice Award" for putting the squad before himself.

Even though Kentucky, which ranked ninth in the final Associated Press poll, had the best record in the SEC, it didn't officially win the conference crown because of NCAA probation. Pitino said after the season that his "rebuilding" team was the biggest surprise of his coaching career because of its tough schedule, which included eventual Final Four teams Kansas and North Carolina. In the regular season, while the Wildcats dropped to North Carolina by three points, they defeated Kansas 88-71, avenging their embarrassing 55-point loss (150-95) to the host Jayhawks in 1989.

During Kentucky's unforgettable run to the Elite Eight during the 1991-92 campaign, Feldhaus basically saw himself in the same role again. As a senior, he was UK's top sixth man, averaging 11.4 points. Pitino liked to call him "the sixth best man in America."

And Feldhaus said his happiest moment as a Wildcat performer came at the Kentucky-Duke game in the 1992 NCAA East Regional finals, even though his team lost in overtime, a 104-103 heartbreaker in Philadelphia. While he and his teammates obviously were disappointed with the setback, Feldhaus said it was also a happy moment for him even if he saw his UK career ending. He had just seen a complete transformation at Kentucky as it went from a losing team to NCAA probation to a winner during his college days.

While he only scored five points, grabbed one rebound and had five assists in 37 minutes against the Blue Devils in what many described as "the best college game ever," he said that was probably the most satisfying game of his Wildcat career. "You don't know how many people know you from that game, and you look back and say what a great game that was," Feldhaus said. "It feels great to be part of that. Just being a part of that game is really something that I will reflect on more as I get older."

Shortly after the NCAA tournament loss, Pitino said he was more than proud of the effort the four seniors — Feldhaus, Pelphrey, Woods and Richie Farmer — had displayed in their Wildcat careers. An emotional Pitino commented in the post-game news conference, "I told the four seniors, 'You've been part of something that's not only glorious, you've been part of something that has allowed the University of Kentucky never to go through the pains they would have gone through if it wasn't for your presence. If you're crying right now, I expect you to go in the shower, and come out very happy, because no tears should be shed for what you've accomplished. You're not playing the game of life, you're playing the game of basketball. And the game of basketball ended on a high note for you people. Not necessarily with a trip to the Final Four, which could have happened. But you ended with such a great fight.'"

Feldhaus' family, including his divorced parents, attended the heartbreaker which saw UK overcome a 12-point deficit in the second half before Christian Laettner's incredible game-winning basket edged the Wildcats. Of his two older brothers and his dad, Feldhaus said, "I think they were so upset they left (immediately). They drove back to Kentucky."

Meanwhile, his mother, Dottie, and his aunt had to stay overnight at the hotel after the loss. They had airline tickets. So Feldhaus ate with them after the game and got together with some of his teammates. "I don't think I got much sleep that night," he said. "We pretty much just hung out in the hotel room and we talked about the game. We pretty much talked about our career and it was a tough moment. Still there was a lot to be proud of and you know when you lose you usually don't celebrate, but we did some celebrating also." Kentucky finished its memorable campaign with a 29-7 worksheet and a final No. 6 national ranking in the regular season.

It would be six years before Kentucky would face Duke again. They would meet in the 1998 NCAA South Regional finals for the right to play in the Final Four. Just like the last time.

The highly-hyped rematch of 1998 brought back a lot of memories of the infamous 1992 thriller. After Kentucky had demolished UCLA in the regional semifinals, the print and electronic media all had a field day about the rematch. Of course, CBS' Billy Packer, a former Wake Forest basketball player, was excited, too. In its Sunday edition, *Lexington Herald-Leader* ran a full-page article about the 1992 matchup headlined "Unforgettable game" with a complete box score. The story also had a listing of what the former UK and Duke players were doing today.

While the players and the coaches from the 1992 contest were no longer at Kentucky, the red-hot Wildcats, riding a 10-game winning streak at the time, didn't want a repeat episode. And Feldhaus, of course, didn't want to see the Wildcats lose to Duke again. He and two of his buddies even had made plans to travel to St. Petersburg, Fla., to attend the game. But his friends later backed out.

Feldhaus, who now lives in Lexington, instead watched the game on TV in pure excitement as Kentucky surprised Duke 86-84 after overcoming a 17-point deficit in the second half. Afterwards, the ex-Wildcat said he felt good with UK's stunning victory, adding that he hoped people wouldn't mention Laettner's heroics as often.

Since the NBA teams, not surprisingly, had expressed very little interest in Deron Feldhaus, Pitino suggested the Maysville native travel to Japan and play pro basketball. Feldhaus agreed, signing a pro contract worth nearly $100,000 for Zexel, a Japanese corporation.

Pitino is "the one who helped me play in Japan," commented Feldhaus, who had his UK jersey retired after his senior year along with three other seniors. "The coach (Kinichi Okuno) of my team in Japan came to Kentucky my sophomore year. He stayed in Lexington and studied basketball under coach Pitino. So he got to know coach Pitino. I guess in the middle of my senior year he contacted coach Pitino and said he would like for me to come to play in Japan. He liked my work ethic in my sophomore year and he had followed my career. After the (1991-92) season was over, I had a meeting with him and coach Pitino. Coach Pitino felt that would be a good thing for me to do — to continue playing. And that's what I wanted to do."

While in Japan, where Feldhaus competed against ex-Wildcats Reggie Hanson, Gimel Martinez and Kenny Walker, the club paid much of his expenses, providing free housing and roundtrip air fares. "I had an apartment every year and they kept it year round for me," said Feldhaus, who has a degree in education. "I'm only over there six and one-half months, but when I come home they keep it the five months while I'm gone. They treat me great. Airfare expenses and stuff like that are paid for."

On pro basketball in Japan, Feldhaus said each club "is sponsored by a corporation. It mostly had Japanese players. Most teams have three Americans and two of them can play on the court at the same time. I think basketball is really growing over there. Ever since I have been there, the salaries have really gone up. I think the corporations are starting to put more money into it and the fan support is getting bigger and better.

"In talking to other players who have played in Europe and other places, a lot of them want to go to Japan because they treat you so well. You get your money on time. In Europe, you're fighting for every pay-check to get your money. And the Japanese people are great. It's really a good league. It's been a good situation and a great experience for me in five years."

 In about a seven-month period (usually from August to March), his Japanese team usually plays around 25 games. "Being over there six and one-half months, that's not too many games," Feldhaus smiled. "It's kind of like playing about once a week. I've got a lot of free time and that's not good being in Japan, but you know I go to Tokyo a lot. I'm like a hour away from there and there's a lot of things you can do in Tokyo. I've adjusted well."

Living in Japan may be an interesting cultural experience, but it's sure not a bed of roses, according to Feldhaus. It wasn't easy for him to communicate with the natives. Did he learn any Japanese?

"I probably haven't picked up as much as I should," Feldhaus said. "I haven't studied that much and I've wanted to take a class while I'm over there. But in the town I'm in, I've never been able to take a class. Just from having friends and stuff, I have picked up on my own and every year I pick up more, which really does help.

"Their culture is so different. The language barrier was the biggest problem being in Japan — not being able to communicate to people. But on my team, my head coach speaks pretty good English, some of the players speak English, and my assistant coach went to school at Tennessee-Martin so he speaks perfect English. He helps me out a lot."

Feldhaus admits Asian food was another problem. "I get tired of eating rice and the same stuff all the time," he said. Sometimes he eats pizza. "I love pizza, but it's nothing like the American pizza."

With his communication problems and no relatives around, the former Wildcat said he sometimes got lonely in Japan, especially during the holidays. His first year as a pro player was the hardest. "Yeah, I get lonely," Feldhaus said, "but every year gets better and better. I picked up more language. I got more friends. In my first four years, I didn't get to come home for Christmas. I'm so close to my family and friends, I was really homesick then. The last season I got to come home for Christmas for about 10 days in the middle of the (basketball) season. It meant so much to me to see my family and friends, and it just like cut the monotony of being there to get to come home. Yes, I get lonely, but that's part of my job."

While in Japan, Feldhaus said he tried to follow the Wildcats. However, he hadn't been able to watch the entire Kentucky game on cable TV. Not even UK games which were televised on ESPN. "I get some highlights from ESPN news sometimes, but I get tapes," he said. "Friends and family send me tapes of some of the good games so I get to watch them that way. And I keep in touch with people on the phone so they keep me informed.

"I get 50 minutes of sports news every night and that's it. Just the highlights and mostly it's professional sports. So it's not much college sports. I make a point of getting a newspaper every day and they have some articles in there."

Besides getting the videotapes of UK basketball games, he also got tapes of his favorite TV show occasionally. He enjoyed watching *The Young and the Restless*. "My mother sent me the tapes," Feldhaus smiled. "I have followed it all these years and it's the show I like and, yeah, I get teased. I get teased by friends but I still watch it."

Unlike UK's highly-publicized basketball program, there isn't a lot of media coverage on his Japanese team. "The media is not around that much," Feldhaus said. "I see the coach talking to some people at interviews, but that's about it. There's a basketball magazine that has some articles in it, and local papers might have some articles." Were they good or bad? Feldhaus had no idea. Why? Because he couldn't read them. "I see my pictures sometimes and that's it," he laughed.

And unlike college or pro basketball in the United States, his Japanese squad doesn't draw large crowds. "We just go all around Japan and play in smaller towns and play in smaller gyms," Feldhaus added. "In a lot of our games, we don't play home and away games. We might have 2,000 people there (on a good night). Other games we might have 1,000 or less, but every year since I've been there the crowds have grown. You have a lot of kids there."

Feldhaus' father didn't see his son play in Japan. "He didn't really encourage it," said Allen. "He didn't think we really would like it that well."

While over 6,000 miles apart, the father and son frequently stayed in touch by phone. They usually talked twice a week. Their phone bill wasn't as bad as some would think as they had a special rate for international calls.

Since he no longer plays pro basketball in Japan, the younger Feldhaus is now considering a career in business with a possible option in coaching.

Deron comes from a basketball-rich family. Besides his father, who had a very successful coaching career in the prep ranks before retiring in 1991, the younger Feldhaus also has two older brothers who played college basketball — Allen Jr. at Eastern Kentucky and Willie at Morehead State. They are currently coaching together in the prep ranks.

Allen Jr. is the head coach at Madison Central High in Richmond with Willie serving as an assistant. Willie had been the head coach at Pendleton County High before moving to the Richmond school. Both had "always talked about how they wanted to do this together and the opportunity came up," said their father. "There was an opening so he (Willie) quit his head coaching job to go to Richmond and be assistant coach with Allen, and they really enjoy it." During the 1997-98 campaign, Madison Central's quest for Sweet Sixteen fell short when it dropped to powerful Lexington Catholic 82-62 in the 11th Region finals, finishing with a season mark of 23-9.

 With his father and brothers active in hoops, it forced Deron to be competitive when he was growing up in Mason County. "Being the youngest, it seems like I always was trying to keep up with them and they made it hard on me," Deron said. "So that really made me competitive. I've been competitive all my life."

With the elder Feldhaus coaching at Mason County, Deron said it was definitely an advantage to play for his dad. Since the father-son duo were together on the same team, they spent a lot of time together. Practicing. Traveling. Watching basketball on TV.

"We talked basketball a lot," commented Deron. "And I was always watching the Cats play on TV or any basketball game that was on TV. We would always discuss games so it was definitely an advantage (in having dad as the head coach)."

At the age of 50, his father retired from coaching as well as teaching in 1991. Allen posted an overall record of 511-220 in his 31-year career as the head coach at Russell County and Mason County, making him one of the all-time winningest basketball coaches in Kentucky prep ranks. He also sent four teams and three sons — all at Mason County — to the Sweet Sixteen in the 1980s.

Although Allen Feldhaus has been out of coaching for several years, some high schools have inquired about his availability. They have asked him if he would come out of retirement and coach basketball again. He turned all of them down.

"I'm done," said Feldhaus of his coaching tenure. "No, I would not (consider coaching). It wouldn't be fair to the youngsters and the administration. It wouldn't be fair because I just don't have that desire and drive."

Feldhaus finds it hard to believe that many prep coaches older than him are still active. "I really appreciate guys like Guy Strong (Clark County) and Doug Hines (Union County)," he said. "I really have a lot (of respect) for those guys who can stay in and keep that enthusiasm up." Lake Kelly of Fleming County is another veteran mentor who has been around for many years.

All three have ties with UK. Strong played on UK's 1951 national championship team. In the early 1960s, Hines spent one year as an assistant to Rupp, while Kelly served as an aide to coach Joe B. Hall in the early 1980s.

 One of the major reasons the elder Feldhaus quit coaching was that he and his wife, Leeanne (Deron's stepmother), wanted to see Deron play college basketball as a senior. While Allen had already seen most of Deron's games at Rupp Arena, he wanted to follow him and the Wildcats on the road.

"We didn't go on road trips when he was a sophomore and a junior except maybe when my team wasn't playing," Allen said. "We really regret that because that was such a great experience going on road trips. He had some great games on the road. I missed (one of his games) and I think it was Deron's sophomore year. We (Mason County) had a basketball game and they (Wildcats) were playing in Indiana. Deron had a great game. Deron would like to have played for Bobby Knight if he couldn't have played at Kentucky. He really liked Bobby Knight. He always played well against Indiana."

In the 1989 UK-Indiana contest held at Indianapolis, Deron led all scorers with 23 points and grabbed five rebounds in Kentucky's 71-69 loss. The thrilling matchup, which almost saw UK pull one of its biggest upsets in the series, marked Pitino's second game of his UK career.

And it was that game which forced the elder Feldhaus to consider retirement in the near future. Allen recalled, "I remember sitting on the school bus and we were going to Bourbon County to play and I had a little transistor radio. I was listening and I said right then if I ever get in this last year or two so I can retire, I will watch him play every game his senior year. So we, Leeanne and I, went on the road trips and stuff his senior year. Very enjoyable. I'll never forget it."

In addition, Allen wanted to spend more time working outdoors such as operating Kenton Station nine-hole golf course in Maysville where he and his wife own some interest after retiring from coaching.

"I think after my boys graduated, I lost a little something and I don't think you ought to stay in coaching unless you really are motivated to coach," said Allen. "It's a motivation game. I think if I lose my motivation to coach or whatever my job is, the people who are under me are going to lose their motivation, too. It all goes back to the head master type thing if you know what I'm saying. So I was ready to get out and I bought a golf course and I got interested in that. I wanted to do something maybe a little more financially rewarding than coaching.

"I have never looked back (in coaching). I've never missed it. I think of all the good times and of course you always think about some close games that you lost that you wish you had won. But if I had my life to live over again, I don't see many changes I'd make."

 When Allen Feldhaus graduated from Boone County High in northern Kentucky in 1958 where he was a multi-sport star, Kentucky didn't show much interest in him. The Wildcats didn't offer him a basketball scholarship. They felt he wasn't good enough to play for them after coach Adolph Rupp had sent one of his assistants to take a look at him in one of Boone County's games. So the player was set on going to Morehead. The school had agreed to let Feldhaus play all three sports in football, basketball and baseball.

That all changed in the summer when Feldhaus participated in a series of all-star games in the eastern Kentucky mountains. He did extremely well and the Wildcats offered him a scholarship after Rupp's assistant, Harry Lancaster, had seen him play in the series which attracted the state's top performers.

"There used to be an East-West All-Star Game played in eastern Kentucky and you played three games," recalled Feldhaus, who also was named to the 1958 Kentucky All-Star squad in the Kentucky-Indiana series, joining future Wildcat teammate Larry Pursiful of Bell County. "You played one in Pikeville, you played one in Hazard and one in Paintsville. I was selected to play in the all-star games. The first game was played in Paintsville and coach Lancaster was there. I had a decent ballgame. Then we went to Hazard to play and I ended up scoring like 32 points. It was one of those nights. I wasn't a great shooter, but everything I put up that night went in.

"At the time I really wanted to go to Morehead, but when I told my parents I had been offered that (UK) scholarship they said, 'Well, that's the thing to do,' and they were right. It was the place to go. It turned out okay. That was a great experience."

Although he didn't play all three sports at UK, Feldhaus managed to earn letters in basketball and baseball. "Baseball, back then, was my first love," he said. "I loved baseball."

While a sophomore at Boone County High, Feldhaus got to make a memorable trip to the state basketball tournament as the regional champs in 1956. His team, however, lost in the first round of the Sweet Sixteen. Yes, the same tournament which featured incredible performances by legendary King Kelly Coleman of Wayland High at UK's Memorial Coliseum in Lexington, scoring 68 points against Bell County and 50 versus Shelbyville. Rupp praised the coal miner's son, calling him the best high school player he has ever seen.

And Feldhaus has attended almost every state tournament since then. He said the annual tourney brings the folks from all walks of life together to enjoy the games and talk basketball.

 While everyone calls his son Deron "The House" because of his last name, folks refer the elder Feldhaus by a different nickname. They call Allen "The Horse." Some fans believe his nickname was given at UK because of his rugged defensive play and rebounding. However, he said that's not the case. Feldhaus earned the nickname in a prep football game.

"I got that in high school," said the elder Feldhaus. "My high school coach's name was Rice Mountjoy. (He was a) very successful high school coach and he coached at Centre College. I was just a good, old farm boy and he really helped me. Not just as an athlete, but in a lot of parts of life. His assistant coaches (also helped).

"And we were playing Beechwood and their head coach was Edgar McNabb. Beechwood was a smaller team at that time. Anyway, I kept getting into their quarterback and their ends were real small. I was playing defensive end. And at halftime, coach McNabb said (to the team), 'You all have got to stop No. 88.' Evidently the guy who was trying to stop me said, 'Coach, I can't stop that big horse. He runs over me every time.' Well, coach McNabb (later) told coach Mountjoy that and that's where the nickname came from and it stayed with me."

 When the 6-5 Feldhaus arrived on the UK campus, the Wildcats were coming off their national championship season of 1957-58. Popularly known as the Fiddlin' Five, the Wildcats had beaten Seattle and future NBA star Elgin Baylor 84-72 in Louisville for the NCAA title. It was Kentucky's first appearance in the Final Four since the point-shaving scandal hit UK and college basketball in the early 1950s. The Fiddlin' Five players, whom Rupp had thought in preseason wouldn't amount to anything spectacular, included Vernon Hatton, John Crigler, Johnny Cox, Ed Beck and Adrian Smith.

While playing on his freshman team which went 6-3 in a limited

Deron Feldhaus (left) and Allen Feldhaus in UK's publicity photo shots.   University of Kentucky Media Relations

schedule, Feldhaus got to see the defending champion Wildcats in varsity action. The 1958-59 Kentucky team — which finished at 24-3, including a stunning NCAA tourney upset loss to Louisville — featured Cox, a 6-4 senior star forward, and 6-3 sophomore guard Billy Ray Lickert, the state's former "Mr. Basketball" who would make All-SEC three times in his UK career. A native of Hazard, Cox was the only holdover from the Fiddlin' Five clan. The other standouts on the team included a pair of junior college transfers — guards Bennie Coffman and Sid Cohen, 6-7 junior center Don Mills, 6-9 sophomore center Ned Jennings, and 5-10 sophomore guard Dickie Parsons.

In his sophmore year, Feldhaus started the first two games of the season before Rupp replaced him with Mills. However, he continued to see a lot of playing time as a key reserve. Rupp liked Feldhaus' rugged defense and rebounding.

"I couldn't shoot," Feldhaus said. "If I had just been a little better shooter, I might have gotten to play a little more. I could rebound pretty good and I could play defense fairly. I wasn't a shooter at all and that hurt. I shot a lot of bricks. Back then it seemed like you had more people on the bench. There might be 13 or 14 or 15. I was always in the top eight and really that's about all coach Rupp played. And I always managed to stay in that top eight."

Interestingly, in the now-defunct University of Kentucky Invitational Tournament, Feldhaus was the one who broke the nose of All-American guard Jerry West of West Virginia, who later starred for the Los Angeles Lakers in the NBA, in the tourney's championship game.

"Well, I get credit for that," Feldhaus said of West's broken nose. "That was a funny ballgame. Jerry West's nose was probably broken I don't know how many times. I mean that wasn't something intentional. You know, for some athletes you just touch their nose and it does that. He broke his nose and had blood and all that. Of course, they had to take him out of the game and we go in at halftime. We might have been a point or two up. It was close at halftime. Coach Rupp was pretty enthused. He said, 'Well, you know we got him out,' and blah blah."

Well, Rupp was wrong. "He comes back out the second half and the best I can remember he scores like 28 or 30 points in the second half with cotton in his nose and all that stuff," Feldhaus continued. "So that's the way it turned out. I think it might have been the worse thing ever happened when I broke his nose. I think that just motivated him. You know he was the best player that I ever tried to defend. You could play him tight or you could stand away from him, and it didn't make any difference. He wouldn't necessarily penetrate around you. He could shoot anytime he wanted to. He was just a great shooter. Of course, he proved that later on in his career, too." West finished with 33 points in leading West Virginia to a 79-70 UKIT championship victory at Memorial Coliseum.

Over a week later, Kentucky played host to eventual national champion Ohio State, which had future NBAers Jerry Lucas, Larry Siegfried and John Havlicek. Bobby Knight, a 6-4 sophomore guard, was also on that team. In an exciting offensive battle, UK won the matchup 96-93. Feldhaus said, "That was probably the game I remember the most because people were throwing money on the floor. The crowd was just really, really into it. We beat them and of course Billy Ray Lickert had a tremendous game and so did Bennie Coffman. I got to play all the second half of that game. That was really exciting."

When Kentucky's 1959-60 campaign ended without an appearance in the NCAA tournament, Rupp had his worst record as UK boss since 1941 as the Wildcats went 18-7.

Kentucky wasn't much better in Feldhaus' junior season. The 1960-61 Wildcats, who tied for second in the conference (with Vanderbilt at 10-4 mark), lost a couple of more games than they did in the previous year. They finished with a 19-9 record, which at the time was the worst of Rupp's long coaching career at UK.

Despite the poor record (by UK standards), Feldhaus said there wasn't a lot of public criticism of the Wildcats or Rupp. "None, whatsoever," he said. "(Rupp) was the exception. He was an institution, you know."

In the mid-season, Kentucky encountered a three-game stretch in the South when it went into a rare slump, losing to Vanderbilt, LSU and Tulane on the road. UK's record dropped to 7-6 after the trip. "We should have beaten LSU, but they beat us and that's the first time in LSU history that they beat Kentucky," Feldhaus said. "And that wasn't very pleasant. We didn't play hard, it seemed, at LSU. Then the next night we went to New Orleans and played Tulane. They were pretty good. We played real, real hard, but we got beat.

"We thought after the game, 'Boy, we are in for a bad one when we get home.' But he (Rupp) said, 'You guys played hard tonight!' I was really surprised. We all looked at each other like maybe he's not going to kill us when we get home (in a tough practice). So I think he realized that we were just down a little then. But we came back some at the end of the year, too."

Feldhaus, a strong forward who always had to fight for playing time during his Wildcat career, remembers one particular incident when the Wildcats were facing Auburn. He believes it took place during his junior year when he and his teammates got a good tongue-lashing from an irritated Rupp in the dressing room during the halftime. The angry coach was visibly upset with his team's performance. He didn't like what he saw in the first half. He was even upset with Feldhaus who hadn't played at all.

"If you went in (the locker room), you'd almost fight not to be the first guy on the bench or whatever you were going to sit on because he'd start (yelling) and go right down the line and just chew on everybody," recalled Feldhaus. "Well, I was clear in the back. I had been the first one in the dressing room. So, I thought, 'Well, he is not going to get on me tonight. I haven't been in the game.' Then he started to chew on me when he came down to my turn and I was bristled up."

At that moment, assistant coach Harry Lancaster interrupted the fussing coach, saying, "Coach, Feldhaus hasn't been in the game."

"Well, I don't give a damn. He still hasn't done anything to help us," replied Rupp.

Feldhaus still sat, thinking about the Baron, and said to himself, "Maybe if you put me in, I could help you."

 During his coaching career, Rupp limited the media's access to his players even though there were no cable television outlets and specialty publications back then. The coach had a policy that if a sportswriter or a radio/TV guy wanted to talk to one of his players, he had to get permission from Rupp. The coach was fearful that some of his immature players might say something that he would later regret. To many sportswriters in Kentucky, Rupp was an intimidating, but colorful figure. He practically controlled the press, especially on the local level.

"That's definitely correct," Feldhaus said of Rupp's policy. "And back then if coach Rupp wanted something put in the paper, he would ask the sportswriter (to publicize it) if he felt like a player had been playing well and deserved some publicity. I know that happened.

"If you were a local writer, I don't think you'd want to write something about Rupp that he didn't like because I'm sure he would ban you from anything he had anything to do with. That's the way he was. That's all changed a lot. Coach Rupp, I know, if you did something well, he gave you your due credit. And if you didn't do things well, he would go on the other side, too."

Well-respected Knoxville sportswriter Ben Byrd, who is now retired, has an interesting story which took place in the 1960s or early 1970s when the Baron had just lost to Tennessee in Lexington. Byrd said Rupp sometimes wasn't a gracious loser. So when the visiting writer entered the team's dressing room after the game, Rupp noticed him.

"What are you doing in here?" Rupp exclaimed.

"I came in here to talk to you," Byrd replied.

"Well, you should have come out there to my post-game interview on the radio."

"Adolph, I've been coming in here for 20 years to talk to you after every game, and now you lose one and ain't gonna talk to me?"

"Okay, sit down. What do you want?" said the coach.

He was all right in that interview, Byrd later said of Rupp.

Another Rupp story. While Byrd was on a football-related assignment in Lexington he decided to drop by Memorial Coliseum and visit Rupp. Byrd saw the coach who was just getting ready to start one of his preseason basketball practices. The coach invited Byrd to watch the team practice. Byrd was very honored and pleased. "I went in, sat down and watched him and Harry (Lancaster) go through their act out there," he recalled. Rupp later came by and sat down with the writer.

"Adolph, who's gonna be your other guard this year?" questioned Byrd, who wanted to know which of the UK players would play in the backcourt with star Mike Casey. "Is it (Jim) Dinwiddie?"

"No, not Dinwiddie," Rupp answered.

"It's (Kent) Hollenbeck," Byrd said.

"No, no, it won't be Hollenbeck."

And about that time, a player came nearby, dribbling past them. Rupp stood up, pointing to the player, and said, "It's that little fart right there."

So Byrd still didn't know what the player's name was. "Adolph had gotten to the stage where he couldn't remember names," explained the former writer, who still regularly attends UT games in Knoxville.

One of Feldhaus' UK teammates during the 1961-62 season was Cotton Nash, a promising 6-5 sophomore who finished the 23-3 campaign as the SEC's top scorer with a 23.4-point average. One of UK's victories came against a weak Tennessee squad in a 95-82 verdict at Knoxville. That was the year before flamboyant Ray Mears became the UT boss and overhauled the struggling Vol program.

And it was that Tennessee game when Nash and Feldhaus got involved in a skirmish with a Vol player. "That was a lonely feeling," laughed Feldhaus. "I had just come in off the bench. I thought I should have been in earlier. So I wasn't in the best of mood when I went in the ball game and it was a jump ball (situation) on our end of the floor. The benches were on the end back then. As the official threw the ball up in the air for the jump, this guy took an elbow. I mean he just let Cotton have it and sort of bent Cotton over double and I said something to him. He said something back to me and we sort of went at it.

"Then he takes off running for his bench. Well, I took off running after him. When I got to the free throw line, I saw all these Big Orange sweaters with T's on them. That's their football players. Their football players used to sit behind their bench. They were sort of coming down and looked out to see who was going to help me. I didn't see anybody. So I turned around and went back to our bench. It was one of those spur of the moment things."

 Besides Nash, the other UK standouts on the 1961-62 team included guard Larry Pursiful and center/forward Carroll Burchett.   All three made All-SEC teams.   Scotty Baesler, a 6-0 playmaker, and 6-4 forward Roy Roberts also contributed to the team's success as Kentucky placed third in the final poll. And Feldhaus, of course, came off the bench and sparked the Wildcats to several victories as a senior, including a 16-point performance against Florida at the 7,000-seat Florida Gym, better known as "Alligator Alley."

While at UK, Feldhaus and three of his teammates — Burchett, Baesler and Pursiful — all roomed together at one time or another. While the group had good times, they were very close. The roommates once slept on old bunk beds with exposed springs. And Feldhaus has a good story about Baesler, who later became the mayor of Lexington and U.S. Congressman.

"I slept on the top bunk and Scotty was underneath, and there were only like three slats that held my box springs," he said. "At nights, we would go to bed and he would stick his feet up there. He would push me up in the air and then let it back down. And one morning about four o'clock, I fell through on him. It scared me to death and of course it scared him to death, too. We got the lights turned on and I got him from underneath there and his face was all bleeding where the box springs had hit him in the face and everything.

"You have to know Scotty to appreciate anything because he was always doing those kind of things and that was probably one of the fun things."

On Pursiful, Feldhaus said, "We roomed together all four years. I have been to his home at Four Mile (in Bell County) and we were close. We roomed together even at all-star games that summer (in 1958 after high school). What you see of Larry Pursiful is what he is. If he tells you what he is going to do, he is going to do it. He is just a great person."

 While Rupp, who was known as a "dictator-type" coach, guided the basketball program with unquestioned authority, Feldhaus said his team practices weren't that difficult physically, contrary to what some folks believed. The team scrimmaged a lot, but the coach primarily used psychology to keep his players mentally tough.

"I'll tell you something about coach Rupp. Physically, he wasn't that hard to practice under," Feldhaus commented. "He was more of a mental (type of coach). All the time he was working up here on your head. His practices were more routine. (He was) a great fundamentalist. He ran fundamentals after fundamentals. We scrimmaged a lot where coaches don't do that today — game situation scrimmages — and I and most of the players really looked forward to going to practices."

 Feldhaus was not only a basketball standout, but he excelled in baseball at UK. As a catcher, he earned All-SEC honors. After the roundball season ended, he and several other basketball players, including Dick Parsons, Cotton Nash and Larry Pursiful, would play baseball for head coach Harry Lancaster.

"The best part about baseball was when basketball was over, we went straight into baseball," Feldhaus said. "We started playing games. We didn't have to go through training and stuff."

The pro scouts liked Feldhaus, especially his aggressiveness. During his sophomore year, the Philadelphia Phillies offered Feldhaus a generous contract when the youngster, sidelined with a broken arm, sat in the stands with the Phillies scout during a UK baseball game.

"He offered me a pretty good contract and he said, 'I will fly you to Philadelphia and you talk to a Mr. Carpenter (of the father-son tandem which once owned the Phillies organization for many years) and maybe he will give you more,'" Feldhaus said. "Coach Lancaster found out he (scout) was there and ran him out, and he had a good talk with me about finishing college. He was correct."

Then during his senior year, Feldhaus broke a small bone in the wrist of his throwing hand. Since he was a catcher and couldn't throw, Lancaster placed him in the outfield. Playing hurt, he struggled. But

Feldhaus' promising career in pro ranks, for practical purposes, eventually disappeared. "The scouts lost a lot of faith in me then and my stock went down," he said. "So I sort of lost a little zest after that because it was a sort of bad luck thing."

Feldhaus, however, got another chance to play pro baseball after his UK career. While coaching and teaching at Russell County High during the school year, he played in the Washington Senators' minor league system for two summers. But things didn't work out and he decided to concentrate on his family and coaching career.

"I wasn't playing well," he said. "I didn't think I was going to make the major leagues. I already had a coaching job and a family, and I thought it was time to get back and get down to the basics of life and go to work. So I had to drop it (baseball). But I love baseball. That is my first love. I don't believe I could have made it. If I would have gone on and signed out of high school, which I could have, I might have (made it). But I wouldn't trade my experience with playing baseball and basketball at the University of Kentucky for that either."

 In basketball, Rupp and Lancaster had a long productive working relationship as they served as UK's head coach and top assistant, respectively. To be exact, Lancaster was Rupp's No. 1 assistant from 1946 to '69. They were good friends as well.

But their friendship began to deteriorate when Lancaster became the school's athletic director. Rupp's former assistant had become Rupp's boss. It was nothing bad, but their already-strained relationship hit a boiling point around 1970. One day at Memorial Coliseum, Rupp — who was approaching the university's mandatory retirement at the age of 70 — was seen yelling and complaining to a staffer about Lancaster and the school's athletic department. His boss didn't like what he saw and confronted Rupp about it.

As a result, they didn't speak to each other for several years other than an acknowledgment. And that bothered Feldhaus, who played for both men. "It was sad," he said. "I knew those guys. I knew their social life. They were socially close. It's a shame as successful as they were. Whatever the situation was, (it happened) after coach Lancaster took the athletic director's job. It still breaks my heart as much as those guys did together. I understand that right before the death (of Rupp), that maybe they patched up some things. I just think coach Rupp didn't want to quit coaching and I think he just bounced off everybody whom he thought could have kept him in the situation. He just did not want to give up that position and probably, you know, maybe it was time for him to give it up. That's hard to say."

Even though Feldhaus and Rupp actually didn't discuss the player's possible career in coaching while at UK, it was Rupp who helped the youngster land his first coaching job at Russell County High. Feldhaus had been working at Square D in the summer and was playing softball for the sponsoring store.

"I'll tell you how my first coaching job came about so young," Feldhaus said. "I think the superintendent at Russell County had called coach Rupp's office to see if any of the former players who had graduated were going into coaching and coach Rupp gave him my name. So I went to Russell Springs for that interview and that's how I ended up at Russell Springs."

Feldhaus remained there for several years before he quit. While he loved the beautiful south central Kentucky area, he felt that he should have been more successful with his basketball program even though several of his teams had posted 20 wins or so. Getting out of coaching, Feldhaus moved his family to Frankfort where he worked for the state government.

However, after four months, he and his family weren't too thrilled with their home life in Frankfort in the 1970s. The kids weren't particularly happy with school. So when the father, who at first wasn't interested in going back to coaching, told them about a coaching job offer from the superintendent of Mason County Schools, they encouraged him to say yes.

And the rest is history. "It turned out real well," Feldhaus said of his coaching days at Mason County High. As far as his sports career, including UK, is concerned, he wouldn't change it for anything else. "The opportunities in sports and the friends I made out of it are unbelievable and that's the best part of it. You know, financially, we overrate finances and we overrate a lot of things, but realistically the friends I've made through sports has meant the world to me and I wouldn't trade it for anything."

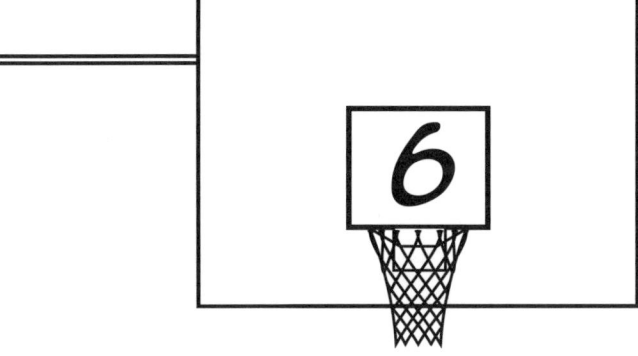

"PROFESSOR POPE"

Visiting the President at the White House is an once-a-lifetime experience that Mark Pope and his teammates will never forget. It all happened on May 20, 1996, exactly seven weeks after Kentucky's national championship victory over Syracuse. In a special ceremony honoring the NCAA champions, the Wildcats got to chat with President Clinton and Vice President Gore. Pope, on behalf of the team, presented President Clinton a special gift — a Wildcat uniform that had the President's name on the back and the jersey number 1. Vice President Gore also was given a UK jersey by Pope's senior teammate, Tony Delk. The jersey had No. 2 and Gore's name on it.

"It was really fun," said Pope about the White House meeting. "It was an amazing experience sitting in there waiting in this (East) Room in the White House and, over the loudspeaker, all of a sudden came this voice that said, 'Ladies and Gentlemen, the President of the United States will be arriving in five minutes.' So everyone kind of hushed down and you know, here you are in the White House.

"This voice comes over the loudspeaker again and said, 'Ladies and Gentlemen, please stand for the reception of the President of the United States.' All of a sudden the doors open and the band starts playing. Everybody stands up and starts clapping, and President Clinton, the Vice President and their attendants walk in. It was quite an amazing experience.

It was really exciting to be able to walk up to the podium and say a few things and be able to shake the President's hand. Just because the office that he holds and the respect due to that office, it was a great experience for all of us."

Did President Clinton, an avid Arkansas Razorback fan, recognize Pope? "Yeah, I think so," Pope said. "I know that the President, for example, watched the championship game. So, I'm sure that he recognized the players and you know he follows athletics. He's been extremely supportive of athletic endeavors whether on college or professional level. He follows the game closely."

With Clinton and Gore standing nearby at the ceremony, then-UK coach Rick Pitino joked that the nation should re-elect the Clinton/Gore team for another term since the SEC has commanded the Final Four for the last few years. The red-faced Clinton laughed so hard that he had to wipe his eyes.

The Wildcats, by the way, were not the only team participating at the White House affair. The Tennessee Lady Vols attended the ceremony as the women's national champion. It marked the first time a single conference — or the SEC for that matter — had both men's and women's NCAA basketball champions in the same year since 1982 when the NCAA began sponsoring the women's tournament.

 At UK, Mark Pope was not a typical basketball player. While he was a 6-10, 235-pound center and enjoyed basketball, he had many other interests. He also loved to read. He loved to write essays. He loved cycling. He loved milking cows. He was nominated for a prestigious Rhodes Scholarship and he received his bachelor's degree in English. Unlike some players, Pope didn't allow his Wildcat popularity to cloud his proper perspective on life. As you can tell, Pope, a devoted Mormon, is just one of those unique people who doesn't let basketball dominate his life completely.

In 1995, during his senior year, a very pleased Pope was honored when the school nominated him as one of two Rhodes Scholarship candidates on the UK campus. His professors saw Pope's enormous potential and they encouraged him to apply for the Rhodes Scholars program. According to Pope, it was an interesting experience just to go through the process.

"I had a couple of teachers who had said, 'Listen, this is something

An attentive Mark Pope listens to then-coach Rick Pitino in their earlier days at UK.

Photo by Chris Jones

you should really seriously consider,' and I did," said Pope, who was one of the more likable players on the team. "I went through this whole long drawn out process — I had to write a full-length essay, get recommendations from teachers on the campus and go through a series of interviews on campus — and then when I was chosen to do that, I was thrilled. I was really excited. It's one of those things that I can't imagine anything else that I would look forward to more. Of course, it didn't work out, but the procedure itself was interesting and I learned a lot from that. It was something to actually represent the university."

When his professional basketball career is over, Pope isn't very sure about his career options, but admits teaching is a very good possibility.

"I'm not absolutely sold on any course yet," Pope said. "But my preference probably would be to teach college English. You know, I just really have a passion for that and really enjoy it. I love the college atmosphere. Of course, to do that (teaching at a four-year university) you have to go out and get your Ph.D., which is another heck of a process. That is something I would look forward to doing in the future."

An Academic All-SEC selection and third-team GTE Academic All-America pick as a junior, Pope said that while he took some literature classes, he learned not only so much about himself but also about cultures and peoples around the world. He loved these classes. "I think it's fantastic," he said. After a practice, Pope would often lie down on his bed and read. "It's a great leisure for me," said the Bellevue, Wash., native who transferred to Kentucky after a couple of seasons at Washington.

 Born in Omaha, Nebraska, Pope played prep basketball at Newport High School in Bellevue, Washington (near Seattle), where he was regarded as the best big man in the state. Pope also received player of the year honors for the state of Washington from *Seattle Times* and McDonald's, among others. A highly-recruited standout, he eventually signed with Washington of the Pacific-10 Conference even after Kentucky's Rick Pitino visited the player at his home on a recruiting visit. Besides Washington and Kentucky, Pope was mainly interested in Utah, California (at Berkeley) and Arizona. He liked Syracuse, too.

Pope said Pitino's two-hour visit to his parents' home in Bellevue during the 1990-91 campaign was "the first time I had met the coach. I remember I was extremely impressed with coach Pitino. How could you not be? I mean anybody who's dealt with him would be impressed. He's a really charismatic guy. He presents himself well and has great stories to tell because he has been around.

"I just listened and listened to what he had to say. I honestly didn't know much about Kentucky at the time. Kentucky had been on probation so you didn't hear a lot about them in the national media. They hadn't been in the NCAA tournament. So I just didn't know too much.

"Coach was extremely impressive. He had just come from the (New York) Knicks and had been successful with Providence. I really enjoyed what I heard. But you know I didn't really start to appreciate the coach. You can't really start to appreciate him until you work with him everyday. So it wasn't until I got here (at UK in 1993) and had to deal with him every day, that I started to understand him a little better and I really started to have a great respect for him."

While he considered Kentucky and Syracuse, Pope said he concentrated his collegiate choice among the schools from the west coast. "Those were the schools I was most familiar with," he said. "I really like the west coast and you know there were some good programs."

Since he was very comfortable with the school and its basketball coach, Pope ended up signing with the Washington Huskies in his hometown of Seattle. Interestingly, Pope's mentor at Washington had some connections with UK. Lynn Nance once coached at UK as assistant under coach Joe B. Hall for a couple of seasons in the mid-1970s.

 When Pope began his freshman year at Washington, Nance and the basketball program were still struggling to bring the Huskies into the upper echelon in Pac-10. Nance was just beginning his third year at Washington after posting an overall record of 26-31 in his first two years at the Husky helm.

In his first year at the university, Pope showed promise when he was voted the Pac-10 freshman of the year. He led Washington in field goal shooting, hitting nearly 58 percent of his shots, and in rebounds with 8.1 rpg, which was good for fourth place in the league. He also was the only Pac-10 rookie to start every game.   As in its previous two years, Washington, however, still struggled in 1991-92 as it didn't show many signs of improvement.

Nance got involved in a local controversy involving racism. "There was a big deal about a couple of players who had gotten kicked off the team," Pope said. "(They) claimed they were kicked off for racial reasons. So all of this kind of stuff started getting thrown around and the university did not support coach Nance. It was just an unfortunate situation."

About a year later, Nance eventually stepped down from his Washington job after a so-so 13-14 campaign (7-11 in Pac-10). While the racism charges certainly played a key role in Nance's leaving, the coach reportedly resigned because athletic director Barbara Hedges had rejected his request for a contract extension. According to published reports, Nance, who had one year remaining on his contract, received over $100,000 from the school in a settlement.

Because of Nance's ugly departure, the Huskies lost Pope after his sophomore year when he decided to leave the campus. In 1992-93, he averaged 12.2 points and 8.0 rebounds. Pope, who had a season-high 22 points against arch-rival Washington State, also led the league in free throw accuracy with an 86.2 percentage.

While Pope admitted the team should have done better on the floor, he believes Nance's firing wasn't done properly. "I didn't believe it was handled fairly and I didn't want to be there if he wasn't there," Pope commented. "The whole situation with coach Nance and him being fired and all the stuff that went on in Seattle was really tumultuous. It was a difficult experience to deal with. It was a tragedy. I was really disappointed and decided that I was going to leave Washington."

Nance, a former FBI agent who compiled a four-year mark of 50-62 at Washington, was replaced by Bob Bender, an ex-Duke assistant who was the head coach at Illinois State. Bender, a former guard who once played against UK in the 1978 NCAA Finals, scoring seven points, also tried to talk Pope into staying. However, the player said no.

Pope said he and Nance still keep in touch. In the summer after UK's 1996 NCAA championship, Pope visited his former mentor at Southwest Baptist University in Bolivar, Missouri, where Nance was serving as the head coach. Nance and his wife Sally are both graduates of Southwest Baptist, a former junior college.

"I went out and spoke at his camp and we had a great time," said Pope. "He is a real special man and he has meant a lot to me. Coach took me to the barber shop because that's where all the important citizens in town hung out."

And the local folks asked him about his national championship experience. "It doesn't matter where you go, whether it be in the United States or Turkey, people want to ask you about that because it's such a big deal and it's published worldwide and everybody knows about it," Pope said.

After two years at Washington, many people thought Pope would be heading for Utah where he had many relatives, especially on his mother's side, since Utah had been Pope's second choice while in high school. Utah's personable coach,

Rick Majerus, was still there. Majerus, who had unsuccessfully recruited the player hard, still sought the transfer from Washington

"I really liked coach Majerus," Pope said. "He loves the game. The man is single. He lives in a hotel. He just lives for the game and he does a great coaching job. Unfortunately, he hasn't been able to recruit very many athletes to Utah and that's hurt him. But he has done a great job there and you know he really treats the game and his players with respect. His players really improve under him."

While his relatives encouraged him to transfer to Utah, Pope wanted to think it over. But not very long because Washington was "a pretty hostile environment as far as the press was concerned how they were dealing with me. So I needed to make a quick decision, " explained Pope.

Therefore, he concentrated on only two schools that he was interested in while in high school. In addition to Utah, he liked UK. "Kentucky had been in my top five out of high school," he said. "It was the last visit I had planned, but decided not to take it out of high school." Nance even talked to Pope about Kentucky, too.

After visiting UK, Pope fell in love with the program and the campus. No single person or factor persuaded him to sign with the Wildcats, he said. He liked just about everything at the school. He liked the coaches. He liked the players. He wanted to be a part of school's strong basketball tradition. He was impressed with the team's ardent fan support.

"I really liked coach Pitino and loved his coaching staff," Pope recalled. "I really enjoyed the little time I had to spend with the players and was very impressed with them. I loved the situation that they were in. They all lived together (in Wildcat Lodge) and just spent time together. Coach Nance obviously had influence on me, his being here (at UK one time) and knowing what Kentucky was like. He was excited about the prospect of me playing here (in Kentucky).

"I don't know if there was one thing that stood out above the rest (in choosing UK). It was just the whole deal. I was excited to be at a school where you're playing the best schedule. I mean I was excited to be in the best program in the country and I kid you not."

Utah's Majerus wasn't surprised when he lost Pope to Kentucky. "Once they get a look at Kentucky, they don't come back," said the coach in *The Seattle Times.*

 Because of transfer rules, Pope had to sit out the 1993-94 campaign. He practiced with a young Kentucky team that had to play without All-American Jamal Mashburn, who left UK after his junior year for NBA. The Wildcats, nevertheless, adjusted well. They captured their third straight SEC tournament title and advanced to the NCAA tourney's second round before dropping to coach Kevin O'Neill's Marquette squad in a disappointing 75-63 setback. Under the guidance of senior playmaker Travis Ford and a group of talented sophomores, Kentucky finished with a 27-7 mark and a No. 7 national ranking.

For Pope, it was a very difficult season not being able to play in regular games. However, it gave him an opportunity to learn the new system at UK. "It was great for me," he said of his learning experience. "At Washington, I had played a half-court style of play. That was all I had ever been used to. I didn't know anything about pressing or running or anything like that. The year that I spent sitting out gave me an opportunity to kind of become acquainted with the system, acquainted with coach Pitino's style and acquainted with the carnival atmosphere in Kentucky and all those things. So it was really an important year for me." After Pope spent one year on the sidelines, Pitino praised the player's work ethics, calling him "by far the hardest worker I've come across in my 20-year coaching career."

 In his three years at Kentucky, including the one he sat out, Pope has seen several incidents involving Pitino. Pope said the most remarkable thing he has seen about Pitino occurred when the coach blasted the team for cheating during the UK-Vanderbilt game at Nashville in 1994. Three Wildcat players — seniors Travis Ford and Gimel Martinez, and sophomore Jared Prickett — participated in the free throw scam in Kentucky's 77-69 win over the Commodores. As a result, Pitino suspended these three players for one game.

"You know that is hard to narrow it down to just one thing," he said of Pitino's memorable incidents. "(I remember) we had just played Vanderbilt down there and there was the free throw scandal. Coach called an emergency meeting and he just yelled and screamed at us for 45 minutes. He was not talking about winning or losing which a lot of people think he is obsessed with. He is driven to win, (but) there are things that drive him that are more powerful or more meaningful than that. He was talking about integrity, honesty and respect for the game. He was furious. I mean he was just in a rage. It was one of the early experiences I had that first year I was sitting out that really won me over to him.

"My respect for him really grew because it was one of those moments where you see, while the guy is a great coach, he is a better man than he is a coach. That was really exciting for me and it was a great experience in dealing with him day to day and seeing how hard he works. He really, especially during the season, just dedicates all of his time to the game. I think he might be the most talented coach in the country not just because of his Xs and Os, but because he has a great scheme and of how he deals with the players. He's a great people person."

With three suspended players staying in Lexington, a very thin Kentucky team traveled to Knoxville and surprised everyone when the Wildcats found a way to beat the Vols. Kentucky, which once fell behind 14 points, scored its last 10 points on free throws to defeat Tennessee 77-73.

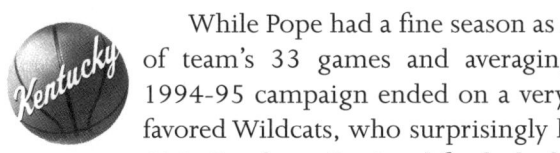 While Pope had a fine season as a junior, starting eight out of team's 33 games and averaging 8.2 points, Kentucky's 1994-95 campaign ended on a very disappointing note. The favored Wildcats, who surprisingly lost to North Carolina 74-61 in Southeast Regional finals, had been expected to advance to the Final Four. While the contest featured an ugly confrontation in the first half between UK's 6-9 Andre Riddick and North Carolina's 6-10 Rasheed Wallace, a future NBA lottery pick, it marked Kentucky's worst shooting performance of the season. As a result, UK finished with a 28-5 worksheet, including a thrilling 95-93 overtime victory over eventual Final Four participant Arkansas in the SEC tourney's title game in Atlanta.

Shortly after the NCAA tourney loss which saw ice-cold Kentucky hit only 28 percent of its field goals, the team returned to its hotel in Birmingham, Ala., and painfully watched the game they had just lost on tape. Pitino was furious. He sincerely believed that his players really blew a once-a-lifetime chance to win the national championship in Seattle, the site of 1995 Final Four (and Pope's hometown).

"Coach made us all come back to the hotel. We sat there and watched the video for about three hours of the game," said Pope, who had one point in 13 minutes of action. "That was devastating. Coach's reaction

Linda Pope proudly looks up to her son, Mark, in an emotional pre-game ceremony honoring UK seniors in 1996. The Wildcats later capped the Senior Day festivities with an easy 101-63 victory over hapless Vanderbilt.

Photo by Jamie H. Vaught

was really devastating. The coach just yelled and hollered the whole time. We had just lost, and all our hopes and dreams had been crushed. The season was over. It was devastating for me personally because the Final Four was in Seattle and I would have been able to go home."

A visibly-torn Pitino, however, was still in a lousy mood the next morning, a Sunday. He ordered a one-on-one meeting with his players and severely criticized them for not being mentally prepared for the regional finals. "Coach had us all come down and meet with him individually," Pope said. "He said some extremely harsh things to us just one-on-one."

And Pitino left his players madder than ever, including Pope, after the meeting. The players were fuming at the coach. Pope commented, "We got back (to Lexington) and I remember talking to Tony Delk about two weeks after the loss. We were both really angry at the coach. You know we were hurt. We were devastated and yet the coach had to go on and magnify all the hurt and despair a hundredfold with his harsh criticisms and incisive comments for hours after the game. And we were pretty angry with him."

Looking back, Pope said Pitino's scathing comments had a purpose. Using one of his motivational techniques, the coach was preparing the players for the future. He warned them that they had better be ready for every game or face the consequences. To this day, Pope said he is still hurt by Pitino's behavior.

"In hindsight, we realized that coach Pitino, as it's usually the case, was preparing us for the future," said Pope. "I really believed that it was coach's reactions to that loss to North Carolina that enabled us, for example, to go through the entire SEC regular season undefeated (16-0 in 1995-96), something that no team had done in 40 years.

"Because of what the coach had ingrained deep into our souls, and I still hurt today, he made that such a profound experience in our lives that we would never again go into a game not prepared to go 100 percent. We knew that whether we were playing the best team in the SEC or maybe not such a good team in the SEC, we had to come in and play as well as we possibly could every night to win. I think coach used it as a great learning experience, however difficult it was, and taught us a lesson that helped us to win the national championship the next year (in 1996)."

On the post-season loss to North Carolina, Pope agreed that the Wildcats were not 100 percent ready. "It wasn't only that we weren't ready to play, but we were not in top condition to be prepared to win that game," he said. "We were not at our very top level mentally. We were not at our top level execution-wise with what we were doing on the floor."

Before UK had won the national crown in 1996, Pope once mentioned that his greatest moment in sports took place in a practice session at Memorial Coliseum when Pitino interrupted practice and angrily screamed at the player in front of his teammates. "I was in practice one day and I can't even remember what we were doing, but I said something," Pope recalled, "and coach just stopped the playing, yelled at me and said, 'Would you stop talking so much? You're wasting your oxygen! Save your oxygen!' Coach would say strange things every now and then. He would come up with some great lines and you know that was the kind of things that happen when you're in such an intense atmosphere.

"We practiced twice a day, every day, and during the winter we practiced sometimes three times a day. After the first practice in the morning, you are so tired and you don't think you can even walk to class. You got to walk to class and come back and have another full-blown practice. So, working that hard together and spending that much time together, funny things are bound to happen. You know you're under this intense scrutiny. There's so much pressure and you're so tired and busy all the same time. You're just squeezed in this little area and it's bound to cause strange things to happen. So those are the times that you really treasure.

"The guys were giving me a hard time about it. But the thing is that coach gets on everybody. What coach does is he makes you stronger."

 During Kentucky's 1995-96 national championship season, *Sports Illustrated* ran a cover story, "A Man Possessed," about Pitino in its February 26, 1996 edition. Authored by senior writer William Nack, the 12-page article, including several unflattering illustrations of the coach and his wife Joanne, described Pitino as a man obsessed with winning basketball games. The story upset Pitino so much that he asked for an apology from the magazine. *Sports Illustrated* balked, standing behind the writer and the article. Pope wasn't too pleased with the story, either.

"I was really disappointed," said Pope of the article. "I was disappointed by the pictures, but also just by the article. You would expect a comprehensive or at least fair-minded article. I didn't think it was fair at all. It talked about coach's obsession with winning and losing, and with the things in his life."

Before the article was published, Pope spent nearly an hour with the writer. They discussed Pitino at length. "When the reporter was spending time on campus, I sat down and talked with him for about 45 minutes," Pope added. "We talked about that very thing (Pitino's obsession). I remember making the comment to him several times that, yes, coach is obsessed with winning and losing.

"There's a side to him that is deeper than that and it is more important and must be kept private just because that's a sacred side of him. This is something that we talked about at length. This author choose not to be fair, or try to be understanding and not to say a word about that at all.

"You know, I'm not a journalist so I don't know. But if you're talking about a man's life, you're talking about it on a national scale. I think that you owe it to the person that is being discussed to at least give a fair evaluation. At least give the full scope. If (the writer) wants to have somebody saying all that matters to coach Pitino is winning and losing and nothing else in his life matters, that's fine. But if you're going to do that, you should also have the other person who is saying, 'Listen, there is more to the man,' and I know because I spent every day with him for three years. So that was disappointing to me."

Ex-Wildcat Cameron Mills had heard the article was very disturbing. "To be honest, I never read the article," he said later in 1998. "From what I heard about it, I would say it's probably inaccurate. I had seen the pictures in it. The pictures were not good. But coach Pitino is a man who loves his family and is not possessed. He is obsessed with winning basketball games. I don't think he would necessarily sacrifice his family because he loves his family more than anything else. His kids will walk in, his wife will walk in practice. He leaves practice for a second to go talk to them and give his kids hugs and you can just tell he loves his family to death."

While an ambitious Pitino obviously believed the one-sided article unfairly painted him as some type of maniac, he told his players not to say anything about the story. The coach, who let his own actions speak for themselves, didn't want the controversy to escalate and create unnecessary distraction for the squad. It was his problem, not the team's, he said.

Said Pope: "All coach Pitino said was, 'Listen, guys, just don't make any comment about it. I'm going to let my own actions and my friends speak for themselves. I don't need to come out and get all angry and upset about this.' And that's just his style and he deals with things like that so well because he teaches us to stand up and not be discouraged by tough situations or events or criticism."

 Pope, meanwhile, had launched his senior year on a good note. In a season-opening Hall of Fame Tip-Off Classic against 14th-ranked Maryland, he scored what would be his career-

high 26 points and grabbed six rebounds in top-ranked Kentucky's come-from-behind 96-84 victory at Springfield, Mass. For his outstanding effort in the nationally-televised matchup, Pope received the MVP trophy.

"I don't know if it was my best game," Pope said of his UK career. "It was my best game as far as scoring. As far as things that we look for in a game, I don't know if it was my best game or not. Midway through the season I had two or three double-doubles. It's hard to rate your games because it just depends on what you are looking for."

Coming off the Wildcat bench, Pope had a couple of outstanding games in February. In UK's 88-73 home court win over Arkansas, the Wildcat center posted his first double-double of the season as the reserve center had 11 points and 11 rebounds. Tony Delk scored a game-high 21 points for the winners. Pope also had another double-double in UK's next game. He starred in the Wildcats' 86-73 victory over new coach Tubby Smith and his Georgia Bulldogs at Rupp Arena, scoring 16 points and snatching 11 rebounds, both game-highs.

According to Pope, who finished his senior year with an average of 7.6 points a game, February is "the time when the team starts to get a little bit tired. That's the time when your starters start to wear down a little bit. It was up to guys coming off the bench, like me, to put up a real good effort to maintain our intensity because it's a long season for a college kid going to school and everything. So there were some good games there."

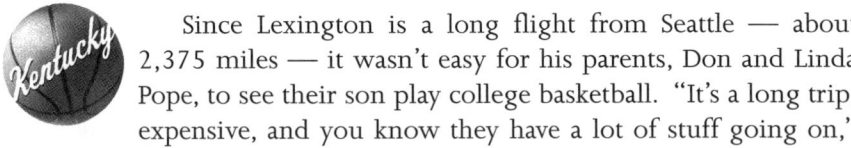

Since Lexington is a long flight from Seattle — about 2,375 miles — it wasn't easy for his parents, Don and Linda Pope, to see their son play college basketball. "It's a long trip, expensive, and you know they have a lot of stuff going on," said Mark Pope, who has three older brothers and two younger sisters.

Still, his folks managed to make one journey to Kentucky during the 1994-95 season when Pope was a junior. During his senior year, they made a couple of trips in the regular season, including the Senior Day festivities. His parents also saw him play in post-season action — the SEC tournament and the Final Four. Although the younger Pope wished his parents had attended more Kentucky games, he said he's thankful that his parents saw "enough where they got see what Rupp Arena was like and what it was like in that game," he said. "That was important to me. They had the opportunity to understand what the whole thing (atmosphere) was like."

"My folks are great. They participated in my athletic career and were supportive all along, and that was one of the most difficult things for me coming to the University of Kentucky because it is so far away from home. My parents were not able to see the games with the exception of watching them on TV and some infrequent visits. I wish my parents had been able to attend more games. It was a little bit tough, but they were so grateful on their visits they could really see how well people here were taking care of me, in particular, and the team as a whole. They were extremely appreciative of the people here and (they) knew I was in a great situation. You're forced to have this team as a family and the people in the community are great. You can't go anywhere without someone willing to offer help."

 Pope said his dad, a retired executive from a natural resources firm, is the primary inspiration as far as his sports career is concerned. "He is the quintessential example in my life," he commented about his father.

Many years ago, when the elder Pope realized his son had potential to be a good basketball player because of his size, he started to encourage him to participate in roundball. The father wanted his son to have the opportunity to play basketball.

"Dad was always encouraging," Pope said. "He loved to see me be successful in that and it was really exciting for him. Of course, he never pushed me into anything that I didn't like. He, as well as my mom and all of the extended family, just appreciated the fact that I was being successful and having a great experience with it."

Before he concentrated solely on basketball when he went to Newport High School, Pope ran a lot. "When I was young, my favorite sport was track and field," he said. "I loved the running. We got into that point where we would do it all summer long and travel all over the country, going to meets. We had a great time. Once I got into high school, though, I kind of set everything else aside and just played basketball."

Pope today is also a bicycle enthusiast. He rides every chance he gets. His favorite sports figure is someone who is not even involved in major sports like basketball, football and baseball. Pope's favorite is cyclist Miguel Indurain of Spain, who has won Tour de France several times. "He's probably the greatest cyclist who ever lived," he said. "He might be the most conditioned athlete around."

 Many of Pope's relatives in Utah aren't all that pleased with Kentucky's recent success against Utah in the NCAA tournament. His grandfather and uncle held season tickets at Utah's home games. Since the 1993 NCAA tourney, UK is 4-0 against the Utes in post-season action, including a 101-70 victory during Pope's national championship season as a Wildcat senior.

"They are definitely not big Kentucky fans," Pope smiled. "It has been really frustrating for them. My entire family on my mom's side all live in Salt Lake City. My mom had seven brothers and sisters, and all of them had big families. It's a lot of people.

"Out of high school, when I was being recruited, Utah was my second choice behind Washington. Then, when I decided to transfer, it was Kentucky and Utah and I got a lot of family pressure for Utah (he laughed).

"It was especially poignant playing Utah in the tournament my senior year. All of my family, of course, were excited for me, but they were also die-hard Utah fans. So, (they were) a little bit torn there. It was interesting."

In UK's 31-point victory over Utah in the 1996 Midwest Regional semifinals, sophomore sensation Antoine Walker led the Wildcats with 19 points, eight rebounds and six assists. Teammate Derek Anderson followed with 18 points, including a perfect 8-for-8 from the line. Pope had five points and two rebounds in limited action.

 Pope, who for two years served as one of the team's three captains, didn't really preform well in Kentucky's national title game with Syracuse. He scored only four points, hitting one of six baskets, and committed four turnovers in 27 minutes of action. The Wildcats, however, had enough manpower to defeat the Orangemen 76-67 as Tony Delk (24 points, including seven three-pointers) and freshman Ron Mercer (20 points) guided the school to its sixth NCAA title.

"In the national championship game, I didn't play well at all," admitted Pope. Of course, he wasn't proud of his performance, but he didn't get real discouraged during the game. Why? Because Pitino had coached the player and others to be mentally tough, and stay focused on the game plan.

"That's something that coach really works on," Pope said of Pitino's coaching tactics. "Had I been playing that bad in the past, I would have gotten down on myself. And you know that would have been the end of it. But coach had been so tough on us that we would never be that tough on ourselves. The media or anyone else couldn't be any tougher. So you are used to it.

"For example, in that (NCAA title) game, I had been so conditioned that even though I was playing bad, I could still stay focused and stay with the game. At the end of the game I ended up making a steal and hit two free throws. It is just a small little thing, but it is a thing that maybe you couldn't do if you're not that mentally tough.

"It's not fun to just be yelled at and berated and embarrassed in front of your teammates or in front of anyone else. And coach doesn't do that to humiliate you. He does it to make you stronger. It really works and it shows. It's a gift that he has given to us so that whether it be in games or in the rest of our lives that we can stand up and be confident in what we are doing and not be distracted or discouraged by negative events or personal failures, but just keep pushing forward."

After the championship victory, a jubilant Pope celebrated with his team on the floor, hugging everyone in sight, and operated a camcorder to capture rare moments of a picture-perfect conclusion of Kentucky's 34-2 campaign.

 Not long after UK's 1996 NCAA title, Pope had an eye-popping experience during an autograph session at a Lexington shopping mall. At this special moment he will never forget, he began to realize that UK's high-profile basketball program was bigger than he had previously thought.

"I was at a mall signing and going through the line and all of a sudden coming at the front of the line was a man who must be have been 40 or 45," said Pope. "His skin was just leathery hard and he had a beard. His clothes were kind of dirty and he had a real, real thick eastern Kentucky accent. Tears were streaming down his face. This man had worked harder than any of us probably could ever imagine for his whole life just doing manual labor. A hard, strong man who was just sobbing just because of the whole idea of Kentucky basketball, the tradition and the championship. It means so much (to the fans). Stories like that I could just tell for hours.

"That's where you really see what Kentucky basketball is about.

You can see it in those people's eyes. That's the only way you could ever understand what this whole thing is about. That's the only place you can find it. This is about the state of Kentucky and this is about people's pride. This is about a love for the game and it is so much bigger than any individual. That is the great thing about this program. As great as some of the superstars that we've had at Kentucky, they're not Kentucky. Kentucky is the people in the state, knowing the pride that they have. It's an extraordinary thing. The longer that you're here, the more you can kind of get a grasp of what it's all about. It's amazing.

"I remember when I was deciding to transfer here, coach Nance told me all kinds of stories. I would kind of listen to the stories and kind of shake my head, thinking he's exaggerating. Here in Kentucky, it is something that you can't believe until you see or experience it for yourself. Each year I have learned a little bit more how amazing it was."

 Now that Pope has graduated from UK, he has become friends with Pitino in more comfortable surroundings. They are no longer in a player-coach relationship, which was at times, rocky. After a pro basketball stint in Turkey, Pope returned to the UK campus and stayed at the Wildcat Lodge for a few weeks in the spring of 1997.

"It has been really fun for me being an ex-player and seeing my relationship with coach Pitino because that is something he also takes very seriously," said the ex-Wildcat, who posted a cumulative 3.7 grade-point average at UK. "After you graduate, suddenly this player-coach relationship is gone and so now you just have real friends. He is such a great friend that he will really do anything for you. So if you need a favor or you need some advice or you just need a good word, you can always be in contact with coach.

"He always wants to know how things are going with his players. I remember every once in a while he would bring a letter in from a former player and read it to us before practice. It wouldn't be about basketball. It would be about how this person's life had gone after college and how things were going. You could tell that those things were always extremely important to him and this is one of the things that I did not know about the coach when I decided to come here. That's been a huge bonus. It's just that he takes so much interest in his players' lives after their careers are over. So the coach has the whole spectrum.

"You know he is not perfect. He makes some mistakes, but he's the best coach I've ever been around and one of the best men that I've ever been around. He knows how to motivate people and how to understand people and how to push the right buttons. Not manipulatively, but in a way that is going to bring out the best in them. And he really cares about them."

On Pitino's relentlessness, which eventually landed him a lucrative contract with the Boston Celtics, Pope said, "He's got a great drive and enthusiasm. He just keeps a torrid schedule. He is extremely busy. He is trying to take every moment of life and every little bit that he can. He always talked to us about the precious moment and he really follows his own example. He really does grab everything that he can, which is the way it should be."

Although the Indiana Pacers selected Pope as the 52nd pick in the 1996 NBA Draft, he opted to play pro basketball overseas in Turkey after holding frank discussions with Indiana officials, including president Donnie Walsh. The Pacers felt Pope needed to improve before the player would have a chance to make the NBA team. So he signed a one-year pact with Efes Pilsen, a squad based in Turkey, with an eye toward the NBA in near future.

Pope didn't disclose the financial terms of his contract, but he admitted that the Turkish team took very good care of him. In addition to his salary, the club provided him an apartment and a car. Asked if his pay was very similar to the NBA's minimum salary of about $250,000, Pope replied, "Well, there is the potential to make a lot more," he said, "because of those benefits — you don't have to pay any expenses. You don't have to pay taxes. Taxes are the big thing. I ended up having to pay about three or four percent (in U.S. income tax) or something like that, instead of 40 per-cent, which just makes an amazing difference. Those are some of the ben-efits.

"Because of the way FIBA (Federation of International Basketball) works, the team not only pays your taxes, but it also pays your agent. So, supposed the team is paying me $500,000. If I was playing in the States for that $500,000, I would pay $220,000 for taxes and pay $40,000 to my agent and then pay another $100,000 for my living expenses or whatever. But in Europe you just get that ($500,000) in your bank . They pay your agent and your taxes, and they pay all your expenses. So that's one of the benefits. The drawback is that you're stuck in Turkey."

 Besides Turkey, the Istanbul-based team also played in other regional countries such as France and Spain. Its schedule usually called for games twice a week, according to Pope. As his squad prepared for the opening of the basketball season in the fall of 1996, Pope encountered an extraordinary cultural experience. It took place on what he calls the "Media Day."

"The third or fourth day I was there we sacrificed a ram and it was our media day," said Pope, who was the only American on the team. "We were all dressed in uniform and we circled around this ram. They killed the ram, collected the blood in a bucket and splashed some across us. (The event) was almost like our Midnight Madness or something.

"It is just a different world. Turkey is on the other side of the world. It's a completely different culture. It's an Islamic country. It was hard because my teammates didn't speak English very well and the coach didn't speak English at all. So I had an interpreter and that was a challenge.

"But it was also exciting to be able to travel all over and to be able to live actually in Europe, especially in a place like Turkey that is very different. They have (prayers) five times a day in every neighborhood. Five times a day you hear over the loudspeakers calling for prayer and you'll see people at the public fountains washing before they go pray."

Because of language barriers, Pope often got lonely during his adventurous six-month stay in Turkey. "It's just you," he said. "You couldn't talk to anyone. There's people all around and people know who you are because they see you on TV but you couldn't (communicate to them). For example, I remember we went to Moscow (in Russia) and I was standing in Red Square, right in front of the Lenin Tomb. The Kremlin was in the background. I mean this was like the seat of some of the most amazing history we've ever had and I was just sitting there in awe. I was looking for someone to turn to and say, 'Look at this.' And there's no one. So it is just a different experience."

He also didn't find any UK games on television and that made the problem even worse. "I didn't get to see any of the Kentucky games," Pope commented, explaining that he didn't have the ESPN cable sports channel. "The only (English-speaking) channels they have are CNN and the NBC super channel, which don't show anything. And then they also have BBC (British Broadcasting Corporation.)"

After he was released from Efes Pilsen with an injury in early 1997, Pope returned to the United States and did a brief stint as celebrity journalist for Lexington's WLEX-TV (Channel 18) during Kentucky's NCAA tournament run.

"I definitely didn't do any real news stories," he said. "I don't know that I helped the (TV) ratings or anything. All I did was get on camera and goof around. It was a blast and it was fun. For me, it was particularly interesting to see the tournament from the eyes of somebody other than a player. When you're a player, you just don't see all the stuff going on outside because you're focused on what you are doing and you just don't have time. It was great to kind of just be around the atmosphere outside of the game. That was really neat."

During the NCAA tournament, many UK fans asked the former Wildcat if he would have liked to play for another national title as Kentucky nearly won it for the second straight year before losing to Arizona in the championship game. Pope said he had mixed feelings about that.

"You know you always want to play, but in another sense I was blessed to come away my senior year with a championship. So when you go out like that, you feel fulfilled. It was so exciting to go (to the NCAA tourney in 1997) and almost relive that experience from a different perspective."

When Pope returned to the U.S., he didn't have to worry about finding a NBA team who might be interested in the former Wildcat center. He wasn't a free agent as the Pacers still held the rights to the player. However, he was a borderline NBA candidate. His NBA chances weren't all that great. Pope participated in the summer tryout games for Indiana and did extremely well, leading the Pacers in scoring in the Atlanta Summer League with a 12.3-point average. And new coach Larry Bird liked his attitude and his size, placing Pope on Indiana's opening-day roster.

While Pope isn't complaining about his opportunity to play in the NBA, his 1997-98 salary wasn't anything to brag about when compared with his high-salaried teammates. But he had to take whatever came since he was a "bubble" player. According to the team payroll figures compiled by *The Indianapolis Star* and *The Indianapolis News*, Pope earned $242,000. Superstar Reggie Miller earned over $9 million in a four-year deal worth $36 million. At the time, the Pacers had the league's sixth-highest payroll with about $39 million. The Chicago Bulls, meanwhile, had a payroll of nearly $62 million, the highest in the NBA.

Other than a mid-season knee injury, which forced him to miss some action, Pope had a memorable NBA rookie season with the formidable Pacers, who finished with a 58-24 worksheet, making them the fifth winningest team in the league. Sometimes the ex-Wildcat would find himself playing against Bird in a one-on-one matchup after practice. At other times they would have shooting contests. It was something that Pope will never forget — a living legend who would take the time to play with a rookie who didn't see much action.

During the regular season campaign, Pope — who had his head shaven along with his teammates to show unity as the team headed for the playoffs — averaged nearly seven minutes in 28 games, scoring 1.4 points a game. His NBA career highs came against the lowly Toronto Raptors in separate games with seven points in one contest and five rebounds in another.

However, Pope earlier had been philosophical about his NBA chances. He knew he had worked very hard in the summer and that was all he could do. If he didn't make it, fine. If he did, great. He was mentally ready one way or the other. Pope said his basketball career has already done wonders for him. "I've gotten more out of it than I could have ever asked for or wished for," he concluded.

THE
FLOOR GENERAL

After former Wildcat standout Travis Ford had finished playing his character role as a short, red-headed Irish player in a "PG-13" movie entitled *The 6th Man*, released in the spring of 1997, he didn't anticipate coaching a college basketball team right away especially since he had no coaching experience.

"I was somewhat surprised," Ford said several weeks after he was named the men's head basketball coach at Campbellsville University, a private Christian school (with approximately 1,500 students) located in south central Kentucky. "But I think this is pretty good timing to be able to be my own boss and be a head coach in my first coaching job. I met with the president (Dr. Kenneth Winters) several times before he offered me the job. It took me several days to finally agree if this is what I wanted to do. He had enough confidence that I could do it and I had enough in myself."

Ford was 27 when he took the Campbellsville post in the summer of 1997, replacing veteran coach Lou Cunningham who had died of complications from colon surgery. Many folks questioned Campbellsville's gamble in hiring a person without coaching experience at any level.

While Ford understood their concerns, he didn't spend much time worrying about what they thought. To compensate for his lack of coaching experience, he took advantage of his basketball knowledge he already obtained from his coaches, including Don Parson at Madisonville-North

Hopkins High School, Norm Stewart at Missouri and Rick Pitino at Kentucky, during his younger days as a reliable playmaker.

"I always knew that I learned under some great people," said Ford, who had played at Missouri before transferring to UK after his freshman year. "I used my knowledge of the game to help me be successful and hopefully that will make me a good basketball coach. There are no promises. I was the type of player who always studied the game and somebody who just loved the game of basketball. I wasn't an athletic player. I was a coach on the floor."

Ford said he would like to duplicate the coaching success of ex-Indiana star Steve Alford at Southwest Missouri State of the Missouri Valley Conference. Like Ford, Alford came to Southwest Missouri without any coaching credentials.

"You've got to look at somebody like Steve Alford who had never coached before who's been very successful. So hopefully I can be like him," said Ford, a native of Madisonville who finished his first season in 1997-98 with a 16-17 record at Campbellsville, including an upset 92-90 victory over top-ranked and eventual national champion Georgetown. (After the 1997-98 season, Campbellsville was hit with sanctions by the National Association of Intercollegiate Athletics for using an ineligible player. The university, however, strongly appealed NAIA's ruling as this book went to press.)

 Coaching is something that Ford has always wanted to do. He thought about coaching when he was younger. And he grew up with a couple of coaches in the family. His parents. They were both head coaches in the prep ranks. "I've had basketball in my blood all my life," quipped Ford.

His dad, Eddie Ford, a former coach at Cuba and Webster County High Schools, is well known in Kentucky for his active involvement in AAU and summer all-star basketball activities for many years. His mother, Pat, coached the girls' varsity team at Webster County High in the early 1970s. Actually, Ford's mother, who was a physical education teacher, got the coaching job by accident.

"They figured since my father was a high school coach, she had to know something," Ford said. "She had never coached basketball before and never played it. So, it's kind of funny. She had some very, very good teams.

"But the story is, my father and I would sit up in the stands. I was about three or four years old. We would sit and watch the women's game and he would write down notes. I would run them down to my mom during the game and she would read them and do whatever my father had written in the stands. So I was the notetaker and I guess that was the first experience of a coach I had at about three years old."

During Ford's basketball career, including his days as a star player at North Hopkins High School, where he averaged nearly 32 points and eight assists as a 5-9 senior guard, his parents, along with his older sister, were his biggest cheerleaders. They were always there to give support. He hasn't forgotten their never-ending support and is very appreciative of all the things they have done for him.

"My parents are probably my two biggest fans," said the younger Ford. "I give them all the credit in the world for anything that I've accomplished. My father taught me the game of basketball from a very young age. My mother was always there in the stands rooting for me and she was the one who cooked all my pregame meals in high school and took care of me. There is no way you can thank your parents, especially the way I feel. There is nothing in my lifetime that I could do to repay them."

When Ford later played at Missouri and Kentucky, his parents also attended every game. It didn't matter where his team was playing. "My parents never missed a game, home or away," he said. "If we were playing in California during the week, they would make arrangements to get a plane ticket and watch us play. In Hawaii, they went to the Maui Classic (in 1993). They never missed a game in my career. They loved the game. Like I said, they were my biggest fans and biggest supporters."

On the Hawaii trip, his parents definitely got their money's worth. Not only did they see UK defeat Texas, Ohio State and Arizona to win the Maui Invitational, but they also saw their son win the tourney MVP honors as well.

 In the late 1980s, when Ford guided North Hopkins to three consecutive appearances in the state tournament, he heard many unflattering comments about his size. Some people said he would never amount to anything in college. At 5-9, they thought he was too small to play on the collegiate level.

Ford, who began his high school varsity career as an eighth grader, said the comments never bothered him. "It made me work that much harder," he explained. "The thing that always motivated me was everybody saying that I couldn't play at the next level. When I went out in my back-yard and practiced every single day, that's what I thought about, people say-ing, 'He can't do it. He's too small. He's not fast enough.' That's what motivated me.

"I always tell my players you've got to find out what motivates you. For some people, money motivates them. Wanting to be the best motivates some people. Wanting to impress their girlfriend motivates them.

"But that's something that never bothered me. I never got upset about it one bit. I used it to my advantage. If you look at me, you would think 'how could he ever play?' and I agree. You've got to prove yourself. I always used it as a motivational tool."

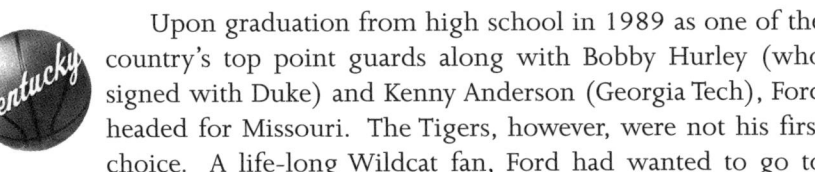 Upon graduation from high school in 1989 as one of the country's top point guards along with Bobby Hurley (who signed with Duke) and Kenny Anderson (Georgia Tech), Ford headed for Missouri. The Tigers, however, were not his first choice. A life-long Wildcat fan, Ford had wanted to go to Kentucky. But there really wasn't any room for him on the UK roster when then-coach Eddie Sutton had Richie Farmer, Sean Woods and Sean Sutton (who eventually left after his dad resigned from UK) in the backcourt. Had Ford gone to Kentucky, he wouldn't have seen a lot of playing time.

"It would have been a tough situation for me coming in and I real-ly didn't want to go to Kentucky because they had all those point guards," Ford explained. "I wanted to step into a program and play right away whether that be at Campbellsville University, Kentucky Wesleyan, University of Missouri, Duke, Arizona or all of the other schools that recruited me.

"I was going to go to a school where I could learn under maybe a senior guard, back him up, but still play a lot of minutes. And that's what I saw in the University of Missouri. They had a team that was going to be ranked in the top five preseason. They had one point guard who was a senior, a very good point guard in Lee Coward. That's the main reason I went there. I knew I would get a lot of playing time my freshman year."

So Ford began his collegiate career in Columbia, Missouri, where the talented Tigers faced high expectations. Missouri had four talented players, including Doug Smith and Anthony Peeler, returning from its

1988-89 team which finished with a 29-8 worksheet. And he found himself a solid contributor to the team as he started seven games. Averaging 6.4 points and 3.5 assists a game, Ford was named to Big Eight Conference All-Freshmen team.

"I just got very lucky that when I went to Missouri, we were rated No. 1 for like seven straight weeks and I was starting every one of those games," Ford commented. "The first one was because our point guard did get hurt. He broke his ribs. So it was my job. They threw me in there to learn as the season went along. That was valuable experience for me and it couldn't have worked out any better. I loved it at Missouri. I don't have anything but great things to say about Norm Stewart and the program at Missouri."

Things soon began to change. Missouri started to have problems with the NCAA with apparent rules violations. Since Ford didn't like what he was seeing in the program, he asked for a release from veteran coach Norm Stewart in the summer of 1990. Obviously, the coach wasn't too happy about that.

"He was disappointed because we were going to have a very good team coming back," Ford said of Stewart's reaction. "I was going to be the starting point guard and we really didn't have that many players coming in, but we did have a great returning squad.

"Then on the other hand, I think he did understand that they (the Tigers) were going on probation and at that point in my career it was very crucial for me to play on TV and to play in a post-season tournament. Those sorts of things were important to me. He was always courteous when I asked for my release. He told me the reasons he thought I should stay, but then he said if this is your decision, then that's what you should do. I don't think he ever tried to talk me out of this, but once I told him this is what I wanted to do, he understood. I never had any problems getting released."

Several schools, including Kentucky, began to recruit Ford for his playmaking skills. In addition to UK, Ford seriously considered LSU (which had future NBA star Shaquille O'Neal) and North Carolina.

When then-LSU mentor Dale Brown learned of Ford's decision to transfer, he immediately contacted the point guard about the possibility of wearing the purple-and-gold uniform. "I remember him calling me on the phone and saying, 'Well, I'll have the jet there in about three hours to pick you up so you can came down here and see the campus,'" recalled

Ford. "He had Shaq call me because Shaq and I played together (in the 1990 U.S. Olympic Festival)."

Because of Brown, Ford came close to signing with the Baton Rouge, La., school. He got to know Brown as they spent a lot of time together in the Olympic Festival in Minneapolis. Ford (and O'Neal) played for Brown's South squad.

"I spent about a whole month with him, every single day with him being my Olympic Festival coach," Ford said. "He's very unorthodox. Getting you ready for a game, talking to you before a game was like nothing I've experienced. He has more stories. He brought people in before the game that have been through all these tragedies and this and that. They will talk to you right before you go out on the court.

"And he's a master at mind games and preaching. I call him the preacher man. I thoroughly enjoyed being around coach Brown and that is the main reason I even considered going to LSU. (He is) somebody I admire and respect a great deal. I really enjoyed playing for him."

In the Festival, 7-1 sophomore-to-be O'Neal practically overshadowed Ford's outstanding play when he dominated the event with his thunderous performance, averaging nearly 25 points, 14 rebounds and seven blocks a game in leading South to a gold-medal finish. Ford averaged 22.2 points and five assists for the winning team.

Several weeks later, Ford overcame Brown's charming personality and announced his decision to play for the Wildcats. The player had begun to feel the heat from the Wildcat faithful as he narrowed his collegiate choices. "I started getting a lot more pressure to go to Kentucky because they had coach (Rick) Pitino," said Ford, who canceled his planned visits to North Carolina and LSU after Pitino offered him a scholarship. "I just wanted to come and play for him."

Transferring to UK meant Ford would have to sit out the 1990-91 campaign. He didn't like the idea of not playing in real games, but he had no choice because of NCAA transfer rules. It was the year that Pitino's ninth-ranked Cats had posted a SEC-best 22-6 record. The surprising Cats were good enough to go to the Big Dance. But they couldn't go because of NCAA probation.

Sitting out was tough for Ford because he wanted to play so badly. "That was a very, very hard year because I had never really had to sit out a

Wildcat playmaker Travis Ford (5) searches for an open teammate against Florida at Rupp Arena.

Photo by Rogers Photography

year in basketball competitively," he said. "Of course, I got to practice everyday but that just wasn't the same because I enjoyed the competitive part of the games and preparing for the games. It was very, very tough."

He also talked to ex-UK star and current Morehead State head coach Kyle Macy, who was one of his boyhood heroes, about the situation. "When I got here, he talked to me a little bit when I had to sit out," Ford commented in a 1992 interview with the author which appeared in *The Cats' Pause* magazine. "He had to sit out when he got here (in 1976 from Purdue). He really helped me a lot. So he's really been somebody I look up to.

"I was always pretending I was him (Macy) when I got on the playground. Especially when I was at the line (shooting free throws), adjusting my socks — that sort of thing. He's one of the great free throw shooters of all-time. I loved that and tried to copy him."

While Ford sat out the actual games, he and his teammates were involved with individualized instruction sessions with Pitino's assistants, including future Wildcat head coach Tubby Smith. These practice sessions sometimes were held very early in the morning before the players attended the 8:00 or 9:00 classes on campus.

Ford got to know Smith. One particular thing he will always remember the most about the assistant coach: "When he worked with us in individual instructions, he always hated to rebound basketballs because they would be knocking everywhere," Ford recalled. "They would be going to half court and he would have to run after them and get them back to us. I don't think he ever particularly enjoyed the eight o'clock or the seven o'clock individual instructions."

Although Smith left UK after the 1990-91 season to take his first head coaching position at Tulsa, Ford was nevertheless very impressed with the assistant even though they practiced together for only one season.

"He was one of the most personable coaches I've ever played for," Ford said of Smith. "He knew how to relate to the player and I think that is very important. He is going to find out there are so many outside things going on at Kentucky the players are exposed to that he'll do really well because he is so personable and he can keep a handle on that."

Ford began his first year of eligibility at UK as a sophomore benchwarmer in the 1991-92 season, playing behind the likes of seniors Sean Woods and Richie Farmer. Slowed by a nagging knee injury suffered in a preseason scrimmage, he saw action in 33 of team's 36 games, averaging about 13 minutes a game, as UK went all the way to the NCAA East Regional finals where it lost to Duke in a classic 104-103 overtime thriller.

One of his season's highlights came during the SEC tournament in Birmingham when he gunned in three three-pointers for nine points in a 80-74 victory over Dale Brown's LSU Tigers. Ford also had an outstanding game against Florida at Rupp Arena with eight points and eight assists as he sparked UK to a 21-point victory margin.

With his bothersome bad knee, Ford was never 100 percent on the court. He had some good days and bad days. He often couldn't move around very fast. "He was playing on one leg," Pitino explained. Ford said his first playing season at UK "was much more difficult than the year I sat out."

Consequently, Ford underwent a successful knee surgery in the off-season. He became a "new" player at the beginning of the 1992-93 campaign as he lost 15 pounds on his 5-9 frame. He had no problems with his knee. With his weight loss, he became quicker. Obviously, Pitino was pleased with Ford's summer workouts and the coach expected a great year from the playmaker. The point guard declared that he was ready to assume crucial leadership roles as a junior after the departures of four key seniors, popularly known as "The Unforgettables," from the previous squad — Woods, Farmer, Deron Feldhaus and John Pelphrey.

The Fab Five of Michigan.

They were the ones who spoiled the 1992-93 Wildcats' quest for a national title in an 81-78 overtime thriller in the national semifinals at New Orleans. Led by a pair of juniors in Ford and 6-8 Jamal Mashburn, Kentucky had reached the Final Four for the first time under the dynamic leadership of Pitino since he assumed the UK post in 1989.

Even though Kentucky didn't win the national crown, the hoopla surrounding the Final Four trip, not surprisingly, is the highlight of Ford's UK career. "If I was going to a Final Four, New Orleans couldn't have been a better place to play in the (Louisiana) Superdome in front of 64,000 people. I think that was probably the most glaring moment," said Ford, who was also named the Southeast Regional's most outstanding player. "If I had to think of a best moment, I think (it was) when the final buzzer went off (in UK's 106-81 win over Florida State) and we knew we were going to the Final Four."

Today Ford still believes had Mashburn not fouled out in the overtime loss to Michigan, Kentucky would've come out as a winner. "We were on a roll as a team playing very, very well. Michigan was probably the most talented team I've ever played against from top to bottom. We had some very untimely injuries and untimely circumstances where (senior guard and defensive specialist) Dale Brown was having the game of his life and on fire. He was the only person who was scoring at will. He dived for a ball out of bounds (when he injured his shoulder in late second half.) That was the first big mishap.

"Then we go into overtime with our best player and Jamal Mashburn picked up a very questionable fifth foul. Then it was tough for

A beaming Travis Ford meets well wishers after a news conference in 1997 when he was named the head basketball coach at Campbellsville University.

Campbellsville University Office of Public Relations & Marketing
Photo by Joan C. McKinney

us to score because Jamal created a lot of shots for me because they would double and triple team him, and he would kick it out and I would knock it down (for a field goal).

"I think those two timely things were the turning points in that game. If Jamal hadn't fouled out, I think we would have had a different outcome because we had the game in pretty much in hand, even in over-time while he was playing and then when he went out, we couldn't score."

Like Mashburn, freshman starter Jared Prickett also fouled out in overtime. Kentucky, consequently, had to play without three of its starters most of the extra period.

Mashburn, who earlier in the season had announced his intentions to turn pro after a three-year UK career, led the team with 26 points. Brown gunned in 16 points, including four three-pointers, with Ford contributing 12. Michigan's Chris Webber took the game's scoring honors as he scored 27 points. He also grabbed a game-high 13 rebounds.

Kentucky finished the memorable campaign with a 30-4 mark.

The team didn't stay around in New Orleans to watch the championship matchup as coach Steve Fisher and his Fab Five team — which included Webber, Juwan Howard and Jalen Rose — dropped to Dean Smith's North Carolina squad 77-71.

During Kentucky's run to the 1993 Final Four, Pitino had said there weren't many basketball junkies on the team. The coach lamented that most of his players would rather do something else, like listening to music or watching MTV. However, Pitino said Ford is an exception. Ford is a true basketball junkie who regularly watches the games on ESPN.

Ford didn't argue with Pitino, saying he himself doesn't miss many games on television. "I guess if there's a basketball junkie on this team, I'm it," smiled Ford in 1993. "All the other guys like playing Sega or Nintendo in their spare time — I'm happy sitting down and watching a good basketball game."

During his senior year, Ford encountered a couple of very interesting moments during UK's 27-7 campaign, both good and bad.

UK's stunning comeback victory over LSU in Baton Rouge is a game Ford will never forget. The nationally-televised matchup, which began late at 9:30 p.m. (EST), saw LSU blow a 31-point lead in the second half as red-hot Kentucky miraculously ended up winning 99-95, snapping a rare two-game losing streak.

"It was definitely the most unbelievable game I've ever played in," recalled Ford, who was one of UK's four seniors (along with Jeff Brassow, Gimel Martinez and Rodney Dent) on that squad. "It might have been the most exciting game. It's something that it's hard to explain when you're out on an opponent's floor and you're down 31 points with 15 minutes to go.

"I can remember calling the players together because we'd already lost two games before that at Syracuse (93-85 at Carrier Dome) and Arkansas (90-82 at Rupp Arena). We're looking at the third loss in a row. I can't remember the last Kentucky team to do that. We might not have gotten back into Lexington if we had lost. I can remember bringing the guys together and saying we will not leave this building until we win.

"Things started to click. Everybody stayed positive. Coach Pitino stayed positive. (He) started telling stories about comebacks, this and that. To be a part of that is definitely something I will always remember. Being a part of one of the greatest comebacks ever in college basketball was unbelievable. Just a feeling in the locker room of everybody celebrating together.

"What was so impressive about the comeback was that everybody contributed. Chris Harrison, who never played, came in and hit two big three-pointers. Jeff Brassow scored 14 points. I scored 10. Walter McCarty hit a big three-pointer at the end (with 19 seconds remaining to give UK a 96-95 margin). Tony Delk scored nine. Everybody contributed. So that's what made it so great. It was a total team effort and that game definitely gives me chills to think about it." McCarty led Kentucky with 23 points and eight rebounds, while Ford had 12 assists. Four other Wildcats also scored in double figures.

Because of the game's late starting tipoff and its apparent blowout, most of the national television audience in the eastern part of the nation, including UK fans, went to bed, figuring LSU had the game won.

"A lot of people didn't see that game," Ford said. "A lot of people went to bed. Everybody I talked to went to bed and even my parents, who never missed a game at home or away, almost got up and left. Luckily they stayed and saw one of the best comebacks ever in college history."

Asked if he looked at losing coach Dale Brown's face after the game, Ford replied, "I really didn't. I was too busy celebrating with my teammates to even pay any attention to that. Believe me, that was a heck of a celebration in the locker room after that game."

An emotional Pitino told the reporters the comeback was "the most unbelievable thing I've ever witnessed. I have never, ever seen a comeback on the road like that in my life. Nothing has ever come close to this."

 After their stunning victory over LSU on Tuesday night, the Wildcats played their next game against Vanderbilt in Nashville on a Saturday afternoon. And Kentucky won the regionally-televised contest, beating the Commodores 77-69 behind Ford's 22 points.

It was that February game in which three of the UK players — Ford, Jared Prickett and Gimel Martinez — later admitted that they cheated by sneaking better free throw shooters to the line, creating a front page controversy. "I instructed someone else (Walter McCarty instead of Andre Riddick who was supposed to shoot) to get on the free throw line," Ford explained, "and then at another point in the game, Jared Prickett and Gimel Martinez switched free throws which I didn't have anything to do with."

Pitino, as a result, placed the players on a one-game suspension after learning of the free throw flap. Pitino "was upset with us and maybe the maddest I had ever seen him," Ford recalled. "Coach Pitino was not happy. He did not know what went on during the game and he had no idea until the next night on his coach's show when people were calling in and asking about it. He was a little surprised and he wasn't happy at all."

Without the help of three suspended players, the Wildcats and their thin bench defeated Tennessee on sophomore Rodrick Rhodes' late free throws in a 77-73 thriller held in Knoxville. Rhodes hit seven of eight critical free throws in the last minute. Sophomore guard Tony Delk was UK's top pointman with 21 points.

"I felt bad," remembered Ford of his suspension. "I felt like I was letting the team down because I was a senior. I was a captain. All three of us had to stay back (in Lexington). I felt bad because we didn't have a lot of players that year and we were going down sort of empty especially with three guys not going, two starters. It was tough sitting back and watching that game, praying they would win.

"Luckily they went down there and played a wonderful game. I got the other two guys together and I said, 'Let's go out to the airport and meet them when they get back.' So we went and as soon as they got to the airport, coach Pitino was the first one off the plane. We were waiting at the bottom of the stairs. He gets off and says 'Hey, guys, how you all doing! Great to see you all. Great to have you all back.' "

Ever since Pitino and the team arrived at the Bluegrass Airport that night, Ford said the coach hasn't mentioned the free throw incident to him again. "That's one of the things that hopefully as a coach I can take on," Ford said. "He never kept a grudge and never stayed mad very long. Not another word was ever spoken about it again. If you messed up, he would let you know, but he'd forget about it.

"And that always made me feel good that I knew he was upset, but as soon as he stepped off the plane and we had won, he was like 'Great to have you back. See you tomorrow at practice and I hope everything is going good.' That is something that I always appreciated."

Not surprisingly, the free throw controversy in the Music City is the most embarrassing moment Ford had encountered while at Kentucky. What made him do it?

"It was a pretty close game," Ford said. "We were up about 10 points. Andre Riddick and Walter McCarty were going for a rebound against a Vanderbilt player. The Vanderbilt player goes over their back. The referee blew the whistle and called a foul on the guy going over their back. And I saw the referee running to the scorer's table. I knew the referee did not know who the foul was on. I knew he did not know who was going to the line. I knew he did not pay attention and I had no idea which one was supposed to (shoot), either.

"I knew which one I wanted at the free throw line. I did not know which one got fouled. I really didn't know that and a lot of people don't believe me, but I would swear to it to this day, I did not know which one got fouled. But I knew which one I wanted — Walter McCarty — at the line. So I went and told Walter to shoot the free throws. When you go back and watch it on tape, it was Andre Riddick who got fouled. (It was) just bad circumstances.

"It was a mistake. It was in the heat of the moment. You don't think about what you're doing. It is something that I think it's probably made my coaching mentality go into work again. 'Hey, this is what I want done and you're not (actually) thinking about what you're doing.' I don't really think it was something that you're saying you're trying to cheat another team. It's something that happens in every single basketball game. It wasn't something where I was trying to cheat. It was the heat of the moment, but we ended up winning the game. So I don't think it was something that at all made the difference in the outcome of the game."

UK went on to finish the regular season in a tie for first place in the SEC Eastern Division (with eventual Final Four participant Florida). Ford won SEC's second straight free throw shooting title with 91.2 percent, which was the highest in the league since 1980.

In post-season action, the Wildcats also captured their third consecutive SEC tournament championship in Memphis by beating Florida 73-60 in the title game. Ford, by the way, took the tourney's MVP honors for the second straight year.

Ford's Wildcat career came to an end in the NCAA tourney's second round when coach Kevin O'Neill's Marquette squad, with its tough defense, stopped seventh-ranked UK 75-63. A St. Petersburg, Fla., crowd of 25,830 saw Kentucky shoot a horrible 31.6 percent in the disappointing loss. Like UK, Ford couldn't hit a thing, making only two shots in 11 tries for six points before fouling out.

In the classroom, Ford was considered the team's top student. After all, he earned Academic All-SEC teams for three years in a row (1992 to '94). And he interestingly was UK's lone representative on the league's academic squad during those three years. His final grade-point average was about 3.4 (on a 4.0 scale), according to Ford, who has a bachelor's degree in communications.

"I didn't enjoy going to class, but I enjoyed the pride of getting good grades," Ford said. "That's the only thing that kept me going to class every day. I wanted to be the best student. I wanted to outdo everybody on the team. I wanted to have the highest grade-point average. Every year I was there I got the Academic (All-SEC) award. I didn't like studying, but I enjoyed being the best and I enjoyed making good grades."

As far as academics are concerned, Ford said it definitely wasn't real easy to stay motivated. When he is speaking to a group of high school or college students, he tries to tell them that education is very important and that studying wasn't an easy task for him during his younger days.

"I went and spoke to a big high school group yesterday," Ford said. "I told them, 'Hey, I'm just like you are. You don't like getting up in the morning and going to school, but you got to go. You don't have a choice. Find out what motivates you and then go from there.' So I think everybody just has to find out what motivates."

While at UK, Ford and his teammates got to meet several celebrities. Famous people like Ashley Judd and Spike Lee attended UK games.

Judd is arguably the biggest Wildcat fan of any non-athlete celebrity. A popular actress who graduated from UK with honors in 1990, Judd can be seen at many Kentucky games, cheering for the Wildcats. When she can't come to the games, she watches them on television. Wherever she goes, she will talk about UK at every opportunity. For instance, as the 1997-98 season unfolded, Judd gave the Wildcats a nice plug in her first appearance on *Regis & Kathie Lee* television show. They briefly discussed coaches Rick Pitino and Tubby Smith, among other topics. In December of 1997, Judd and her older sister, Wynonna Judd, a country music star, were spotted on the front row in UK's 79-76 upset loss to arch-rival Louisville at Rupp Arena.

"The most interesting celebrity (I met) while at UK? Oh, gosh, there are several," smiled Ford. "Ashley Judd always came around. Spike Lee came and talked to us before one game. He sat on the bench with us." A filmmaker, Lee was in Lexington for a speaking engagement on the UK campus.

Not only Lee sat on the Wildcat bench, Judd did, too, at one of UK's games. So did Muhammad Ali. "I think the most interesting person that I met was Muhammad Ali. (He is the one) who I remember the most. He always had his people around him but he came in the locker room and he spoke as well as he could. He was somebody whom I always admired." A famed boxer from Louisville, Ali currently suffers from Parkinson's disease.

 As a UK player, Ford had a lot of publicity. There were hundreds of articles about him. He regularly had interviews with the television and print media on the state and national level. While the coverage was mainly positive, there were some articles or interviews that he didn't appreciate.

"I'll never get into names," Ford said. "There were times that I thought some writers wrote something that they did not know about. I guess that's their job. There are always articles that you don't agree with, or sportscasters that you don't agree with. But I never let it bother me at all."

Ford also doesn't particularly care for radio and television call-in shows, which have grown dramatically over the past several years. "I never listen to the call-in shows," he commented. "That's a money thing and that's all it is. Nobody likes doing them. Coaches don't like doing them. It's for the fans to call in and maybe learn a little bit behind the scenes, but I never pay any attention to them. I never listen to them."

 With Ford's physical shortcomings, many NBA teams were not comfortable with the 5-9 playmaker. They thought he was too short and too slow to play in the league. So they didn't select him in the 1994 draft.

But at least one NBA team liked him. The Golden State Warriors, then coached by Don Nelson, signed him to a free agent contract in mid-September. Ford played through the exhibition season, including the team's European tour, before he was waived.

"I was with the Warriors for about two months trying out," he said. "It was an unbelievable experience. We played in Barcelona, Spain and I got to travel to Paris with the Warriors. Then we came back and played in all the NBA arenas.

"I was disappointed (in being cut from the team), but I knew that I had given it everything that I had. There was nothing else that I could do to make that team. I knew it was a long shot, but just to have that experience was great."

 After his unsuccessful NBA stint, Ford went back home to Kentucky and pondered his future. He wondered if he should continue to play basketball. If he did, it would be either pro basketball overseas or the CBA (Continental Basketball Association).

Once Ford made his decision, he opted for Europe. Still, things didn't work out. On the very day Ford had planned to leave for Europe, his agent called and advised the player, saying, "I don't think you should go there because we just found out the team isn't paying. Some of the players haven't got paid the amount they were supposed to get. So it may not be a good situation."

Said Ford, "That got me very discouraged about overseas. That didn't make me happy and then I didn't really want to go to the CBA."

He remained in Kentucky, living in Bowling Green for several months. "I was the spokesman for a couple of companies in Kentucky and that kept me busy," Ford said. "I did that for awhile. (Later) I decided maybe I wasn't going to play right now and went for my stockbroker's license. That took me about six months (to study and get his license). And the day I passed my stockbroker's license, I got a call from Touchstone Pictures and Disney executives asking me to be in this major motion picture."

So Ford, in a temporary career move, headed for Los Angeles to study acting and auditioned for a role in a basketball-oriented comedy. He became a first-time actor, playing in *The 6th Man*, as a point guard.

"I never dreamed of acting and never wanted to act," he explained. "It was just a situation where they called and said we knew you from Golden State, we knew you from Kentucky and we think you'd be perfect for this role.

"It wasn't something that they just gave to me. I had to go out and audition against several other actors. Lucky. I got it and I had a leading role in this Touchstone (Pictures) movie. It was a surprise and the experience was something that I'll always keep with me.

"I met some great actors who are major stars in Hollywood. I lived in L.A. for about six or seven months. We shot the movie in Vancouver, Seattle and L.A. Just to see how a movie is made and be a part of that was just unbelievable."

While Ford held a significant role in the movie, the major stars were Kadeem Hardison (from NBC television series *A Different World*) and Marlon Wayans (whose family headlined in Fox's *In Living Color*).

While Ford enjoyed his movie stint on the west coast, he knew an acting career was a long shot. He loved basketball too much to stay away from it very long.

"I think it was good for me to get away from basketball a little bit," said Ford. "I always knew I'd get back, whether it was refereeing or something. Basketball is in my blood and that is what I know."

Call him Coach Ford.

THE QUIET
THREE-POINT
BOMBER

A humble Tony Delk wasn't exactly the most talkative player at UK. He was basically a shy person who avoided bright lights whenever possible. The former All-American guard and the 1996 SEC Player of the Year liked to do some things in a quiet way. He didn't like a lot of attention. He wanted his performance on the hardwood to do all the talking as far as the press clippings were concerned.

He couldn't do that, however, especially during his senior year. He had to face the media. Because of Kentucky's highly-publicized 1995-96 NCAA championship run and his outstanding play as the team's leading scorer, he was the guy the news media wanted to interview. He was cooperative but usually did not say much. He answered their questions without going into details. He did his job.

But when Delk first arrived at UK, he was so painfully shy that he stayed in the training room as long as he could to avoid the media after the games. He didn't want the spotlight.

"I would say probably Tony Delk was the shiest (player) until he became a senior," Brooks Downing, UK's associate media relations director, said. "Early on when he was a freshman and sophomore, he'd be hiding out back here in the training room. He'd be disappearing. He just didn't want the exposure. I think it was his personality. I think he just kind of shied away.

"But by the time he was a senior, he had a lot of confidence and felt really good about himself. He started to feel more comfortable in those type of media settings and did a great job for us."

Said veteran sportscaster Tom Hammond, who has covered the Southeastern Conference games on regional TV networks for many years, "(Delk) doesn't say much and you can imagine on television when you get guys like that they only answer with one or two words to every question. It's pretty hard to carry on (the interview), but you have to because you're on live television."

One of Delk's teammates at UK was Travis Ford. They played together for a couple of years. "Tony was very shy," Ford remembered. "He was a very quiet mature person. That's just his makeup. He doesn't go out of his way. He is not really a wildly outspoken person. He is the type of player who came to practice, did his job, and went home and did his thing. But he was one of the most talented players I ever played with."

Ford also said part of Delk's shyness during the latter's freshman and sophomore years may have come because the Tennessee native didn't really know how to fit into his new surroundings at the UK roundball camp. Delk perhaps didn't want to take the spotlight away from older players who had already established themselves at the school.

"Tony came into a situation where in high school he was averaging 39 points a game," explained Ford. "He was the man. Getting all the publicity. McDonald's All-American. And when you come into a situation where you're playing with players like myself, Jamal Mashburn, Gimel Martinez, Rodney Dent and some other really good players who are ahead of you, you tend to (stay in the background). Some players don't know how to react. It took him a little time to adjust, a little time to mature."

A popular student who once was voted "Mr. Haywood High School," the 6-1 Delk comes from Brownsville, a small town of approximately 10,000 citizens in rural western Tennessee. It's a short drive to Memphis — less than an hour.

Interestingly, it's the same place where pop vocalist Tina Turner was born. Delk said although he has yet to meet the famed entertainer, he looks forward to the day he meets her. "She doesn't come back a whole lot," he said in Charlotte, N.C., in 1997 when he was with the NBA's Hornets. "If she did, I would meet her."

Turner grew up in nearby Nut Bush. Before she moved to St. Louis

UK All-American guard Tony Delk (00) looks for a pass as he battles for a position under the basket against Tennessee. A native of southwest-ern Tennessee, Delk is currently the school's all-time fourth-leading scorer.

Photo by Rogers Photography

at the age of 16, Turner even played on the girls' basketball team and was a cheerleader at the old Carver High School, then an all-black school in Brownsville.

 Delk comes from a large family. He is one of Leslie and Florence Delk's eight children. Born on January 28, 1974, he was the quiet baby who basically grew up alone with his parents because all of his siblings were a lot older and had their own lives.

Some of his brothers, however, visited him regularly and they played basketball. One of them was Ricky, who was an All-American at Lambuth University in Jackson, Tenn. He is the reason Tony still wears No. 00 on his jersey, which was Ricky's number at Lambuth. When Tony was younger, he revealed to his family and friends that he wanted to play in the

NBA some day. That was his lifetime goal.

Tony's basketball playground battles with his brothers eventually paid off. He became a highly-recruited star at Haywood High. While at Haywood, he once scored an eye-popping 70 points and led the state of Tennessee in scoring for two straight seasons. As a senior, he averaged 38.6 points and was chosen the state's Class AAA Mr. Basketball in leading his team to a 29-5 mark in 1991-92.

In the November early signing period during his senior year, Delk announced one of the biggest decisions of his career, picking UK over Arkansas. Several other big-name schools — Memphis, Notre Dame, Tennessee, Oklahoma, Pittsburgh and Wake Forest — also sought his services. They all loved his scoring machine, especially his NBA shooting range.

While Delk liked UK's tradition and its enormous fan support, then-coach Rick Pitino's NBA reputation was a big factor in Delk's decision. Delk's attendance at UK's Big Blue Madness in Lexington— along with prep superstars Rodrick Rhodes, Walter McCarty and Jared Prickett — certainly didn't hurt. With UK-LSU football game on Saturday afternoon, the players had a great time with the campus' festive weekend atmosphere. Pitino's recruiting gamble in the annual preseason event worked like a charm as he later got all four in UK fold, making the recruiting class the best in the nation, according to well-known recruiting experts.

Delk remembered Pitino's first visit to his Brownsville home. He said the coach talked like a salesman making his pitch. "He was one of those guys who goes to their (recruit's) house and sells his program as well as himself," commented Delk. "Of course, having (his former) players who are veterans in the NBA helps out a whole lot. The guys want to go where they have a chance to go to the NBA. Kentucky is definitely that program to go to (before the NBA)."

Then-Kentucky assistant coach Billy Donovan, who is now the head coach at Florida, said he really enjoyed recruiting Delk. "I felt a very, very close relationship with Tony," recalled Donovan in 1997. "Tony is an easy going kid. He was very, very easy to recruit. He always kind of kept me informed about what was going on, what he was thinking about and what questions he had.

"As a coach in recruiting, I think a lot of times you are kind of on the outside trying to figure out what's going on on the inside. And Tony was one of those guys who really, for whatever reason, opened up to me and we became very close. I went into his home and you know, whatever the NCAA rule was back then, we spent as much time as we possibly could there recruiting him."

On Kentucky's recruitment of Delk, then-associate coach Herb Sendek said in an 1993 interview which appeared in the The Daily News of Middlesboro. "That was one of the most enjoyable recruiting processes that our staff has ever had. He was really a pleasure to recruit. Tony's family is a beautiful, close-knit family." Sendek is now the head coach at North Carolina State.

When Delk made his collegiate choice in 1991, there were rumors of Pitino returning to the NBA. Published reports had the coach going to the New Jersey Nets after the season. Was Delk worried? "At one time, we were concerned, but it's not that big of a deal," he said. "I mean, he made a commitment to the guys who came out (with their decision) that he wasn't leaving. He was honest about it."

For instance, Pitino had told Rhodes, who was preparing to ink with Kentucky, not to worry, promising the player that he'll remain at the school for at least five more years when his contract expires. Rhodes signed with the Wildcats several hours later.

As Delk began his rookie season at Kentucky, he had a painful adjustment to make. He had a new position to learn. The coaching staff penciled him at point guard, instead of shooting guard. There were reports that he wasn't too happy with his situation in the Wildcat camp.

Sendek didn't quite agree with that assessment. "It's not necessarily that Tony was unhappy," said Sendek in The Daily News in 1993. "I don't think that I would use that particular terminology. I think Tony was experiencing the frustrations any young player goes through when they are trying to learn a difficult, complicated system.

"I think Tony has come in and worked very hard and, as a result, each day that goes by he seems to improve. He is in the process of making a transition to point guard position, which is probably the most difficult position to adapt to. Tony's attitude is good. He's working hard and we are very much pleased with the progress he is making."

Delk — who played his freshman year as a substitute, averaging nearly 10 minutes and 4.5 points per outing — admitted that playing point guard was much more challenging than he had anticipated. He said at the

Tony Delk shoots one of his patented
downtown jumpers at Rupp Arena.
During his freshman and sophomore
years at Kentucky, he was a shy player
who tried to avoid the media in the
dressing room after the games.

Photo by Rogers Photography

time that he tried to learn his new role as much as he could from guard
Travis Ford, who was helpful.

Toward the end of the season, Delk began to improve and showed
promise. For instance, in UK's 87-66 victory over visiting South Carolina,
Delk came off the bench and gunned in a then career-high 18 points,
including four of five three-pointers. Also, in the 1993 SEC tournament at
Rupp Arena, Delk pumped in game-high 15 points in UK's earth-shattering 101-40 victory over Tennessee.

 Along with his adjustment on the court, Delk, not surprisingly, found the academic environment at UK far different from Haywood High. "(The classes) are a lot harder," he said during his freshman year. "A lot of things that we did in high school are not done in college. College is more of a learning experience. I really find that the professors are a lot different from high school teachers.

"They expect you to go out and do your own work and bring it back to them. In high school, I went and got help from a teacher, and they let you know your grade. In college, they said, 'I'll let you know.' "

But Delk adjusted and made decent grades the rest of his college years. In the summer of 1996, Delk (along with teammate/roommate Walter McCarty) received his bachelor's degree. His major was communications.

 On November 27, 1993, as coach Rick Pitino began his fifth year at Kentucky, Delk, a sophomore, found himself in the Wildcat starting lineup for the first time. As a shooting guard, instead of the dreaded point guard position, he would start the season opener on national television as the No. 2 Wildcats host the seventh-ranked Louisville Cardinals at Rupp Arena. As it turned out, the matchup — won by UK in a 78-70 verdict — would mark the beginning of Delk's impressive streak as a starter. During his last three years at Kentucky, he started 103 consecutive games with the last one being UK's 1996 national title victory over Syracuse.

And when that 1993 Kentucky-Louisville encounter ended, Delk's superb stats showed 19 points, 10 rebounds and five assists. He was named the player of the game as CBS announcers Billy Packer and Jim Nantz praised Delk's performance on the air. They also had him on their postgame interviews with Pitino and Travis Ford.

Delk was on his way to stardom. He had become the outstanding player that his coaches had envisioned him to be. He finished his sophomore campaign as the team's leading scorer, averaging nearly 17 points, ahead of fellow sophomore Rodrick Rhodes' 14.6 points, as UK finished at 27-7.

He also had a real good junior year which saw the 1994-95 Wildcats finish with a 28-5 mark after a disappointing loss to North Carolina in NCAA Regional finals. A third-team All-American choice by

Basketball Weekly, he led the squad in scoring again with a 16.7-point average.

When Delk's senior year arrived, Pitino decided to put him at point guard partly because the player need to brush up his ball-handling skills for NBA. "He'll move over to the point guard position this year which should enable him to be a first-round draft pick," the coach said in 1995. But Delk struggled like he did before as a freshman. Pitino, as a result, scrapped the idea after UK's 92-82 loss to coach John Calipari and UMass in the second game of the season.

The rest is history. With 6-2 junior Anthony Epps moving up as a starting point guard, Delk concentrated on his shooting and defense as the Wildcats became the "Untouchables" en route to the school's sixth national championship in 1996. Pitino later admitted had he not made the changes in the backcourt, the Wildcats probably wouldn't have won the NCAA title.

Nicknamed "TD," Delk said capturing the national crown was especially sweet when the clock ran out. That was his most satisfying moment at Kentucky. "It was something that we had worked hard for all year," said Delk, who received the Final Four's Most Outstanding Player award. "To be a good team, you have to have good individual players and that's what we had and we played as a unit on the court."

In the championship game, Delk paced the Wildcats with 24 points and snatched seven rebounds. His seven three-pointers tied an NCAA championship record set by Indiana's Steve Alford in 1987 and Oklahoma's Dave Sieger in 1988.

Delk completed his storybook UK career as the school's fourth leading all-time scorer with 1,890 points, also the highest ever for a guard in school history. The consensus first-team All-American, who holds UK's three-point field goal records for career made and attempted, also became the first Wildcat to lead the team in scoring for three straight years since Jack Givens did it in the late 1970s.

The Los Angeles Lakers.
The Indiana Pacers.
The New Jersey Nets.
The Atlanta Hawks.
The Dallas Mavericks.
During Pitino's first seven years at Kentucky, they all wanted his

winning magic at one time or the other. They offered him millions of dollars — a lifetime security. Some even sweetened the deal by giving him a piece of the team's ownership. He said no. He was happy at Kentucky.

Delk said he tried to ignore frequent rumors of Pitino's departing the Bluegrass for NBA. "I wasn't even concerned," Delk said of the rumors. "I think he was more concerned with trying to get a championship for the team and you know he wasn't going to sign (a contract) to leave. He had to prove to the people around and to the fans as well as to the players that he could lead his team to a championship and that's what he did." However, after guiding Kentucky to two straight NCAA championship games, Pitino couldn't say no to NBA anymore in 1997.

Like Pitino, after UK, Delk's next stop was the NBA, his lifetime dream. He said during his senior year that he didn't care which NBA team drafted him. As Pitino feared, there was some concern about Delk's size as a shooting guard in the NBA since most of the shooting guards in the league are at least 6-5. Because of that, Delk was likely to play at point guard. While most observers had projected him as a first-round NBA pick, Delk said he could make the roster with the right team. "As long as they give me a chance," he told Middlesboro's *Daily News*. "I'll show them that I can play the game."

On June 26, 1996, the Charlotte Hornets selected Delk as the league's 16th pick overall in the annual draft. Two other Wildcats — Antoine Walker and Walter McCarty — were also drafted. Boston picked Walker as NBA's sixth selection overall, while the New York Knicks tabbed McCarty for No. 19 pick. The top pick went to Allen Iverson, a sophomore from Georgetown, who became the first guard selected No. 1 since 1979 when the Lakers drafted Magic Johnson out of Michigan State.

Delk became a millionaire, signing a three-year pact reportedly worth an estimated $2.8 million with the Hornets. McCarty also did well with the Knicks, getting nearly $2.6 million over three years. What was the first thing Delk did after signing the contract? He didn't do much except play summer basketball. "Actually, I was out in Utah," Delk commented. "We were out there for the summer league so I really didn't do a whole lot. I was out there just enjoying myself and just trying to get better as a player."

 Not surprisingly, Delk found the NBA to be a huge adjustment in his rookie season. Besides playing against bigger athletes and adjusting to his new social surroundings, he had to learn his new position at point guard, which is something that he had tried previously at Kentucky but it didn't work out. After a slow start with Charlotte, Delk began to fit in with the team, becoming a more reliable reserve guard. Several of his best games came during the latter part of the season. He scored a season-high 25 points and had four steals in 25 minutes against Boston in a 136-111 victory on Charlotte's home floor. In another fine game, he had 10 assists against Cleveland. Against Detroit, he also grabbed 11 rebounds .

Charlotte assistant coach Lee Rose, a native Kentuckian who once coached at Transylvania University, said Delk worked long hours trying to improve his game. "He has an excellent attitude," Rose said in the spring of 1997. "He comes in early and he stays late and that is a major plus for him. The most important expectation we had was that he would come in here and work to be a point guard and he is doing that on a daily basis.

"In college he was depended on to score a great deal, whereas in NBA, we are looking at him more as a point guard with scoring capabilities. So he's had to make some adjustments. He is a young player who has many skills — he is very quick, he is very athletic, he can jump, he has great explosion, he is a prolific scorer."

Despite Delk's limited exposure at point guard, Rose said that UK's open-court, pressing game and its big-time college basketball atmosphere made the player's transition to NBA somewhat easier. "The exposure of playing in a major program, with a fine coach, and a system that they had, it benefited him," said Rose, the former head coach who once guided North Carolina-Charlotte and Purdue to the Final Four. "I know they tried him at point guard one time, but it just didn't quite work out. Wherever he'd have gone, he probably would still have been a scoring guard. I don't think that would have changed in his collegiate career."

For the surprising Hornets, who had posted their best-ever record of 54-28, Delk completed his first NBA season with a 5.4-point average, hitting nearly 47 percent of his shots. While he started only one contest, he managed to average 14.2 minutes.

Not bad for a rookie who saw little action as a college point guard. "He played better actually than I thought he would coming into the league because of the size," said ex-Wildcat Jack Givens, who covers NBA through his TV broadcasting duties with Orlando. "I thought he'd have a little more difficult time. It's tough for a rookie coming into the NBA. But he made the most of it. He had some good people to learn from — a good coach there in Dave Cowens who taught him a lot. He played extremely well. He had a great year for a rookie."

 Delk had one of his thrills when the Hornets faced the defending champion Chicago Bulls, who were coming off a historic 72-10 campaign in 1995-96, in an early season game. He got to see Chicago star Michael Jordan in person. He said that was a very interesting experience.

"(Jordan) is somebody you grew up watching," Delk explained. "You know just to be on the court with him has been the most interesting thing. It's something I really enjoy."

Delk also got to see Chicago's Scottie Pippen. While at UK, Delk had listed Pippen as his favorite sports figure in the team's media guide. The ex-Wildcat told Pippen about that. Pippen just smiled. "I normally like Scott," Delk said. "I think he plays well. You know with him being at Chicago and being with Michael Jordan has made him a much better player."

 Delk and Walter McCarty are close buddies. During their rookie year in the NBA, they regularly stayed in touch while living in different cities. They talked four or five times a week, giving support to each other, according to Delk.

And during NBA's annual all-star break, Delk and McCarty headed for Lexington for a brief visit when Kentucky faced Villanova in a nationally-televised encounter. Also joining Delk and McCarty was ex-teammate Mark Pope, who had just returned to the U.S. from Europe where he played pro basketball. "Three of us spent a little bit of time together and that was really fun," Pope said.

While in Lexington, they didn't spend much time with Rick Pitino. They didn't visit Pitino's home for a very good reason. "Actually when we got there, the coach was sick. So we didn't want to be around him and get sick," smiled Delk. "Really (we) didn't have time to go and just hang out with coach."

Instead of staying at the Wildcat Lodge, the campus dormitory which primarily houses the basketball players, they lodged at a Lexington motel. Pope said they didn't really want to interfere with the squad's living quarters. "During the season, you know, this is the team's place," he said. "I mean it's something that's really important for the team that they have their home. It doesn't mean that ex-players are not welcome, but we (understand their) privacy is important."

With Pope looking very casual, Pitino joked after UK's 93-56 victory over No. 16 Villanova that the neatly-dressed duo of Delk and McCarty ought to buy their former teammate a classy suit. "I'm still waiting for that suit to come," Pope quipped a couple of months later. "Those guys are making the big bucks now. You know it's just not my style to really (dress up). I just kind of enjoy dressing casual. But the coach will always rub me for that a little bit, which is great."

Delk said Pope "is not one of those guys who's a flashy dresser. He really doesn't care about what he wears."

 Interestingly, Delk went from one of college basketball's attendance leaders (where UK averaged nearly 24,000 fans during his senior year) to the attendance leader in pro basketball. The Hornets regularly captured the league's attendance championship, averaging over 24,000 fans at the Charlotte Coliseum.

Delk said there wasn't much difference between UK and the Hornets as far as the fans were concerned. "They are pretty much the same," he said. "It's always good to have your fans behind you."

But college basketball overall is more enticing, according to Delk. "I think the college atmosphere is more exciting to me. I mean you have the fans and students who are really into the game. I think the NBA players and the fans are more laid back."

 After seeing limited action in three games with Charlotte at the start of the 1997-98 campaign, Delk had to move. In a three-player swap, he and long-time franchise favorite Muggsy Bogues were sent to Golden State for standout B.J. Armstrong. An unhappy 5-3 guard nursing a sore knee, Bogues had quarreled with coach Dave Cowens and the team officials about his playing time.

Delk became expendable when free agent guard Corey Beck, who played college basketball at Arkansas, impressed the Hornets with his outstanding play. In addition, the team reportedly saved huge sums of money as Beck was earning considerably less than Delk.

That meant Delk went from a championship contender to one of the league's sorry teams. About three weeks later, he and his new Golden State teammates became indirectly involved in a very ugly controversy that will be talked about for years to come. Golden State coach P.J. Carlesimo and all-star guard Latrell Sprewell clashed in a shocking incident at a practice when Sprewell choked and punched his fiery coach, creating a nationwide firestorm.

Announcer Tom Hammond, who also covers the NBA games for NBC, described the incident as "totally unfortunate. I think they (Golden State) did the right thing by suspending him and by terminating his contract (before it was reinstated in legal squabbles). When Latrell played at Alabama, he didn't seem to have an attitude (problem) at all. He was fine. But since he's signed a $30-million contract, it seems that every year his attitude gets more and more intractable. Although he is a fine player and all-star, that kind of behavior just can't be tolerated." On Carlesimo's reputation for verbal insults, Delk said in published reports, "It's not even close to some of the coaches I've had."

After the Sprewell affair, Golden State struggled the rest of the 1997-98 season, finishing with a poor 19-63 worksheet, the fifth-worst in the league. An occasional starter, Delk averaged 10.1 points in nearly 22 minutes of action despite a nagging Achilles tendon injury which bothered him in the last several weeks of the campaign. He had several 20-point games with the most being 26 points — also a career-high — against Portland. His field goal shooting percentage wasn't something to brag about, however. Even though observers said Delk was the squad's best shooter, the former Wildcat only made 39 percent of his baskets. But that wasn't entirely his fault as Golden State, one of the NBA's worst offensive teams, rarely gave him open shots. In addition, playing two backcourt positions at point guard and shooting guard certainly didn't help Delk's performance.

Although the Golden State franchise is over 2,000 miles away from his Tennessee roots, Delk said he wouldn't mind staying in the San Francisco area to help the Warriors rebuild for the future. When his playing days end, Delk mentioned that he would like try his hand in sports broadcasting.

Delk, who still loves to play ping pong and shoot pool in his spare time, said he doesn't miss UK. While he definitely enjoyed his stay in the Bluegrass, he said it was time for him to move on. "I had a good time while I was there," he commented, "but no, I don't miss them. I've been there for four years and some guys are now leaving early (for NBA)."

He attempted to follow Pitino and the Wildcats during his first NBA season. Delk, however, had trouble finding some UK games on television in Charlotte. He would have liked to have seen more Kentucky matchups.

"I didn't get a chance to watch a lot of them," he said, "because down here it is more like ACC (Atlantic Coast Conference) country."

Like most college graduates, Delk does not miss studying. The former Wildcat said that he is awfully glad today that he doesn't have to walk to classes on campus anymore while playing the sport he loves.

Playing in the NBA is nice. Playing for pay is nice. And he doesn't to have to study to stay eligible. "That's the great part about it," he said with a smile.

ON THE AIR

K entucky fans currently know Tom Hammond as the TV announcer who has covered UK basketball for Southeastern Conference's regional networks since the 1979-80 season. However, some fans, especially the ones from the younger generation, may not realize that Hammond has very strong connections with UK.

His ties with the school go way back to the early 1950s when he was a very young kid. His grandfather, Thomas P. Cooper, was a long-time Dean of the College of Agriculture, who served as the university's acting president for one year in the early 1940s. Hammond and his mother, Katherine, stayed with grandpa while his daddy, Claude, was in the U.S. Army. His parents also had strong ties with UK. Dad played football for the Wildcats in the early 1940s, while mom worked at the university for many years.

"My earliest memories are listening to UK football and basketball on the old radio that my grandfather had in that house on Limestone," recalled Hammond, who also works for NBC-TV. "I listened to Claude Sullivan and Cawood Ledford all those years."

And a young Hammond got to meet some of the Wildcat players through his mother's job. "My mother, who got her master's and doctorate degrees in dietary studies, worked at the UK facility for sometime, and I would walk in and meet some of the football and basketball players as they came to eat," the broadcaster remembered.

His favorite players were probably Cliff Hagan and Frank Ramsey, the stars of UK's great teams of the early 1950s, according to Hammond. "In the early years, they were my favorites, I guess. But that was not unusual. They were everybody's favorite in those times, growing up.

"Then I can remember the '58 team that won the national championship. Because I was getting big at that time, I always watched the centers play and, of course, Ed Beck was the (6-7) center. So I remember him. I was able to go up to Freedom Hall and to see that championship game in 1958, which was a thrill. Vernon Hatton, having been from (Lexington) Lafayette High School, where I later attended, was also a favorite player." Cotton Nash, Pat Riley and Larry Conley were also high on Hammond's list of favorite UK players.

 One of Hammond's teammates on Lafayette High's basketball team included highly-regarded guard Jeff Mullins. And their coach was legendary Ralph Carlisle, a former Kentucky standout who earned All-SEC honors in the late 1930s.

With Carlisle coaching Mullins in UK's backyard, many folks figured the player would eventually attend Kentucky. And the Wildcat mentor Adolph Rupp came to many Lafayette games to see Mullins play. He was impressed with the prep star who was named Kentucky's "Mr. Basketball" for the 1959-60 season.

"When I was a sophomore in high school, Adolph Rupp was trying to recruit him when he was a senior," said Hammond, who played center or power forward. "I sat on the bench and he sat behind me a lot of times coming to see Jeff Mullins play. He (Rupp) probably had his knees in my back a few times."

Rupp, however, lost Mullins, who shunned UK in favor of Duke. The 6-4 forward went on to lead the Blue Devils to two consecutive trips to the Final Four (1963 and '64) during his junior and senior years. (As a senior, he was Duke's leading scorer with a 24.2-point average. In the NCAA championship game, Mullins poured in a team-high 22 points before fouling out in a 98-83 loss to then-rising power UCLA.)

On his high school playing days, Hammond said, "I was a better football player actually than I was a basketball player. But I was on some good basketball teams. I did have to guard Jeff Mullins in practice when I was a sophomore and he was a senior. He played guard. I wasn't agile enough to play guard, but I was the only one tall enough to sort of get in his way. In those days I was 6-3 or 6-4 and that was a fairly big player. I did start, but I was not good enough to play college basketball."

In the 1960s, Hammond began his college studies at LSU. But he didn't stay in Baton Rouge very long, transferring to UK where he eventually received two degrees. After getting his bachelor's degree in equine genetics, Hammond thought about a career as a farm manager or a horse breeder.

But things didn't quite go in that direction. "I couldn't really find a very good job," Hammond explained. "So, out of some desperation, I went to graduate school."

While studying for his master's in equine genetics, he began to work for WVLK Radio in 1967 as a part-time announcer, covering horse racing. "I started doing the race results every night on WVLK's 15-minute show making $35 a week," Hammond recalled. "I probably wasn't very good because there was no one else (to take the vacant job). As they continued to have a need for someone to do a nightly sports show, someone to do high school basketball and football games, and someone to do news, I kept volunteering for all those things. After I had been there for awhile, I became news director and then program director."

After gaining some valuable radio broadcasting experience at WVLK, Hammond entered the television world in 1969. He was named sports director at Lexington's WLEX-TV (Channel 18). Interestingly, his first assignment was to cover a Wildcat basketball game at Memorial Coliseum on a delayed telecast. It was a frightening moment for a young man with no TV experience.

"The very first thing I did at Channel 18 was a Kentucky-Kansas basketball game in December 1969," he said. "It was black and white (TV). It was primitive. That was the very first thing I did. I hadn't done a studio show, the nightly sports news or anything. I was scared to death."

For the record Kentucky beat Kansas 115-85 in its second game of what would be a memorable 1969-70 season. It was the year that senior co-captains Dan Issel and Mike Pratt guided the popular Wildcats to a remarkable 26-2 mark and a No. 1 national ranking.

Veteran broadcaster Tom Hammond (right) is shown here resting during a commercial break from an SEC telecast while his partner, ex-Wildcat Larry Conley, studies his notes.

Photo by Rogers Photography

Hammond, however, almost didn't take the TV job. He also had another job offer to ponder. It was from Fasig-Tipton horse sales company in New York. That job offer was more lucrative than WLEX-TV. "It was very difficult decision," said Hammond, "because Fasig-Tipton then was probably even bigger than the Keeneland sales are now. It was the most well-known horse auctioning company in the world with branches all over the United States.

"In the final analysis, I guess I didn't want to leave Lexington. I guess that was the deciding factor. I would have had to gone to New York City, to Long Island actually, and live there."

Rupp also had an influence in Hammond's decision. The coach told Hammond that he would be pleased if the young broadcaster stayed in Lexington and worked for WLEX, which carried the coach's TV show as well as the delayed telecasts of UK games.

There were reports that Rupp and Hammond's predecessor, Cy Follmer, at WLEX didn't have a very good working relationship. As a result, it's believed that Rupp played a key role in forcing the TV station to hire a new sports director.

"Cy Follmer and coach Rupp didn't get along in the best of ways, and I think coach Rupp sort of arranged with his friend, Red Auerbach (of the Boston Celtics), to hire Cy Follmer to come to the Celtics games," Hammond said. "He did the Celtics games on a TV station (WSMW-TV in Worcester) for a couple of years and then I don't know what happened to him.

"But they always said that coach Rupp was kind of glad to see him go and that he kind of forced him off on his friend, Red Auerbach. Whether he had anything to do with me getting the actual job, I don't know."

As for Hammond, opportunities to broadcast UK games and to have a working relationship with Rupp were simply too much for the broadcaster to ignore besides working in his hometown.

 Although Hammond served as WLEX's top sports announcer, he didn't host Rupp's weekly television show which was held during the basketball season. He and Rupp, however, crossed paths many times, and they usually got along well.

"Actually Billy Thompson hosted the coach's show," Hammond explained. "Rupp and Billy Thompson were old cronies from way back. But since he was at our station, there were plenty of times that I could come and do interviews which appeared on the regular sports news at night and things like that. He would call me up occasionally — sometimes to chew me out about something he didn't like and sometimes to praise me for other things. So I had plenty of opportunities to come across coach Rupp."

The Baron was a lot of things. He could be overbearing. He could be funny. He could be hateful. "I think he was all those things," Hammond commented. "He could be mean. He could reduce you to two inches tall. And other times he could be so charming and so funny that you just couldn't help but want to be around him all the time.

"His practices sometimes were brutal. No talking. No one was allowed to talk but him. He would dress a player up. Dress him down. I mean he would absolutely reduce them to nothing with some profane words even I hadn't heard before. At other times he could just make you laugh and be so charming that it was pretty amazing. I think he was a complex character. He certainly was all those things and many more."

As far as one-on-one interviews with Rupp are concerned, they were usually colorful and sometimes unpredictable. "He had that well known gift of gab so you'd ask him one question and he was off to the races," Hammond said. "You'd ask him one question and he would be talking for 10 minutes if you wanted him to. Sometimes it was a matter of cutting him off rather than asking him another question. But he was pretty easy (to interview).

"There were times when you would say something he interpreted as critical that he didn't like, he'd let you know. But I always thought he was sort of testing you as he would anybody else and if you stood up to him well, he respected it. So we got along okay. We weren't the best of friends, but we had a good working relationship. Coach Rupp could be critical. General speaking if he was in a good mood and wanted to do an interview or do something, he was the best. He could just say things that would be charming, enlightening and interesting."

 Hammond comments that today's perception of UK's past and Rupp is very inaccurate and unfair. "It has now become set in stone," Hammond said. "It has now become accepted that Kentucky has a racist basketball past. That is how that has evolved. That is completely unfair, but that is the way the national media looks at it. Billy Reed (of *Sports Illustrated* and *Lexington Herald-Leader*) and I have talked about this before and we share the same opinion that it's an unfair analysis.

"But it's based on a perception that has been blown up and blown up and now guys (news media) who have never met coach Rupp, who were never around Kentucky basketball, and who weren't even born in those days just accept that because that's what has been said in recent years. So now it is entered into the fact aspect of things when it is not fact at all. It is just a perception that has been overblown."

However, according to Hammond, Rupp could've done more to be a pioneer in integration. "To be fair about it, we were not as conscious of race of those days. We should have been better, too. Coach Rupp should have been better," said the announcer. "It is easy to look back on it and say, 'If he had only had the first black player, it would have eased the transition throughout the whole South. For a program of this magnitude to have had a black player early, the first one of the SEC, it would have opened a lot of doors in a lot of places. But he didn't. He wasn't a pioneer ...... A lot of other people could have been and were not. In the South in those days, it was easy to go along without being a pioneer. So it was a missed opportunity on his part .....He didn't go against the prevailing notions of the day, the wisdom of the day, for that he can be criticized. But he wasn't unusual for his time. He was simply a product of his time.

"On the other hand, to call the program under Rupp racist and those kinds is completely wrong. I was there (at UK). I was in school. I was very good friends with (Larry) Conley, (Pat) Riley and (Louie) Dampier and those guys. I know that everyone holds up that 1966 (NCAA) championship game against Texas Western (was college basketball's so-called answer to the landmark segregation case of Brown v. Board of Education). I was there also. Then I was with them before and after the game. They didn't see it as a racial event. They didn't see it as a symbolic game. They saw it as a basketball game. I just think that has been overblown."

 When Hammond did the delayed broadcasts of UK games in 1969-70, he got acquainted with senior All-American Dan Issel. They shared a common interest in horses and horse racing. They also had some mutual friends, including well-known Lexington horseman Tom Gentry, who basically got the duo involved in the thoroughbred business.

"We had a lot of mutual friends and we became good friends," Hammond said of Issel. "Our families were good friends and we have continued."

Later Hammond and Issel also got together for several SEC regional basketball telecasts. "I got him (Issel) started, I think, doing basketball broadcast. (We did) a few SEC games to start with and we were lucky enough to be reunited on the NBA on NBC (in 1997)."

 The lowest point of his WLEX-TV career came before the 1970-71 season — Rupp's next-to-last year at Kentucky — when the station lost the television rights to carry UK basketball games on delayed basis. The unique partnership of Louisville's WAVE-TV, Evansville's WFIE-TV and Lexington's WKYT-TV outbid Channel 18 (along with WHAS-TV of Louisville) for the Kentucky games and that meant Hammond would no longer broadcast the Wildcat matchups for WLEX.

"I was devastated," Hammond said. "That was one of the main attractions of that job — the connection to UK sports that you do the bas-

Tom Hammond's first
television assignment was
WLEX-TV's delayed
telecast of a UK basketball
game in 1969.

Courtesy Tom Hammond & NBC

ketball games — and I was devastated. It really was a painful time.

"I thought about leaving (the station). I never actively sought another spot. But certainly it crossed my mind. I was always hopeful we would get them back, but in reality there was no way we would ever get them back.

"And I sort of had a similar situation at NBC. I had only been working there a year or so when NBC lost the Final Four to CBS. So I was starting to think it was fate following me around. But it was heartbreaking when we lost those (rights) when I was at Channel 18."

While the combined bid offered by the joint venture of WAVE, WKYT and WFIE was greater, the breakup of UK-WLEX television arrangement wasn't without controversy. Even Rupp's involvement didn't keep the rights in Channel 18's hands. *The Courier-Journal* of Louisville reported the top bid was $3,010 per game as compared to WLEX-WHAS' proposal of $2,033.55 per contest.

"They did something that we thought was prohibited in the bid specifications," Hammond said. "But they made it work and as long as it provided more money, I think UK was willing to look the other way on any kind of deal in the bid specs and that was okay with them.

"I'm sure coach Rupp would have been for Channel 18. He was very loyal to them. In fact, he had a show on Channel 18 even after he retired, which was kind of an awkward situation (for then-new coach Joe B. Hall, whose show aired on WKYT and others). I'm sure that he made some comments on behalf of Channel 18, but (it was) obviously not enough. It wasn't enough to get by that big dollar sign.

"So I was left to do just a few Transylvania games every year. That was all the basketball I was able to do after that. When I (later) sent a tape to the people at the SEC network to do the SEC regional (TV) games, I had to send them a Transylvania game. I didn't have anything else to send them."

 While at WLEX, an NBC affiliate, Hammond began to branch out. He spent some time announcing at thoroughbred auctions throughout the country and did occasional stories for the NBC network. In the late 1970s, he also broadcast Saturday afternoon college basketball games for NBC in conjunction with TVS network. With his increasing horse racing and TV duties, he saw his paycheck grow as a free-lancer and left WLEX in 1980.

"One of the main reasons I left was because I began doing Southeastern Conference basketball for what was then TVS network and they were tied into NBC," Hammond said. "As a matter of fact, Joe B. Hall was one of the men who was instrumental in me getting that job at TVS.

"Of course over the years, those (TV) rights holders in the SEC had changed. It has been TVS, it's been Sports Productions, it's been Lorimar and now it's Jefferson-Pilot. So I've been lucky to stay through all those different rights holders."

For nearly two decades, a reliable Hammond had a perfect record of not missing a single beat before bad weather in early February of 1998 forced him to sit out his SEC regional TV assignment for the first time. He missed Kentucky's 63-61 victory over LSU in Baton Rouge because he was stuck in Lexington in nearly two feet of snow.

So instead of calling the game, he had to stay home and watch his temporary replacement, Tim Brando, call play-by-play for Jefferson-Pilot. How did Hammond feel about staying home?

"It was an unusual feeling," Hammond said. "I didn't think I would ever miss one after this long. And what's really odd is Baton Rouge is one of the easier places to get to. Direct air service there (from Atlanta) and you figure that would be one of the best places, but that snowfall just took everyone by surprise in Lexington.

"If I'd known it was gonna snow that much, I'd have left the night before (the game). But I didn't know and it was really an odd experience to be watching a game where you knew you were supposed to be (working) and unusual too after 19 years to finally miss a game. It wasn't a good feeling."

Before missing that regional TV game, Hammond said he had a couple of close calls during his long tenure with SEC telecasts. "I once arrived in Oxford (Mississippi) about a hour before a game," he said. "And I had been there in Fayetteville (Arkansas) probably a hour and a half before the game."

In 1984 he became a regular member of the NBC Sports team as a broadcaster. "NBC hired me to work on the first Breeders' Cup telecast as a horse racing expert," said Hammond, who also owned Lexington-based Hammond Productions, which produced weekly syndicated horse racing programs, at the time. "And at the end of that day, they asked me if I would be interested in doing other things, starting with NFL football (telecasts) and I've been with them ever since." Interestingly, NBC's telecast of the inaugural Breeders' Cup won an Eclipse Award.

A 1995 inductee of the Kentucky Journalism Hall of Fame, one of the few sports journalists so honored, Hammond has year-round network duties, covering NBA games, track and field events, and Notre Dame football games, in addition to horse racing assignments. He had also announced the NFL games on a regular basis before NBC lost its television rights in 1998. The network had televised pro football games for 33 straight years, going back to the days of the old American Football League (AFL).

On NBC's losing television contract with NFL, Hammond said, "It was really a bitter pill because I had gotten to the point where I was doing either the No. 1 or the No. 2 game each week. (Veteran sportscaster) Dick Enberg is nearing retirement age and so you figure if NBC had signed the eight-year contract, I would have gotten to do a Super Bowl sometime in that period and now they lost the contract. (That means) no more NFL football and no chance at a Super Bowl. Football was about the most fun (thing) to do. I miss NFL football a lot."

Beginning with the 1998 season, the NFL is slated to receive nearly $18 billion over the next eight years from four networks — CBS, Fox, ABC and ESPN.

After spending nearly 20 years as a sportscaster in regional or national television events, Hammond has seen the highs and lows. As a TV announcer, Hammond has several memorable moments. They include:

*Tom Osborne's first national championship as Nebraska football coach in beating Miami 24-17 in the Orange Bowl after the 1994 season. "That was a big moment," Hammond said.

*Kentucky's dramatic overtime victory over Arkansas in the 1995 SEC tournament championship game in Atlanta. "One of the finest games I've seen and one of the most exciting games ever," said the announcer.

*Don Shula's record-setting performance when he became the NFL's all-time winningest coach.

*Sprinter Carl Lewis' world records.

*Legendary coach Eddie Robinson's football games at Grambling.

*Track star and gold medalist Michael Johnson's world-record performance in the Atlanta Olympics in 1996. "It was the most electric, most exciting moment that I can remember," Hammond said.

*Kyle Macy's last-second basket in UK's 76-74 overtime win over LSU in Baton Rouge. "An amazing game where he hit the game-winning shot," said the broadcaster of the 1980 thriller.

*NBA playoffs. "At its best, NBA basketball is tremendous," said Hammond.

As a broadcaster, Hammond said if he had to choose a favorite moment, it would be Johnson's phenomenal performance in the 1996 Olympics. "I have one of my treasured possessions at home — an autographed picture of him crossing the finish line with the time showing the world record in the background and with this look of astonishment on his face," he commented. "He autographed (the picture) for me afterward."

What about the lows? What about his most embarrassing moment? Hammond has some stories to tell.

The failure of decathlon favorite Dan O'Brien to make the U.S. team for the 1992 Olympics. Since O'Brien, who was the leading favorite to win the decathlon in the Olympics in Barcelona, had unexpectedly stumbled in the Olympic Trials, Hammond and the network had to make nerve-wrecking, last-minute changes on the air. It was one of the announcer's most unprepared moments.

"When Dan O'Brien failed to clear a pole vault and didn't qualify, we're scrambling to find out why and do the answers," he said. "We're going live on the air to several million people without really knowing it was going to happen. Every game involves some moment of unexpected things that you hope that you're prepared for with your background."

The 1990 Breeders' Cup which saw filly Go For Wand break her leg at Belmont Park. "That was a horrifying moment," said Hammond. "We had three more hours to go in the telecast and we all feel like, you know, we just want to quit and go home because it's not any fun anymore. It is too sad to go on. But you have to go on." Later the filly, who nearly won that $1 million race, had to be destroyed.

Hammond's broadcast partner who nervously fell apart during a live telecast of the U.S. Track and Field championships in 1991. "The first track and field meet I ever did at NBC was the U.S. Championships in 1991. When we opened the two-hour telecast, the color commentator completely lost it," Hammond said. "He couldn't speak. He was so nervous that he just choked up and I had to try to carry him along and then had to do the two-hour show basically by myself.

"It was my first track meet. I didn't know a whole lot about it and that was something that I for sure wasn't ready for. And I felt sorry for him. I had compassion for him because he just could not speak. He was paralyzed. Paralyzed with fear. And (he) started to sob and to cry. I had to carry on two hours live on something that I wasn't that familiar with.

"So that was a difficult moment. A moment for which you can't prepare. More difficult for him than for me, I should say. But you know many things that come upon like that you hope you have enough background to prepare you for. There will always be unexpected things that will happen."

A taped, halftime interview with then-Auburn athletic director and football coach Pat Dye, whom Hammond mistakenly called by the name of jockey Pat Day when he con-

cluded the interview. Hammond said that was probably the most embarrassing moment in his broadcasting career. It took place in the early 1980s. "He (Dye) looked at me like he could just shoot bullets through me and I didn't even know what I had said at the time," he recalled. "He looked at me and I knew something wasn't right. I didn't have the opportunity to correct myself. I didn't even know I had done it until they played it back on tape. And then I felt rather foolish.

"Knock on wood, there haven't been too many embarrassing moments. There have been many times when I'm sure I looked foolish and said foolish things, but none of them humorous enough to recount that I can think of. I'm sure I've done a lot of stupid things, but not too many funny things."

What are the most interesting or memorable interviews Hammond has had with celebrities? For starters, he mentioned a 1936 Olympic great and a presidential hopeful.

"I can remember two of the first ones that I did that were interesting — Jesse Owens and Robert Kennedy," he said of the interviews held in the late 1960s. "I don't know how I ended up interviewing him (Kennedy), but I did shortly before his death (in 1968)."

NFL quarterback Warren Moon also ranks high on Hammond's list. "I always thought Warren Moon was one of the most intelligent, thoughtful, pleasant guys that I ever met in professional sports," said the broadcaster. "He had some domestic problems which really pained me. He had a domestic squabble with his wife that drew some attention. I guess they patched up. But (it) pained me because I never would have thought that from him. He was one of my favorite guys."

Hammond also respects mega-superstar Michael Jordan. "Michael Jordan, without a question, is a good guy and some of my most interesting interviews have been with him," he said. "One of the most interesting times I spent with him, he had just come back from his baseball experience and was not shooting that well. (He) was getting ready to do a game that afternoon at United Center (in Chicago). I was at the arena two and a half hours early and Michael Jordan showed up early to get some extra shooting in because he was having trouble shooting. We were basically the only two people around at that time.

"So I ended up rebounding the ball for him while he shot and we carried on a running conversation the whole time. It was one of the most interesting times that I spent with an athlete."

While he has had a share of good interviews, Hammond has run into problems with athletes who didn't say much on TV or difficult players who didn't want to be bothered with an interview.

"There have been plenty of difficult interviews," he said. "There have been a lot of times when players are shy and want to give you answers with yes and no, and things like that. (Some are) painfully bad in their grammar.

"I tried to interview Larry Bird one time live at an NBA game when I was doing a sideline report. He got on the air and said, 'No, I don't care to be interviewed, but thanks for asking' in a sort of smart aleck way. That was pretty difficult. I'm sure there are many times when those things happen."

 Hammond has covered NBA for several years and he doesn't really like what's he seeing today. He doesn't particularly care for some players who are spoiled and have obnoxious attitudes. They are pampered mainly because of their gigantic salaries, said the sportscaster.

"I think they are getting worse," Hammond said of the NBA players' behavior. "Things like Scottie Pippen disturb me when he bails out basically on his team and on Michael Jordan and Phil Jackson. He promised that he would come back (in 1997-98 after an injury) to try to win another championship at Chicago and then suddenly he says he doesn't want to play anymore. What does that do? You're letting your teammates down. It's selfishness, which is rampant in professional sports, I think. (Pippen later had a change of heart and rejoined his squad.)

"Of course, Dennis Rodman goes without saying. Some of his antics can't be condoned in any way. He is just some sort of freak. But we see in all professional sports that the money is distorting reality, spoiling them. They answer to no one because they have so much money. There is no way to control them. I think it's a problem. At its worst, (NBA) is pretty disgusting. The players' antics. The selfish play. I don't have an answer to it, but I think harsh measures such as the NBA took with Latrell Sprewell are a step (in the right direction for attacking his coach in 1997). But at its best NBA basketball is fantastic."

 Even though he grew up in Lexington and graduated from UK, Hammond likes to point out that he has managed to stay objective when he is covering a game involving the Wildcats, on SEC's regional TV broadcasts. Some SEC fans, however, think he is promoting UK. On the other hand, some Kentucky supporters believe he has gone too far in trying not to seem partial to UK. And despite his UK-flavored background, being an objective voice on telecasts hasn't been very hard, according to Hammond.

"It's not that difficult for me and I don't know how to say that," he said. "It's my job and I consider myself a professional. I just don't find it difficult. I'm able to put all those feelings aside because I know it's my job. But I think if you ask people, they probably would say that I'm not. I've found over the years that people from other teams think that I'm biased for Kentucky and Kentucky fans generally think I'm biased against them. So I figure as long as that is the feeling, I must be somewhere around the middle because they both have differing views. It's such a subjective thing for fans. Fans care so passionately about which team wins or loses. The concept of someone not caring is difficult for them to understand. So they figure if you're not for us, you must be for them.

"I think in my heart that I have been objective and fair the whole time and I want to be because, like I said, that's my job and I'm a professional."

 Another highlight during his college days at UK came when he met his future wife, the former Sheilagh Rogan of Middlesboro. Her father, Dave Rogan, once held the SEC mile run record for many years. And today the Hammonds have three children — David, Christopher and Ashley.

Interestingly, both of their adult sons are following their dad's footsteps by getting involved in some capacity in athletics. David, who played minor league baseball in the Philadelphia Phillies organization, is radio color commentator for the Michigan football and basketball games at WUOM in Ann Arbor. Christopher, a former baseball player at Duke, works for the Montreal Expos organization. Daughter Ashley, meanwhile, lives at home, attending Tates Creek High School.

Hammond, whose faith is Presbyterian, commented he feels lucky that he is able to realize his ambitions of having a network job while living in a small market like Lexington. By making his home in the Bluegrass, he did not have to uproot his family. He got the NBC job in a very unusual fashion. Unlike some sportscasters, he did not move from one market to another to advance his TV career. "My whole career was somewhat governed by not wanting to leave Lexington," he said. "Normally, if you are going to enter TV business on doing local TV, you try to advance to bigger markets all the time. I never wanted to do that. I wanted to stay in Lexington. That's how I got into announcing the horse auctions and so on. I could supplement my income that way and not leave Lexington. So I didn't arrive at the work in a traditional manner by hopscotching to bigger markets all the time.

"I have been fortunate in network television to have started basically at the bottom and to have luckily risen to a spot of some responsibility in getting some good games and things. I mean not many people get to do something that they always wanted to do. What I do is not even like working. It is like being a little kid in a candy store because you're able to do these things that are so enjoyable. Every event is a new challenge. You never get stale. You never get uninterested. It's exciting, satisfying work. And how fortunate I have been able to do that."

CAMERON
AND HIS DAD

U K's 1998 national championship team only had two players from Kentucky — 6-3 senior guard Cameron Mills and 6-9 junior forward Scott Padgett. Mills grew up in Somerset and played prep basketball in Lexington. Padgett hails from Louisville where he played at St. Xavier High School, earning all-state honors.

It is no secret that the rabid Wildcat fans have always had a special relationship with Kentucky-grown players on the team. They just simply idolize them like they did with Kentuckians Richie Farmer and John Pelphrey, to name a couple. "It's a great feeling," Mills said of the fans' admiration. "I think it's because I grew up as one of those fans who watched a few of the Kentucky players come out of Kentucky. I grew up in my backyard pretending I was Rex Chapman, pretending I was Ed Davender, Roger Harden and Sam Bowie. Pretending I was these players and then actually to be on the Kentucky basketball team — that was very special to me."

Born in Fort Walton Beach, Fla., Mills wasn't even two years old when his parents returned to Kentucky where his father, Terry Mills, became the head basketball coach at Somerset Community College in the summer of 1977. The elder Mills, a Knox County native and a former UK hoops standout, eventually left SCC to enter the insurance business. The Mills family lived in Somerset for many years before moving to Lexington for personal and business reasons.

Said Cameron Mills, "We moved from Somerset in the summer before my eighth grade year. I spent, I guess, all of my life until eighth grade in Somerset. I started eighth grade at Beaumont Middle School here in Lexington.

"Dad wanted to be closer to the home or state office of MassMutual. He also felt that he had seen some college basketball potential in me and thought I would have a better chance of getting noticed and getting recruited if we were in a bigger setting where there was more media coverage and better competition."

The younger Mills went on to become a four-year starter on the varsity team at Paul Laurence Dunbar High School under coach Frank Watson. Mills guided the Bulldogs to the Sweet Sixteen championship game in both his junior and senior seasons. As a senior, he averaged 14.7 points a game. When he left Paul Dunbar, his 1,690 career points were the sixth highest in Lexington prep history.

 Mills and his two senior teammates — Jeff Sheppard and Allen Edwards — are members of a very elite group at UK. Unlike hundreds of ex-UK players, they reached the NCAA Final Four three times during their Wildcat career, winning the national championship twice and the runner-up spot once, although Sheppard redshirted during the 1996-97 campaign.

But they almost didn't make the third Final Four trip in 1998 when Kentucky fell behind by 17 points against Duke in the NCAA South Regional finals with over nine minutes remaining. Of course, as history will show, the Wildcats refused to surrender, surprising the Blue Devils by two points at the end. The Final Four also saw UK falling behind in both games against Stanford and Utah before rallying to win the school's seventh national title. Thus, the catchy slogan of the "Comeback Cats" was born. The overachieving team will be forever linked with other great teams like the Fabulous Five (1947-48), the Fiddlin' Five (1957-58) and the Unforgettables (1991-92).

Mills, a tri-captain who was the "heart and soul" of the "Comeback Cats," is clearly very tickled with the way the memorable 35-4 campaign has turned out. "Obviously, it makes us feel great to be remembered in the same area like the Fiddlin' Five, even Rupp's Runts although they never won the championship, the Unbelievables, the

Untouchables and then the Comeback Cats," Mills said. "There is something neat about playing at a school where the successful teams are given a name or a positive nickname at the end of the season.

"I probably couldn't tell you who was on the Fiddlin' Five, but I have heard of them. I probably couldn't tell you all the members of Rupp's Runts, but I have heard of Rupp's Runts. And you know 15, 20 and 30 years down the line, there are probably gonna be kids who have heard of the Untouchables, who have heard of the Unbelievables, who have heard of the Comeback Cats, and not able to tell you who was on that team."

In the Duke matchup, when the Wildcats trailed by 17 points in the second half, Mills admitted that a UK victory was a long shot. He had hopes, but not much. Since he didn't want to end his collegiate career on a blowout loss, he was determined to do his best while the team still had a fighting chance. Interestingly, it was Mills' only basket of the game — a three-pointer — that gave Kentucky a lead for the first time with over two minutes remaining.

"Part of me did and part of me didn't (want to believe the Wildcats would come back and win)," commented Mills, who had five points in 13 minutes. "My mind was telling me we weren't gonna win and my heart was telling me we were. It was very difficult to see us down 17 (points) and to think, 'Is there any way we are going to win this game?' with only nine and a half minutes left.

"I was going through a lot of emotions right there because I kept thinking this might be my last game. I didn't want to go out like this and at the same time I didn't want to even think about that because I wanted to concentrate on winning the game and not even having to worry about that."

Mills said he ranks UK's 86-84 win over Duke as the most exciting one of his playing career along with the NCAA championship victory over Utah. He became very emotional after these two victories. "I was crying just after both games because I couldn't believe what we had done in either one of them," he said. "I couldn't believe we had won the games." In Kentucky's nine-point victory over Utah before a large crowd of over 40,000 fans in San Antonio, Texas, the sharp-shooting Mills gunned in eight points, including two three-point field goals, in 12 minutes of action.

A two-time starter, the former walk-on completed his senior season as a key reserve with a 4.4-point average and missed only one free throw, hitting 22 of 23 from the line for nearly 96 percent. In a mid-sea-

Cameron Mills wore the same UK jersey number (21) his father, Terry Mills, had when the latter played at Kentucky under legendary coach, Adolph Rupp.

Photo by Rogers Photography

son conference game at Rupp Arena, Mills had a hot hand, shooting a career-high 31 points in Kentucky's stunning setback to the Florida Gators. As it turned out, Mills' 31 points were the most scored by a Wildcat player during Kentucky's championship season.

As a junior in the 1997 NCAA tournament, Mills had an unbelievable run, surprising many observers. He averaged 11.3 points in the NCAA tourney, third best on the squad, after a so-so performance in the regular season. He scored a then-career high 19 points against Montana and a week later matched his career-best in UK's 83-68 victory over St. Joseph's.

Asked to explain his suddenly hot performance in the tourney, Mills replied, "I don't know. The easiest answer is just to say it was God because I wasn't doing anything differently. I wasn't practicing more, practicing less or playing any better in practice. I guess I didn't have a name as a shooter. I didn't have a name as a scorer. I wasn't being guarded very closely. I had a lot of open shots. But as far as what I was doing I wasn't really doing any thing (different). It just kind of happened."

His surprising performance gave Mills more media attention than he ever dreamed of. "The more media attention I got the more credit I got to give God," he recalled. "One thing leads to another."

 While at UK, Mills became well-known for his Christian faith, speaking to hundreds of clubs, groups and churches throughout the state. In addition, he was also named college basketball's 1997 Player of the Year by Athletes International Ministries for his commitment to God and for serving as a role model for young people. During the 1997-98 school year, he served as vice president in UK's chapter of the Fellowship of Christian Athletes (FCA) with Wildcat punter Jimmy Carter from the football team as chapter president.

"I started speaking my freshman year," said Mills, who is now a full-time evangelist. "I fell in love with doing it. (I) decided it was something I wanted to do. Then you know it doesn't matter what you want to do. It is what the Lord wants you to do. You are not going to be happy (if you try to do on your own). You know the Lord has plans for your life that are far better than what your plans for your life are. So I started praying about it and just felt the Lord call me into the ministry and say this is what I want you to do. I'm thankful for that because it was something I wanted to do."

Asked what was the most interesting or the most emotional moment he has encountered as a guest speaker or evangelist, Mills' reply was: "They're all incredible. They are all amazing." He also pointed out that watching someone making a commitment to God is much more exhilarating and meaningful than winning the national title in basketball. "Anytime I speak and someone comes to the same realization that I came to when I was seven years old that they need Jesus Christ in their life and they are willing to stand up before a big group of people and say that, that's what is incredible to me. Watching somebody do that is more exciting than winning a national championship.

"I know it is hard for some people to believe, but until you have been through that, until you have been there dealing with that person, crying with that person because that person has come to that point of realization where he or she can't live without Jesus Christ — you just have no idea what that feels like."

 Interestingly, Mills first became fascinated with God and religion on a wintry day when there was no school. In Somerset, with nothing else to do, he was home watching TV with his mother, Lorri.

Recalled Mills, "I was sitting at home just kind of bouncing around the house, having all this energy, and I couldn't go outside. Mom was in her room watching *The 700 Club*, which she always did. But she kind of got tired of me making so much noise and just told me to calm down and watch the show.

"I started watching the show. Pat Robertson came on and started talking about giving your life to Jesus Christ. I had always been raised in the church, but I had never heard it put so plainly. He started talking about how we're all sinners and we all need Jesus Christ in our life. I sat there and listened and listened, and just told Mom, 'Look, it's something I want to do. I want to ask Jesus to come into my life.' So right there at seven years old, I was on my knees and that's when I asked (the Lord to take over my life)."

Other than the Lord, Mills said his parents are the biggest influence as far as religion is concerned. "Both have been very influential in my spiritual life," said the younger Mills, who is a member of Lexington's Southland Christian Church. "I have had so many different people along my life who have just kind of shaped my spiritual walk and just kind of guided me in ways — my youth ministers, ministers, friends, people who have been involved in the FCA, in campus life, at church. You know there are too many to mention, but I say probably the main ones would be mom and dad."

 One of Mills' favorite people is the Rev. Ed Bradley of Henderson, Ky., who has been serving as the basketball squad's unofficial priest for the past several years under the regimes of coach Rick Pitino and coach Tubby Smith. They frequently got together, and held fruitful and spiritual talks.

"Father Bradley is probably one of the nicest men in the world," Mills said. "He never has a bad thing to say about anybody, always saying nice things. (He is) just a sweet man and you know, to me, that is just Jesus Christ coming out in him. He is just a super human being.

"Because he is a priest, we've always had kind of a little thing where both of our love of our lives is Jesus Christ. That is something we have always talked about. It has kind of been our bind between the two of us. I know (sometimes) he was praying for me and he would know when I was getting distracted and upset over practice or something, or at a game."

Ironically, Mills said he and Father Bradley never discussed his future in ministry. "Actually, we never talked (about that)," said Mills. "He obviously was excited when he found out I was going into the ministry. But he never, never really tried to give me advice about it."

As of summer 1998, Mills said he had no definite plans to enter a formal training in ministry, but that's subject to change. "While my name is out there, while everybody knows I'm going into the ministry, I'm just going (to continue speaking)," he commented. "If the Lord calls me back and tells me to go school, I will do it obviously."

 Homosexuality and AIDS are some of the controversial issues that some folks don't like to discuss. These touchy topics make people uncomfortable. Even churches have problems with these issues. Mills has some interesting viewpoints about the society's troubles in dealing with individuals who are gay and/or have AIDS, among others.

"I think the church has gotten itself into a bit of trouble in dealing with homosexuals, dealing with AIDS, dealing with people who are living a promiscuous lifestyle," said Mills, who studied psychology and was expected to receive his degree in August 1998. "It has gotten to the point where it has been blamed with bashing. It has been blamed for not having a Christian attitude. And a lot of churches are well deserved to have this thing stressed upon them because I always live by the saying that Jesus hates the sin, but loves the sinner.

"Homosexuality is wrong. It is a sin, but it is no different than the sins I commit in my life. Therefore, as long as a person is willing to accept the fact that what they are doing is a sin, there is no problem at all. I'm not a person to judge anybody. Obviously, that is one of everyone's favorite thing to do. You know you shouldn't judge (people). Judge not lest you be judged. We aren't to judge, but we are to hold people up to standards. We are to hold people accountable for things. Just like my mom and dad are to hold me accountable to Jesus' teachings. I'm to hold other people accountable to Jesus' teachings.

"If the Bible says something is wrong and I see somebody doing

Cameron Mills' parents, Terry and Lorri Mills, attending a Kentucky Wildcat game at Rupp Arena.

Photo by Rogers Photography

it, I'm going to tell them it's wrong. Just as if I am doing something that is wrong, I expect somebody to come up to me and tell me that what I'm doing is wrong. And that's not judging. Judging is when you hand out a punishment. Well, I can't hand out a punishment for sin. I don't have the power to do that. The only person that has the power to do that is God.

"But I can tell someone when they are making a mistake and I expect people to tell me when I'm making mistakes. Because if you let everybody go and not point out people's failures, no one is going to get any better. No one is going to improve. No one is going to change their lifestyle."

 In 1994-95, Mills had problems during his freshman year at UK, almost quitting the team. He didn't enjoy playing basketball under coach Rick Pitino and his staff. Even though he had a room at the Wildcat Lodge, he frequently went to his

parents' home in Lexington. "I practically lived at home," Mills admitted. He had second thoughts about his decision to attend UK. And he was a walk-on who had turned down a scholarship offer from the Georgia Bulldogs. But it was his faith that kept him going throughout the school year.

"I was miserable," he said of his rookie year. "I wanted to quit. I was tired. I was tired of getting yelled at. I was physically tired, mentally tired. You know the freshman year is the toughest. You are not used to working the way we worked and I came in, not knowing what to expect.

"But I prayed a lot about it and it got to the point where I really felt the Lord had me here for a reason and obviously he did if you look at the past four years. But at that point I didn't see that. I was kind of struggling with what that reason was because it hadn't been unveiled to me yet. And I just wanted to quit because I was absolutely miserable. But I spent a lot of time praying about it and just finally came to the conclusion that this is where the Lord wants me and if this is where the Lord wants me, it's all gonna turn out for the best."

While the 1994-95 Wildcats roared to a 28-5 mark with its final No. 2 national ranking, Mills didn't see much action as a freshman. He saw limited action, logging a total of 32 minutes in eight games. In Kentucky's 124-50 season-opening victory over Tennessee-Martin at Rupp Arena, Mills scored seven points, including a three-pointer, in his Wildcat debut. With his parents looking on from the second row behind the basket, Mills entered the game with less than seven minutes left when UK led 98-45. Mills said after the game he wasn't emotional. "No, actually, I wasn't really (nervous)." But he had butterflies earlier when Kentucky met Athletes In Action in an exhibition contest. "That was the first time I had put on the uniform and that was the game where I got really emotional and got hyper," he said in 1994.

Mills also added that his sophomore year was difficult, too. But it wasn't as bad as his freshman season after adjusting to college life and the roundball program. As a second-year performer, he didn't play much for Kentucky's powerful 1995-96 team which captured the national crown in New Jersey. He averaged less than one point in seven varsity games. "I was going through a hard time, too," Mills said of his sophomore year. "I questioned whether or not I was supposed to be here (at UK), whether or not I made the right decision." Of course, he continued to pray for guidance and eventually realized that UK was the right place for him.

However, he and 6-10 freshman teammate Nazr Mohammed played significant roles for the "revived" junior varsity squad which was coached by then-Kentucky assistant Delray Brooks. Coach Pitino had decided to reinstitute the junior varsity program that season so his reserves could gain valuable experience in game competition as the varsity Wildcats were loaded with talented players. Mills led the jayvee Wildcats in scoring (23.7 points a game), assists and steals.

 Pitino is well-known for his colorful and foul language at games and practices. Many fans have wondered if Pitino's profanity conflicted with Mills' Christian faith. How did the player cope with the coach's language during his first three years at UK?

"Well, it's actually not that big of a conflict," Mills explained. "I mean it does conflict with Christian faith. My language isn't where it needs to be all the time. You can't be in college and not hear (the profanity). You can't grow up and not hear foul language. It is just something you have to get used to and that wasn't a problem for me to get used to. It wasn't a big deal at all."

Comparing Pitino's profanity with coach Tubby Smith's language is easy. Like night and day. Observers like to point out that Pitino's language deserves a rating of "R" while Smith's is given a rating of "PG" or "PG-13."

"Coach Pitino isn't afraid to use profanity and expletives. (This is) not to say that coach Smith doesn't. Coach Smith does," said Mills, who added that Smith sometimes has those fearsome-looking eyes that will pop out, frightening him and his teammates. "But you know you get in practice sometimes and you get so excited or intense and sometimes they (the words) just slip out. I've done it before in practice. You get so upset, so mad and so intense that you just let (the words) fly out of your mouth.

"Coach Pitino was just always so intense and so high strung, especially during practice and I think that is one of the reasons his language was the way it was. Coach Smith is the same way. He wasn't nearly as bad as coach Pitino. But every now and then one would come out of his mouth. Both of them had team practice rules that profanity was not to be used by the athletes. We were not allowed to cuss. We were not allowed to use that kind of language, even though we occasionally did. But when we did a lot of times, we got in trouble for it."

In May 1997, when Pitino announced his decision to leave UK for Boston in the NBA, Mills had a private meeting with the coach. They had a nice conversation. And it was a special moment that Mills will always cherish. That's probably the most touching moment he had seen with Pitino, according to Mills, who earned a basketball scholarship before his junior year. And those moments don't take place very often with Pitino, who happens to be the type of person who fiercely guards his privacy.

Mills said, "He told me how proud he was of me and how excited he was that I had lived out my dream of becoming a Wildcat and actually playing a lot because that was right after I had a little stretch run in the NCAA tournament and SEC tournament."

Another memorable moment Mills had with Pitino took place at a mid-January practice during his junior year. "When I had my concussion — I was back in the training room, just kind of disoriented and didn't know what was going on, I remember he was back there with practice still going on," he said. "That was important to me, too, because I could tell then he was more concerned with my health than he was with what was going on with the team at that particular time." Following the concussion, Mills missed four straight games, suffering headaches and amnesia.

Mills' roommates at UK included Scott Padgett (freshman year), Frank Vogel (sophomore year) and Steve Masiello (junior and senior years). While Padgett and Masiello were better known as the Wildcat players, Vogel was a key member of the UK basketball family. A student manager, Vogel also played on the jayvee team where he averaged 6.5 points as a part-time starter. Vogel is now with Rick Pitino on the Boston Celtics' staff, serving as the head video coordinator.

Mills sometimes comes across as a very serious Christian person. But don't get the wrong impression that he doesn't joke around or have some fun. While Mills sometimes likes to play golf and football, he enjoys listening to music and playing guitar. And he has a good sense of humor. He has a good story about Masiello, the 6-2 walk-on from the state of New York.

"(Coach Tubby Smith) threw Steve out of practice and that was hilarious," Mills said of his roommate. "It wasn't (hilarious) obviously to coach Smith or Steve, but everyone else on the team enjoyed it. That was the only time coach Smith ever threw anyone out of practice that year.

"I remember one time Steve and I were up on the roof of the Wildcat Lodge studying and we were also sunbathing. We both got absolutely burnt. We were always fooling around, always having fun."

Jeff Sheppard, the 1998 Final Four MVP, is also one of Mills' closest friends on the team. And Mills had a role in Sheppard's wedding which was held in London, Ky., the bride's hometown, a couple of months after Kentucky's national championship season. Mills served as one of the groomsmen along with Scott Padgett. Several other UK players as well as team managers took part as ushers. Sheppard's wife, Stacey Reed, is a former UK women's basketball standout.

 Before the NCAA's new job ruling (Prop 62) became effective in August 1998, allowing some scholarship athletes to hold part-time positions and earn up to $2,000 during the academic season, Mills was one of many players who supported a move that would allow players to receive some form of financial support from the school.

"We need some sort of monthly allotment," Mills said in 1996. "We have phone bills, cable bills for our television, and we need money to go out. We don't have time to go out and have a job because playing college basketball is full time. We're already doing something related to college ball.

"Of course, we've got academics that we have to spend a lot of time on. We just need money to spend and pay our bills."

Said Terry Mills, Cameron's father, "I think there should be some way they (the players) can get some money for expenses because it's got to be very difficult for some of them to have spending money if their parents can't give it to them.

"There needs to be some kind of compensation. I know they are getting their books, their education, their room and board paid for, but still there is other expense money that any student would have to have."

Ex-UK star and current NBA standout Ron Mercer thinks college athletes should be paid. "Yes, the schools are making a lot of money over the jerseys and stuff like that," Mercer said in Middlesboro's *Daily News* in 1996. "The players don't get anything besides their education, which is good. But I think (the college athletes) deserve a little bit more. As a result, you see a lot of people leaving school early to get money. Somewhere down

"Comeback Cat" Cameron
Mills goes up for one of his
long-range jumpers at Rupp
Arena. Before becoming the
"heart and soul" of
Kentucky's 1998 national
championship squad, Mills
nearly quit the team during
his first year of college in
1994-95.

University of Kentucky Media Relations
/ Photo by David Coyle

the road, they'll (NCAA) have to draw a line so college players get a little
money from somewhere."

It appears the new employment legislation passed by the NCAA
won't ease some concerns that the players had previously. UK athletic
director C. M. Newton isn't happy with the new job ruling. He doesn't like
the new guidelines because of possible abuses where overzealous boosters
can arrange work for the players.

 It is safe to say that there aren't very many fathers who can
watch their sons play college basketball for two different
schools in their hometown.

Terry Mills, a former Wildcat standout in the late 1960s
and the early '70s, is very fortunate to have both of his sons

stay home and attend college in Lexington. During the winter of 1997-98, the elder Mills didn't have to travel a lot to see Cameron play during his senior year at UK or Collier at Transylvania University where the 6-5 forward was beginning his rookie year. "I enjoy basketball and I have enjoyed being able to follow my two sons," said the father. Both of his sons starred at Paul Dunbar High where both led the Bulldogs to the Sweet Sixteen tournament at different times.

While Terry Mills is usually very calm and doesn't show a lot of emotion, he got a little edgy at times when the sons were playing. That's obviously because he wanted them to do well on the hardwood floor. "I'm not a very emotional person, but I still get a little bit nervous for both of them," said the father, who once coached them when they were much younger. "But you know it's not too bad because I have a lot of confidence that they'll get on the floor and do what they are supposed to do. They both play under control. I don't get too worried about them making a lot of mistakes." Besides their father, Cameron and Collier usually had plenty of family supporters in the stands. Their mother, Lorri, can be seen cheering along with their two adopted sisters — Meredith and Melinda.

Cameron almost didn't stay home and wear the Wildcat uniform. While in high school, he had plans to attend the University of Georgia in Athens where he had a basketball scholarship waiting for him. Then-Bulldog coach Hugh Durham — who once had Terry Mills on his coaching staff as graduate assistant at Florida State — liked Cameron's style.

When fall signing period came around in November 1993 during his senior year, Cameron began to have second thoughts about his collegiate decision. He wasn't sure about Georgia. He and his family earlier had visited the UGA campus during the weekend of Oct. 23, ironically the same weekend when the football Bulldogs faced coach Bill Curry's Kentucky squad, and won in a 33-28 decision.

On Cameron's visit, Terry Mills said, "(Georgia) flew Cameron down before we got there. We just drove down just to spend some time (visiting the campus). The whole family went down for an official visit .... and I think that's when Cameron decided that he wouldn't really be comfortable that far away from home. When it came time to either accept or not accept their invitation to sign early, he decided not to (sign)."

At that point Cameron made his decision that he would like to play for the Wildcats, who didn't offer him a scholarship. And coach Rick Pitino agreed to have Cameron join the team as a walk on, but made no promises. Cameron's lifelong dream to be a Wildcat had just come true. When he was a little boy, he used to pretend he was his daddy and some of the other Wildcats playing basketball at Kentucky.

As it turned out, Georgia was the only major university to offer him a scholarship while in high school, according to the younger Mills. U of L also expressed strong interest in Mills, but it never actually offered him a scholarship.

 While Terry Mills was obviously pleased to see his oldest son going to UK, he was careful not to influence Cameron's decision in the recruiting process. Once Cameron revealed his true feelings about the Bulldog program, the elder Mills stepped in. "When Cameron told me he didn't want to go to Georgia, I said, 'Well, do you want to talk to Kentucky about maybe walking on?' He said yeah," said the father. "So at that point I went to coach (Billy) Donovan to explore the possibility and he said, 'Sure, let me run it by coach Pitino.'

"I think coach Donovan and coach Pitino talked that day and then coach Pitino called me on the phone (to set up a meeting). I went to get Cameron out of school and we drove down that afternoon to meet with coach Pitino and we worked it out that day."

Had Cameron played at Georgia, he likely would have seen significant action during his first two years in college. His dad agreed, but he is kind of glad that Cameron headed for UK, not Georgia, especially because the Bulldogs had fired coach Hugh Durham in a stormy split after the 1994-95 campaign. (Durham, who is now the head coach at Jacksonville, later received a reported $500,000 settlement with UGA.) Said the elder Mills, "Maybe it worked out for the best, you know, that Cameron didn't go down there."

 Before coming to Kentucky in 1966, joining the freshman team loaded with future Wildcat stars Dan Issel, Mike Casey and Mike Pratt, Terry Mills played at Knox Central High in Barbourville where he was a 6-1 All-State guard. He helped his 13th Region squad go to the state tournament twice (1965 and '66). In 1965, he received statewide attention when he starred in the Sweet Sixteen, collecting a two-game total of 43 points and 24 rebounds. He didn't get to showcase his talents much in the 1966 event

when Knox Central dropped in the tourney's first round, losing to star Mike Casey and Shelby County, which eventually captured the state championship.

On his state tourney trips to Louisville from southeastern Kentucky, Mills said, "That was a big-time experience in those days, especially for a school that hadn't been there in many, many years. A lot of people traveled to Louisville. In those days, it was a long way to Louisville because of the highway system. It was a great time."

With his state tournament exposure, especially after his junior year, college scouts started to keep a close eye on the youngster. Some called him a complete player on both offense and defense. And he had over 100 schools which sought his services.

Besides Kentucky, the only schools Mills seriously considered were Tennessee and Western Kentucky. But the Wildcats were, by far, his favorite. "When Kentucky got involved, it was hard to even consider anyone else in those days when Kentucky offered you a scholarship," Mills said. "They (coaching staff) came to visit and watch me play a couple of times. They invited about 12 or 13 of us on a recruiting trip (to Lexington) during our senior years. I think it was after our season was over or toward the end of the season (when the recruits visited the campus). They tried to get us to commit to scholarships that day, which a lot of us did."

While coach Adolph Rupp was impressed with Terry Mills, he didn't visit him at home. Instead, the Baron sent his assistants to Barbourville on recruiting trips. "Coach Harry Lancaster was his assistant at that time and he visited," Mills recalled. "Coach Joe B. Hall was one of the recruiters and he visited. There were no promises made. We knew we would be playing on the freshman team and we would earn our (varsity) spots into the future from that. Of course, as years went on, a few people dropped out and didn't end up graduating from Kentucky."

Unlike today's highly-publicized recruiting world, Mills acknowledged there were many schools which recruited him that he didn't really know much about. Back in the 1960s or earlier, there were no cable television or specialty publications such as recruiting newsletters. Facts about the colleges weren't readily available. "Schools weren't on television as much in those days and you just didn't know a lot of information about some of the schools and coaches," Mills added.

 At UK, Terry Mills is probably best known for his supporting role as a starting guard during the Issel-Pratt-Casey glory years. In 1969-70, Mills, who averaged 8.1 points a game, helped guide the Wildcats to a No. 1 national ranking in the final regular season polls (Associated Press and United Press International). During that season, Mills had some memorable games:

Guarding the unstoppable legendary Pete Maravich in UK's 109-96 win. Mills and his two teammates — Bob McCowan and Larry Steele — couldn't stop the flashy 6-5 LSU guard, who scored 55 points, setting a Memorial Coliseum record. Mills, who poured in 22 points (nine for 13 from the field) in the victory, said many folks, including his relatives, like to tease him about his defensive shortcomings against "Pistol Pete," who is currently NCAA's all-time leading scorer. "That seems to be the joke of our family, especially when somebody is trying to introduce me as who I was," he commented. "You know they'll say, 'Yeah, he held Pete Maravich to 50 points or something one day.' I have been teased more in the last few years about that than I was at the time."

When Rupp earlier informed Mills that he had the nearly-impossible task of guarding Maravich, the Barbourville native responded in a positive way. Mills liked the challenge. He didn't mind at all. "Obviously a player would look forward to the challenge and if he wanted you to guard Pete Maravich, then that would make you feel good because that would make you feel like he thought you were a good defensive player," said Mills. "Maravich was a great ball-handler and a great passer. We didn't expect any one person to be able to guard him one on one and hold him down as far as his points. When we played LSU, there were two or three people who ended up guarding Pete Maravich at different times in the game. You know everything was run just for him and people were picked for him. We knew he was going to get his shots."

Hitting a game-winning shot with 11 seconds to lead UK to an 84-83 victory over host Auburn before a crowd of about 10,000. The win gave the Wildcats a tie (with Georgia) for the SEC lead. Mills, playing as a substitute guard, had four points for the contest, which saw Auburn star John Mengelt gun in 41 points. For the Wildcats, Dan Issel scored team-high 28 points and grabbed game-high 12 rebounds, while Mike Pratt had 20 points and 10 rebounds.

Scoring 18 points against Jacksonville in Kentucky's 106-100 stunning loss in the NCAA Mideast Regional finals before fouling out. Mills said it was probably his best game he's played at UK. The disappointing setback, however, took away the glitter of his outstanding performance. "We weren't expected to lose that game," he recalled. "We were ranked No. 1 at the time and we were expect-ed to go on to the Final Four. So it was just an abrupt end of the season and that was it."

How did Rupp handle the crushing loss? "I don't recall him say-ing a whole lot," Mills said, adding that the Baron kept it to himself. "He didn't make a lot of long speeches after a game. You know he would have a few choice words to say and that was about it. Of course, that was the last game of the season that year and we didn't see much of him again real-ly (until the fall semester) because we didn't socialize with the coaches or anything like that."

The Wildcats got over the setback to Jacksonville quickly, accord-ing to Mills. However, he said the loss "probably disturbed a lot of fans more than it did the players."

 Unlike his son who won two national titles with the Wildcats, Terry Mills had never won the NCAA title during his collegiate days. The elder Mills, who also didn't reach the Final Four, said he has no regrets about not being able to win the national crown in his playing career.

"I was on a national championship team; it just wouldn't be in the NCAA tournament," said Mills of the 1969-70 season. "We were rated number one in the nation. In those days the ratings were a little bit differ-ent than they are now. The final ratings actually came out in those days before the tournament. Of course, now you are not officially ranked No. 1 unless you win the final game." Mills also helped Kentucky capture three straight SEC championships from 1969 to '71. In his second year (1967-68) at UK, when Mills was redshirted, the Wildcats also won the confer-ence crown .

Even before the Cats captured their second NCAA title in three years in 1998, the elder Mills, however, was awfully glad to see that Cameron, then a little-used sophomore, got to experience the excitement of winning the NCAA tourney title. He and his family attended Kentucky's NCAA tournament games as well as the Final Four games in East Rutherford, N. J. "That's a memory he will always have and can always say he played on a national championship team," said the proud father. "He got a nice ring that he gets to wear all the time. He was obviously excited and still is. You know we were excited for him and that was a great team —

Terry Mills during his early days at Kentucky.

University of Kentucky Media Relations

one of the greatest teams I guess that they've had." Mills' family also made trips to 1997 and 1998 Final Fours.

It is a well-known fact that Rupp sometimes had trouble remembering his players' names. But he knew where they were from. So he liked to call them by their hometowns.

"He would call me Barbourville many times," Terry Mills smiled. "He would call you by your hometown sometimes before he would call you by your name. He had a sense of humor and we all enjoyed being around him. You know he wouldn't be as rough and mean to us as maybe a lot of people thought even though sometimes he was. It was more like slapstick than anything."

Asked if he ever talked back to Rupp in practice in a moment of anger, Mills replied, "I don't recall ever talking back. In those days, I think players knew better than to talk back to their coach or anyone actually."

If the players retaliated, they eventually left the team. "I recall a few people talking back, but I think those few people ended up transferring, too, and it was a little bit different than it is today," Mills said. "Young people are different today. They feel like they have as much say so, as much authority as the adults do today, which is not right. But that's the way society has gone over the last 20 or 30 years. I think most of us didn't even consider trying to talk back to any of our coaches then."

Since Mills had so much respect for Rupp, he never caused the coach any serious problems. While the coach was very strict as far as the rules were concerned, Mills obeyed them. "I never did (break the curfew)," he said. "There's some people who did, but I never did. I always tried to follow the rules the best I could."

Mills warned that if the player was late for a meeting or a road trip, he was in big trouble. No matter what. Mills said Rupp and the team once left a player standing at the airport when he was only one minute late. The Baron wouldn't wait for the player even when he saw him pulling into the parking lot. The coach told the pilot to take off.

Despite Rupp's reputation of being rude and mean, Mills pointed out that the Baron was an easy coach to play for. And he sometimes acted like a comedian who kept his players laughing, according to Mills.

While Rupp — who appeared on the cover of *Sports Illustrated* during the year of his famous Rupp's Runts squad — was (and is still) a giant in college basketball circles, Mills believes that the coach's notoriety would've been much bigger today because of the media's explosive coverage, including the Internet. "If coach Rupp were here today and coaching, it's hard to imagine he would even be more popular and more well-known now than he was then because of all the media attention and all the different cable (TV) systems," he said. "He would be even more well-known than he was at the time and people still remember him. I think he had a real good time with the media. He said a lot of things that he knew the media wanted to hear. So I think that's the kind of way coach Pitino is now."

During his college days, an attractive Floridian by the name of Lorri caught the attention of sophomore-to-be Terry Mills in the summer of 1967. No, he didn't meet the coed at UK. They met in Barbourville. "Her father was in music education at Florida State (as a professor) and they were traveling through

Kentucky, going to Columbus, Ohio, for the summer and he stopped to do some work at Union College in Barbourville," recalled Mills. "I ran into her for a few days while they were there."

The couple continued to stay in touch despite their long-distance relationship. They talked on the phone or wrote letters. They always looked forward to their summer gatherings. "I would either travel down there in the summer time to visit her (in Tallahassee, Fla., where Lorri also attended Florida State) or she would come up here to visit me in the summer time," Mills said.

In the summer 1970, the couple tied the knot. Mills was not the only UK player who married that summer. His roommate/teammate Jim Dinwiddie also got married. Teammate Clint Wheeler tied the knot, too. Mills said coach Rupp practically blew his top. "I don't think he liked it very well," laughed Mills. "Obviously, we had to move out of the dorms and we got apartments. They (UK) had to give us a little bit more money for apartment rent — that was legal — and so they had to do that.

"He was upset that three of us got married that summer and I think he just felt like he lost control of us maybe because we weren't right in the dorm every day. I'm sure he felt like being married would interfere with our concentration of what we were supposed to be doing."

After UK, Terry Mills and his wife went to the Sunshine State where he would start his graduate work at Florida State. It also meant Lorri would get to see her family more often.

And Mills had visions toward a career in coaching. So he served as a graduate assistant for then-head coach Hugh Durham for nearly two years. With his master's degree in hand, Mills returned to his hometown, coaching at Union as an assistant for one year.

Then he went back to Florida where he taught and coached at Ruckel Junior High School in Fort Walton Beach for three years. In 1977, Mills couldn't refuse an opportunity to coach at a Kentucky community college. He figured if he was going to stay in the coaching profession, Kentucky, being the basketball state, was the best place to go to. In addition, Kentucky was his home state. He couldn't say no to Somerset Community College, which earlier had fired its popular head coach who had guided the school to a 22-7 record. Many local folks had questioned the college's coaching change in a controversy.

When Mills took the SCC head coaching job, he said he wasn't going to worry about the pressure. "I'll just do the best I can," he told the author in an interview held over 20 years ago.

In his first and only season as SCC mentor, Mills guided the Cougars to a fine 18-6 mark and a Kentucky Junior College Conference title. In the spring of 1978, the school's intercollegiate sports fund-raising organization voted to drop basketball because of financial problems. According to Mills, the group was in debt of approximately $3,000 before it sold the old bus and the uniforms to erase the red ink. "At the end of that year, the college decided that the expense was just too great to keep on having a team," Mills explained. "So that was the last year we had a basketball team at the community college. We did very well that year, but they just didn't have the finances to fund an athletic program further."

While Mills didn't have a basketball team, he continued to work at SCC in various capacities as physical education instructor, intramural sports director, and coordinator of veterans' affairs until 1983. That's when he decided to work full-time in the insurance business.

"There are still a lot of times I feel like I could have been successful in coaching if I'd stayed in that profession and gone on," said Mills. "I enjoyed it at the time but sometimes you have to make a career decision or a career change that benefits the family and that's what I did several years ago."

While his insurance office is located in Lexington, Mills makes frequent trips to Barbourville where he has clients and many close relatives, including his parents. His father, who has been disabled since 1989 with Lou Gehrig's disease, was a long-time homebuilder. "He hasn't been able to even get out of his chair for seven years or so," said Cameron of his ailing grandpa. The elder Mills' mother, meanwhile, worked at a local bank for many years. Terry Mills also has two brothers who are in the teaching profession in public schools in the Knox County area.

"I go back to Barbourville to visit and work," Terry Mills said. "I sell insurance and I have a lot of clients back there. I'll go back and work once a week and spend some time with my family there."

UNFORGETTABLE WILDCAT

S ean Woods was supposed to be the hero. Just like Brooklyn Dodgers' Bobby Thomson who in 1951 hit perhaps the most famous home run called "the shot heard around the world."

After making an incredible shot heard around the country, it appeared Woods was on his way achieving legendary status as the hero who seemingly propelled the Wildcats to their first Final Four berth in the Rick Pitino Era.

His 10-foot basket had given foul-plagued Kentucky a narrow one-point lead with 2.1 seconds left on the clock in overtime. With the game practically over, surely there was no way that Kentucky would lose the NCAA tournament game, arguably the best ever in college basketball history. If Duke were going to win, it had to travel the entire hardwood floor to get to its basket. Could the Blue Devils pull it off? Not with only 2.1 ticks left. Impossible, you might say.

Needless to say, the ecstatic folks back in Kentucky, watching the dramatic game on TV, were buzzing with excitement not felt in a long time. Woods had instantly become a folk hero with his potential game-winning basket, shooting over a star by the name of Christian Laettner.

The celebration, unfortunately, was short-lived as everyone assumed wrong. Yes, after a timeout called by the Blue Devils, they somehow did come back and pulled off a miraculous victory with a turnaround field goal, a 17-footer by someone none other than Laettner.

The nationally-televised contest had found another hero. Instead of Woods, Laettner became one. His stunning, buzzer-beating shot was the one heard around the country, sending Duke to the Final Four.

It all happened on March 28, 1992 in Philadelphia.

And imagine how Woods felt? He had his feelings turned upside down in a matter of seconds. A 180-degree turn. A complete transformation: jubilation to heartbreak.

Several years later, Woods recalled his sinking feeling just moments after Laettner's basket. He took a deep breath and said, "Oh man, I was devastated. Hurt. Lifeless at that particular time. The strength in my legs just left me and I fell straight to the ground, not knowing what to think. Just knowing that I'd never play college basketball again.

"I still haven't recovered from it." He smiled. "That game will haunt me for the rest of my life. You will always (wonder) what if we had won that game. What if we had been national champions?"

In Kentucky's 104-103 setback, Woods hit nine of 15 shots for 21 points and had nine assists. He said he still has the videotape of the game, which saw UK overcome a 12-point deficit in the second half before falling short. But he hasn't watched the entire contest. "Just bits and pieces," he said. "I haven't sat down and really watched it. When you are playing, you don't think about it as some of the best games ever because you are out there competing. So I haven't really taken the time to sit back and look at what everybody is talking about. I have seen a couple of specials, but I haven't seen the whole thing."

On his memorable driving basket, Woods said, "Well, I tried to score, but if it didn't go in I wanted to give us a chance to get a rebound. Fortunately enough for me my adrenaline was flowing a little bit much and I gave it a little push other than what I normally should have. It went off the glass and went straight in."

Woods was asked if he was strategically set to take the shot? "What I was supposed to do was drive and if I could get to the rim and score, that was the thing (to do)," he explained. "If somebody (defender) came to me and somebody else was open, then (I was to) throw it out for a jump shot."

Nevertheless, Woods' field-goal ranked the among the biggest in school history, which includes a handful of memorable shots. His name will always be in Kentucky sports history books even though it didn't lead the Wildcats to a victory.

 What about March 22, 1998, an unforgettable Sunday when Kentucky edged Duke in the NCAA tournament in the next meeting between both schools? Did Woods feel any better?

Woods said UK's two-point victory over the Blue Devils brought a sense of relief for the revenge-minded Wildcat fans. As a true-blue fan, he was happy. However, as a former player, it didn't provide any comfort, though. The ghost of the 1992 game still lingers.

Woods personally didn't see the rematch in St. Petersburg, Fla. He watched it on TV. "I'm happy (to see) these guys beat Duke," he said of the courageous Wildcats who went on to capture the national title. Woods didn't really expect Kentucky, which finished with a 35-4 mark, to go very far. Especially when they appeared lifeless in mid-season and had uncharacteristically dropped three home games. "I didn't think they were a championship-caliber team until the SEC tournament (when they won the tourney)," commented Woods. "They just kept getting better as the year went on."

 Of UK's four "Unforgettables" from the 1991-92 senior class, Woods was the only non-Kentuckian. While the Wildcat fans naturally treated Richie Farmer, Deron Feldhaus and John Pelphrey as their folk heroes, Woods sometimes felt left out.

Woods — who was working for Lexington's WLEX-TV as an account executive when the book went to press — says he understood the situation because he didn't live in Kentucky. The Hoosierland is where Woods grew up and played high school basketball. Born in East Chicago in Indiana near Lake Michigan, where he lived for many years, Woods and his parents made Indianapolis their home by the time he entered eighth grade.

When Woods enrolled at Indianapolis Cathedral High School, he didn't immediately set the world on fire with his roundball play. But he became a solid contributor. He did enough to earn All-State and honorable mention All-American honors. The 6-2 Woods was a two-year starter, and averaged 18 points, four rebounds and 5.2 assists per game his senior season. Interestingly, his high school coach, Howard Renner, played for Indiana coach Bobby Knight when the latter coached at Army.

But Knight and his staff didn't even look at Woods until he heard that UK was very interested in the playmaker, according to Woods. "It was

UK's Sean Woods (11) and Jamal Mashburn (left) apply defensive pressure as Georgia attempts an in-bounds play during Kentucky's 22-6 campaign in 1990-91.

Photo by Rogers Photography

kind of odd how he recruited me," Woods said of Knight. "He didn't recruit me until he heard that Kentucky was high on me. I played in an AAU tournament in Las Vegas and his assistant coach was there and came back and told him about me. They came to a couple of my practices and he invited me up for an unofficial visit to the campus. And my high school coach at that particular time played for Bobby Knight at West Point. So you know there was a kind of special relationship at that particular time."

Besides Knight and Kentucky's Eddie Sutton, there were several other big-name college coaches, especially from the Big 10 and SEC, who liked Woods' playmaking and leadership skills. Denny Crum of Louisville and Gene Keady of Purdue recruited him very hard.

Although Woods eventually signed with Kentucky, he recalls Louisville's efforts, led by Wade Houston, Crum's top assistant then. "When I was in high school, my first recruiting letter was from the University of Louisville," Woods said.

Of all the coaches — head or assistant — who recruited Woods, it was Dwane Casey who had made the biggest impression on the youngster.

"His personality just won me over and I knew that he was a guy or someone whom I could trust," Woods said of then-UK assistant. "You know when you leave home and you are away from home for the first time, you need someone who you think is going to be in your corner no matter what and he was that type of guy."

In addition to Casey, Woods said Sutton and his assistants James Dickey and Jimmy Dykes also visited his home. And Woods liked the fact that Kentucky would be losing Ed Davender, an All-SEC guard who finished his Wildcat career with 1,637 points. That meant Woods would probably get some playing time as a freshman.

"One of the reasons that I chose to come to the University of Kentucky was because Ed Davender just graduated and I knew the spot was wide open," recalled Woods. "And I didn't think that Sean Sutton was better than me at that particular time."

Another factor in Woods' decision to attend UK was his familiarity with the school and its basketball program when he was a little kid. His mother, Vicki, was born and grew up in Lexington, and his grandmother lived (and still lives) there. "I would come down and visit my cousin," he said of his trips to Lexington. "We would always talk about UK. I would watch them on television and I grew to like them. I watched them as much as I could. But in Indiana, you normally got Indiana, Purdue, DePaul and some Louisville games on television. So, I didn't get to see Kentucky that much, but when I did see them I liked them."

But Woods, as he would find out later, began his career at Kentucky on a very rocky note.

 Shortly after Woods inked with the Wildcats in the spring of 1988, the NCAA started to investigate Kentucky after an express envelope addressed to the father of a UK recruit popped open, exposing $1,000 in cash. And the NCAA was all over Woods, asking him all kinds of questions.

"The recruiting violations didn't start until after I signed," Woods commented. "They came to my high school and I wouldn't talk to them and then they met me at my house. They questioned me about what happened in my recruiting visit, this and that. (They were) asking about the $1,000. Did we know anything about the $1,000 that was sent to (recruit) Chris Mills? Quite frankly, we didn't (know). So you know there was nothing that they could say. They didn't have anything on us. We didn't do anything wrong. So after that visit, they didn't come messing with me anymore."

Asked if he regretted his decision at the time to attend UK, Woods said no. "We didn't know what was going to happen," explained Woods, who sat out his freshman year as a Prop 48 academic casualty. "You know a whole year went before they gave us our punishment."

However, Woods had second thoughts after NCAA placed the school on severe probation for rules violations in May of 1989, about a couple of weeks before UK snatched Rick Pitino away from NBA's New York Knicks. "After the punishment I thought about leaving," he said. "I wanted to have a chance to play for a national championship. I wanted to play on television. That was one of the reasons why I came to the University of Kentucky. And for that to be taken away was very devastating to me.

"Another thing (troublesome) to me was the situation that happened with (UK signee and future NBA star) Shawn Kemp. He was blamed for stealing gold chains. He and I came to school together. We were best friends and that was just another blow to me that same year. So I had mixed emotions about staying at the University of Kentucky." The 6-10 Kemp left school before the 1988-89 season began and enrolled at Trinity Valley Community College in Texas. But the Indiana native didn't play at Trinity and was later drafted by the Seattle SuperSonics as the NBA's 17th pick overall in 1989.

Woods' mother, who has worked as a beautician, convinced her son to remain with the Wildcats. "She said, 'Hey, you know, you're going to face problems all along in life. You might as well start facing them now,'" Woods said. "So I listened and I took that to heart. I said, 'Hey, I'm going to try to make something good out of this situation,' and I think I did."

Long-time administrative assistant Marta McMackin of the UK Basketball Office also persuaded Woods to stay put. McMackin and the freshman had a talk, which proved to be fruitful. "After I had a long talk with the secretary, she told me, 'Sean, just stay here. I promise you things will get better and if we get this guy (Pitino), things are really going to get better,'" said Woods. "I believed her and she said some more things that were very personal to me and it sort of hit home. So, you know, I listened to her and things worked out."

Woods, a Prop 48 victim, was not the only player who had to sit out the 1988-89 campaign, which was the worst and losingest season in UK basketball history. A freshman at the time, Woods had company. His teammate's name was sophomore sensation Eric Manuel, who was coming off a fine rookie year, averaging 7.1 points a game. UK officials kept Manuel off the floor as a precautionary measure as they investigated charges of academic fraud involving him.

"I was just lucky enough to have Eric Manuel, who had to sit out too that year," said Woods, who wasn't allowed to practice with the team. "Eric Manual and I were real close because we were the only two who wouldn't be playing that season. So when the guys (the team) would go out of town, it would be just him and me. We helped each other along. It was very rough for both of us.

"(Sitting out was) very difficult. I wasn't able to play basketball for the first time in my life. It was just a dramatic blow to me psychologically because I didn't know what to do with myself. I knew I had to go to school and everything and that was fine. You come down here thinking you're going to be a part of everything and you're not for one whole season. You know it was just very devastating."

With the on-going NCAA investigation in full force, the Wildcats headed for a disastrous 13-19 campaign. It was a horrible season, the one the Wildcat faithful would love to erase forever. "It was a very negative situation for everyone," Woods said. "The guys didn't feel like playing. They had a negative attitude, not with each other, but just on the situation in general. You'd go on the road and people were putting $1,000 bills on the seats. Coach Sutton was under excruciating pressure. So everybody was kind of up against the wall, trying to figure out how they personally were going to get out of this thing."

When the 1989-90 season rolled around with new Wildcat mentor Rick Pitino on hand, Woods was ready to play. Despite the fact he wasn't permitted to practice with the Wildcats the previous season, he had managed to work out, becoming a stronger player. He had been motivated to stay in shape. He knew that he would get to play as a sophomore playmaker. He wanted to be a solid player.

"I didn't want to start the season being out of shape," Woods said.

"I knew there were going to be some ruts because of playing pick-up games, and going out there and playing the actual game is totally different. So I just tried to play as much basketball as possible.

"I hit the weights tremendously. I bulked up. When I came in, I was 163 pounds. My sophomore year I was 175. So you know I gained some weight. I got some muscle and I got stronger and that was what I wanted to do. I just wanted to be ready physically and mentally so when that time came I knew I had to do a job."

In the summer of 1989, Woods had his first one-on-one meeting with Pitino. The coach warned him that the team would run, run, and run, and that he hoped the promising player was ready for the new challenges.

"It was a great meeting," Woods recalled. "I had just got back from the Olympic Festival. He was a very kind person. He just asked me if I was in shape. And I said, 'Yeah, you know I just got back.' He told me to be ready to play ball. He told me that he would have to count on me a lot for what we had. And the last thing he said was, 'Can you run two miles in 12 minutes?' I said I think so. He said, 'Well, I hope you do because that is what we will be doing once everybody gets back (when the fall semester begins).'

"I was happy (when Pitino was hired). I liked his style of play. I knew I could get up and down. That was the way I liked to play. I saw him coach in New York. And (when) I was in high school and a young kid, I saw him (coach) at Providence. I have always been the type of guy who liked to play defense, too. So I thought he and I would be a perfect mix."

In Pitino's first year at Kentucky, Woods played a key role in UK's stunning success when it posted a .500 record, with only eight scholarship players. At point guard, he started 27 of team's 28 games and led the SEC in assists, averaging 5.9 per game. He also averaged 9.1 points a contest.

But Woods believed the Wildcats could've done better that season. "I thought we should have won some games on the road that we lost," he said. "That was the only thing missing in that season. We just couldn't win any games on the road. We could win at home. If we had stolen a few more games on the road, I think we'd have been all right. It would have been a very, very good season."

He was referring to some of Kentucky's narrow SEC losses on the road, including setbacks to Mississippi State (87-86 in overtime) and to Tennessee (102-100). While the Wildcats could win only one conference game on the road, their SEC home mark was a remarkable 9-0.

The following winter (1990-91) saw the run-and-gun Wildcats, still on NCAA probation, improve to 22-6 during Woods' junior year. He had another fine season, averaging nearly 10 points. The junior playmaker also led the squad in assists and steals. In UK's 88-71 victory over Kansas at Rupp Arena, Woods had a solid performance, scoring in what would be his career-high 25 points along with eight assists and six rebounds. With the win, the Wildcats had avenged their embarrassing 150-95 loss to the Jayhawks in the previous year.

"Those two seasons were great for us," Woods said of his sophomore and junior years during UK's banishment from NCAA and SEC tournaments. "I had something to prove and all of my teammates had something to prove. We didn't want to be (on the losing team). People were doubting us and we were always fighting an uphill battle. We weren't as talented but we knew that we were good enough to win ballgames and we kept motivated with coach Pitino's help. He kept us focused and gave us goals we tried to meet."

 In an 83-82 road loss to Mississippi State in 1991, Pitino — who was in his second year at the Wildcat helm — was visibly upset, very angry, especially at Woods, whose critical mistake had cost Kentucky a possible victory. The junior guard, not realizing his team needed a three-point field goal to tie the game, made a meaningless layup at the buzzer as the Wildcats dropped for the second straight game.

Pitino "threw a shoe at me right after the game," Woods said, adding the last play "was something; I just mentally lost it. I don't know what happened. We had to start at their end of the basket and I dribbled the length of the court (for the layup). The play was designed for me to penetrate and kick it out for somebody for a three. But they knew we needed a three and they were just going to let me penetrate and let me get a two-pointer and I did." Despite his game-ending blunder, Woods dished out 10 assists and scored 12 points.

Woods said that was probably the most embarrassing moment of his Kentucky career.

 Remember the Clifford Rozier recruiting controversy that nearly got Kentucky in hot water with the NCAA in May of 1991?

The controversy came about when Woods took Rozier, a 6-10 player who was leaving the North Carolina Tar Heels program, to a Kentucky Derby party in Louisville, breaking an NCAA rule, which bans an institution from entertaining a recruit more than 30 miles from the campus during an official visit.

It all happened while UK was still on probation from the scandal in the late 1980s, creating some fear in the basketball camp that the school could face the death penalty imposed by the NCAA. To avoid any further sanctions by the NCAA, Kentucky ceased recruiting Rozier, who eventually signed with Louisville.

"It was very embarrassing," Woods said of the episode.

And Woods initially lied to Pitino and his staff to cover himself after being asked about television reports that Woods and Rozier were spotted together at a post-Derby party in Louisville. Wildcat standout and Woods' roommate, Reggie Hanson, who had just completed his senior year, also attended the same party, which took place on a Saturday evening. Hanson had told Woods about the party.

According to Woods, the party was held at the home of one of Dr. Rudy Ellis' four children. When Woods saw the late Dr. Ellis, who was a well-known, respected team physician for the Louisville Cardinals' basketball team, at the party, he got scared.

"As soon as I saw him, my eyes got big," Woods recalled. "I knew him from being in the Derby Classic." And according to Woods, their conversation went something like this:

"Doc, you know, you've got to promise me you won't say anything. You can talk to Cliff all you want to about coming to Louisville....but just don't say (anything)," Woods said.

Dr. Ellis replied, "Aw, Sean, I won't say anything."

So Woods and Rozier stayed awhile at the party, and they drove back to Lexington late in the evening. And on Sunday Woods traveled to his hometown of Indianapolis. He received a surprise phone call from one of Pitino's assistant coaches.

"Sean, is there any chance that you and Cliff Rozier went to Louisville?" wondered Herb Sendek, who was trying to get to the bottom of the growing controversy.

"No, coach, I didn't take him to Louisville," said Woods, thinking there was no way Pitino and the assistants, or the media will ever find out about the recruiting violation."

"Okay," said Sendek.

"Why?" commented Woods.

"Well, it was on the six o'clock news. Are you sure you didn't take him to Louisville."

"No, coach, " replied Woods, the team's best recruiter among the players.

After the assistant hung up, Woods became very nervous. He said he was "scared to death" and called Hanson for advice. Woods spent the rest of the afternoon and evening hanging out with his friends, trying to forget the entire episode. But he couldn't get it off his mind.

When he returned late to his home, his mother, who was up, told him that he needed to call Sendek right away. "He's called here about 100 times," she told Woods. "Tell him the truth."

Woods dialed Sendek and said, "This is Sean. I lied to you. I apologize. I did take Cliff Rozier to Louisville. You know there is nothing to do on Saturday in Lexington (during the Derby weekend). You know everybody was in Louisville and I thought we could go there and nobody would find out about it."

Sendek told the player to call Pitino. But before Woods called Pitino, he got in touch with Hanson and the duo discussed the situation in a conference call with the head coach.

"What the — — wrong with you? Are you out of your mind?" said an angry Pitino.

Replied Woods, "Coach, I know I'm wrong. I said there was just nothing to do in Lexington. Everybody was in Louisville. He (Rozier) just really wanted to go out somewhere. I apologize and I'm sorry for lying."

"I want you back here at 3 o'clock tomorrow," said a very perturbed Pitino, who had preached the importance of having integrity in the school's basketball program after its troubles in the late 1980s.

So Woods drove back to Lexington and met Pitino on Monday (May 6) in what was described as a very unpleasant meeting. Woods said Pitino was so mad at him that he didn't want to talk to him for a couple of months.

Consequently, UK issued a statement to the media, admitting an NCAA violation had taken place, and that disciplinary action would be taken as more facts became available. Less than 24 hours later, UK decided to halt its recruitment of Rozier, who had made a verbal commitment to the Wildcats over the Derby weekend.

Woods immediately went back home to Indiana and stayed in great shape during the summer. "I just worked out tremendously by myself because I knew that he (Pitino) was going to be hard on me a little bit of which I can understand," recalled Woods.

When Woods arrived in Lexington for the fall semester to begin his senior year, Pitino took a disciplinary action. The coach made the youngster pay for his poor judgment. "I had a meeting with him and he told me that I had three punishments," Woods commented. "One, I had to do 20 hours of community service. Two, I couldn't practice in Midnight Madness because I lied and three, I had a curfew at 10 o'clock. Believe or not, having curfew at 10 was the worst punishment of them all (he laughed)."

Since it was Kentucky which reported the rules violation and ended the recruitment of Rozier, NCAA didn't issue additional penalties as the violation was termed secondary, not major.

 Despite his costly error at the Mississippi State game in Starkville and the Rozier controversy, Woods said he has had no hard feelings toward Pitino. He liked the coach and his blunt approach with the players. Woods also pointed out that he has never talked back to the coach.

"I had a lot of respect for (Pitino)," he said. "I really respect coaches who were harsh. But you could see the result with him. He didn't have any doghouses. If he fussed at you, (then) you know it was over with. He didn't have any grudges and he was fair. That's the only reason I didn't have any problems with coach Pitino. You can only have more respect for a coach who is fair and who is going to tell you the way it is and that's what he did. Everything that he said to me, it came out to be right. And I was never the type of kid that talked back to my coaches or elders. I always respected old folks."

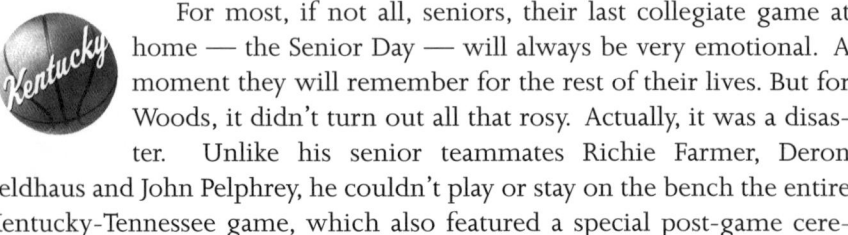 For most, if not all, seniors, their last collegiate game at home — the Senior Day — will always be very emotional. A moment they will remember for the rest of their lives. But for Woods, it didn't turn out all that rosy. Actually, it was a disaster. Unlike his senior teammates Richie Farmer, Deron Feldhaus and John Pelphrey, he couldn't play or stay on the bench the entire Kentucky-Tennessee game, which also featured a special post-game cere-

mony honoring Cawood Ledford, who was retiring as the "Voice of the Wildcats."

In the late first half, the officials had ejected Woods and Tennessee's Jay Price for fighting. So the players, who shook hands and made up, watched the second half together on television in the media room as Kentucky prevailed 99-88. But that was an unpleasant moment for Woods, who already had six assists in 12 minutes of action with no points. He now wished the incident hadn't happen.

"Oh man, I had 25 family members in the stands," Woods said. "They all came from Tennessee, Detroit, everywhere. My cousin told me he went out to get some popcorn or something. (When) he came back and (saw that) I am not in the game and didn't see me on the bench, he asked the guy next to him what happened to me. They told him I got thrown out. I'm embarrassed now. I wasn't embarrassed then.

"When coach Pitino finally saw the tape (after the game), he knew that I wasn't at fault. I was just trying to protect myself. It was an unfortunate situation that it was on Senior Night and you know I'm probably the only player in UK history to be thrown out on his Senior Night."

For the record, sophomore forward Jamal Mashburn paced the victorious Wildcats with 30 points and 10 rebounds. Farmer and Feldhaus added 15 and 13 points, respectively.

Woods — who is now fourth on the school's all-time assists list with 482 (behind leader Dirk Minniefield, who had 646 assists, No. 2 Anthony Epps and No. 3 Roger Harden) — had hopes of playing in the NBA some day. In the summer of 1992, he tried out with three teams as a free agent — the Washington Bullets (now the Washington Wizards), Seattle SuperSonics and Indiana Pacers. But he had no luck. He came home disappointed.

"To this day, I still feel like I was good enough to play," he said. "It was a bad situation. I was always at the wrong place at the wrong time and the agent that I had, he really didn't help me out as much as I thought he could have. But you know that's life. It taught me something."

He later found work in Lexington. WLEX-TV hired the former Wildcat as an advertising representative. Woods does some sports shows as well. "I'm happy with what I'm doing now and I've always been a guy who pushed for success no matter what it was," he said. According to Woods, who now has a degree in social work, his future goals included an opportunity to be either a coach or a television color commentator. He would like to stay involved in sports. In 1997, Woods expressed an interest in becoming an administrative assistant on newly-hired coach Tubby Smith's staff. Smith, however, retained Simeon Mars, who was hired by ex-mentor Rick Pitino to the post in 1996. Mars was also Jamaal Magloire's high school coach at Eastern School of Commerce in Toronto (Ontario) in Canada.

Woods has some thoughts about a couple of issues involving college athletics.

Should college players be paid? "Without a question. If you tally up the education that you get from the university and all the money that they make off you while you're playing at a university, it's no comparison. Education can only take you so far and with education you're still not promised a great future — you know with the economy the way it is and the competitiveness out there in the world today. I think that since the university makes X amount of millions of dollars, why shouldn't this guy be able to have some money to put clothes on his back, take his girlfriend out to eat, have a decent little allowance month to month. I don't see anything wrong with that at all."

Although many observers believe college freshman athletes should be given a year to adjust to academics and social life before playing for the varsity squad, should they be allowed to play as freshmen? "Yeah, without a doubt. Some freshmen are ready. It might take you a little time to learn the system, but talent-wise, you're ready. You know the way guys come in (to pros) out of college right now, they're not staying four years (in college). They're just that good right now. So it's (freshman ineligibility) just slowing up the process.

"Socially, it hurts. You don't get the full effect of the college life because you are so busy. You don't have time to go to those parties all the time. You don't get time to socialize because you're in class, you got practice, you got study hall, you got to eat.

"Academically....I don't think it's a burden because you got tutors and people like that who hang around and are going to show you the ropes anyway. Academically, I don't think it hurts (the freshmen), but socially, yeah, because you don't get the full effect of what college is like."

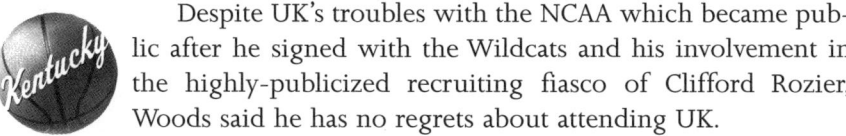

Despite UK's troubles with the NCAA which became public after he signed with the Wildcats and his involvement in the highly-publicized recruiting fiasco of Clifford Rozier, Woods said he has no regrets about attending UK.

"From my standpoint the University of Kentucky has been a great experience and if I had to do a lot all over again, I'd still have chosen the University of Kentucky," said Woods, whose jersey was retired along with his senior teammates in 1992. "I think I had a pretty decent career here at the University of Kentucky."

DEREK
AND HIS UNCLE

Derek Anderson was one of the most exciting players in college basketball. He hopes to do the same thing in the NBA. Just like Michael
Jordan, his would obviously be a tough act to duplicate.

There are a lot of similarities between the former Wildcat standout
and the legendary Chicago Bull. They are both versatile players who can
jump through the roof. They display admirable work ethics. They wear No.
23 on their jerseys. They are nearly identical in size with Anderson at 6-5
and Jordan 6-6. They love to dunk.

But that's not all. They became business partners. Well, sort of. In
July of 1997, shortly after signing a three-year contract reportedly worth
about $3 million with the Cleveland Cavaliers, Anderson had one of the
biggest surprises of his life. When the then-NBA rookie walked into a conference room at Nike's corporate headquarters in Beaverton, Ore., he saw
Jordan along with Nike board chairman and chief executive officer Phil
Knight. He knew something big was going on. He was excited, but very
curious.

And Anderson became dumbfounded when he learned that Jordan
had plans for him (along with four other players) to endorse his Nike
product lines, including basketball footwear, especially when the superstar
retires. Jordan wanted someone to carry on his likeness on the floor.

*Wildcat star Derek
Anderson soars for a
slam dunk in a 1996
contest at Rupp Arena.*

Photo by Rogers Photography

Someone who could play. Someone who worked hard. Someone who
could jump. "It was shocking," Anderson said in the *Akron Beacon Journal*. "I
went to the meeting and he (Jordan) was there. I had no idea. I thought
I was just going in for another interview with Nike. They told me the
scoop and it was a shock."

Needless to say, it was a remarkable year for Anderson, who later
finished his initial pro campaign with an 11.7-point average in the regular
season, despite a mid-season knee injury which forced him to sit out five
weeks. It was a year he will never forget. A dream come true for the lik-

able young man from Kentucky.

Anderson's dream-come-true odyssey began in Louisville where he was born and grew up with his uncle and aunt. Born on July 18, 1974, Anderson learned about not only basketball during his growing up years. His uncle, George Williams, who is also his legal guardian, stressed the importance of education in life and took the youngster to many interesting places, especially in the summer. That meant Anderson had to skip some basketball camps. Uncle George wanted the youngster to be a good citizen, instead of being only a basketball player.

"He needed to (be exposed to different things)," Williams said in an interview in Louisville. "You know as well as basketball you need to get exposure to all elements of society and I wanted him to be able to mix basketball with education. We traveled a lot and we went to different cities where he played basketball. We went to museums, zoos and different things so he could get a well-rounded feel of society and life."

One of their eventful trips was a visit to Atlanta, Ga. "We went to (Rev.) Martin Luther King Jr.'s grave site," Williams recalled. They also visited the church in Birmingham, Ala., where a bomb exploded, killing four black children, during the civil rights movement in the 1960s.

In the late 1980s, when Anderson was about 14 or 15 years old, he showed signs of becoming a dynamic player. But he was very raw. "I could tell he had something different," said Williams, who once played basketball at Paducah Community College and Roanoke College (in Virginia) in the early 1970s. "You know he had to refine it, but I could tell definitely he had a special talent."

Anderson played prep basketball at Doss High School in Louisville. As an All-State senior in 1991-92, he averaged 24 points and nearly 10 rebounds, leading Doss to a fine 29-4 mark. He wasn't a big-name star, but he was invited to participate in the annual Derby Classic matchup in Louisville. Before a Freedom Hall crowd of nearly 11,000 spectators, Anderson — who hadn't announced his collegiate decision yet — put on a decent performance, hitting five of eight field goals for 10 points, for the winning Gold team, which also included three UK signees — Tony Delk, Walter McCarty and Jared Prickett.

It was the game that marked the beginning of Anderson's friend-ship with Delk and McCarty. Anderson and McCarty, who is from Evansville, Ind., also met again in the annual Kentucky-Indiana All-Star series as opponents. "He had really built up a relationship with the play-ers," Williams said. "They had built a bond."

But the threesome didn't go straight to the same university. Only Anderson didn't go to Kentucky. Why? "Well, I think they came in late and made a last ditch effort (to sign Anderson)," Williams said of the Wildcats. "They were recruiting real talent like Walter McCarty and Delk. And I think Derek wasn't everybody's household name. You know a lot of people were looking at blue-chippers instead of players that play between the lines."

Anderson, instead, picked Ohio State where he enjoyed a special "father-son" relationship with head coach Randy Ayers. Coming off a pair of outstanding seasons (27-4 and 26-6) with two consecutive Big Ten Conference titles, the promising Buckeyes were a program on the rise and Anderson wanted to be a part of it. And the basketball experts termed Ayers' recruiting class of 1992 as one of the best in the country. In addi-tion to Anderson, the freshman class included a couple of Mr. Basketball titlest — forward Charles Macon (Indiana) and guard Greg Simpson (Ohio) — and 6-11 Nate Wilbourne (who later transferred to South Carolina). On Ohio State, Williams said, "The program was first class. Ohio State to me is the Kentucky of Ohio. It's a great program — facilities, the people and the environment. Everything was first class."

Many folks questioned Anderson's decision to attend Ohio State since the school already had signed several prep superstars. But OSU wouldn't have gotten Anderson if one of its players hadn't told Ayers about the Louisville standout. "Most people wondered why Derek came to Ohio State because everybody else who came there was a Mr. Basketball and nobody (at OSU) had really heard of him," Williams said. That's until superstar guard Jimmy Jackson discovered Anderson and told the coach to scout the kid. Ayers liked what he saw in Anderson. He found the young-ster to be likable and coachable. They immediately formed a long-lasting bond. "He was great," Williams said of Ayers.

 Like UK, Louisville lost Anderson too. Many Louisvillians had wrongly assumed that Anderson was a lock for the home-town Cardinals. U of L, however, didn't make an in-house visit. As a result, Anderson didn't really consider the Cardinals.

"Louisville was like, I guess, a hands down but we had one policy — in-house visit," Williams said. "No in-house visit (by U of L) was made to talk academics as well as athletics. It then pretty much eliminated them. And I made that (policy) known to the public. I guess a lot of people didn't take me for my word and Derek for his word because we made that one of our rules (in the recruiting process)."

Was Williams disappointed that U of L didn't really make a sincere effort to recruit Anderson? "Well, I'll put it this way. I knew what Derek was gonna be able to do," he said. "I knew whoever missed out for whatever reason they would be sorry later. I wasn't disappointed. I didn't think that Derek would have to worry about 'Would he stand out?' wherever he went. I knew he had the capabilities." Anderson also considered Syracuse, among others.

In the recruiting process, Williams played a key role. He attempted to help his nephew to make the right choice by serving as a consultant. "We looked at different teams," Williams said. "We looked at what conferences that a lot of people would be looking at and which had the better media exposure and things like that. Then it was left up to him to see who he would like to play for and we evaluated coaches. We looked at the coaches who fit his style and that's the way we did."

As far as OSU is concerned, Anderson's first year, however, didn't turn out all that well. After losing Jackson to the NBA, the Buckeyes were sorely lacking experience. They had seven new players. As a result, Ohio State dropped to 15-13 (8-10 in Big Ten action). Ironically, one of Anderson's teammates included 6-9 standout Lawrence Funderburke, who had been a key figure in NCAA's investigation of UK in the late 1980s. Anderson nevertheless finished his rookie year on a very promising note, averaging 10.2 points, good for third best on the squad, after missing the first six games of the season. He had suffered a broken bone in his hand in a pre-season game against the Russian national team. Anderson, a part-time starter who was chosen to the Big Ten All-Freshman squad, also led OSU in steals with 43.

By the end of Anderson's freshman season, Ohio State became the center of controversy when it admitted NCAA rules violations in the recruitment of prep star Damon Flint. And that was the beginning of the turbulent downfall for OSU and Ayers.

Early in the 1993-94 campaign, when Anderson was a sophomore, the Buckeyes traveled to exotic Hawaii to play in the Maui Invitational. There he got to face Kentucky, his future team, in the tourney's second round. Anderson impressed coach Rick Pitino and his Wildcats with his 23-point and seven-assist performance, both team-highs, in an 100-88 setback to UK. "When they played in Hawaii, coach Pitino got a chance to see what they (had) let (a top player) leave the state," said Williams. Anderson "sent a message to the state of Kentucky" that he was a rising star.

Anderson was on his way to a great season when he suffered a late-season knee injury which required a reconstructive surgery. The sophomore had averaged 15 points, while starting all of OSU's 22 games. He missed the team's last seven contests. His injury was a severe blow to the Buckeyes, who finished with a 13-16 mark.

There were personality problems among his OSU teammates during the season. They didn't play well together. Some of them eventually left the team for various reasons. In addition, the school faced a likely probation by the NCAA. In other words, there were many distractions in the roundball program and Anderson didn't like what he was seeing. His grades weren't too good, either. He thought about departing OSU, but he didn't want to leave Ayers in real bad shape. Still, he was loyal to Ayers. The coach was like a second father to him.

During the summer of 1994, Anderson agonized about leaving the Buckeyes before he made perhaps the most difficult decision of his life. He waited until late August before he asked for a release from his scholarship in a meeting with OSU athletic director Andy Geiger so he could transfer to UK at the beginning of the fall semester. Not only was UK interested in Anderson's services, but other major powers inquired about the Louisville native as well.

"At that point, he didn't have to call anybody," Williams said. "When he was ready to transfer, he was a big-time recruit. So, you know, Kentucky got a good deal. I talked to every school, big and small, from UCLA to the east coast. They knew him and everybody wanted him to come. They had seen what he could do."

Williams said Ohio State "just had a bad run, a rash of things that happened immediately to them. I don't think that could happen to another school in a hundred years, but it happened to them. It was a misfortunate thing to happen to any program. But you know Derek's (transfer) had turned out to be a blessing in disguise."

Williams supported his nephew's decision to leave the Buckeye country for another reason — a major one. He wanted Anderson to get his college degree. "I wanted him to leave because of the way he was on line academically," he commented. "First of all, it (academics) was probably 75 percent (of the reasons) that I wanted him to transfer to UK. I wanted Derek to graduate. When I found out how the academics were and that he wasn't on line for graduation, I stepped in. We sat down and we evaluated the teams. I thought there were two schools that he could go on with. It was UK or North Carolina. That's just my opinion. North Carolina never looked at us." And a delighted Pitino welcomed Anderson with open arms and called him a "steal" for the Wildcats.

 So Anderson became the first black Louisvillian to wear the Wildcat uniform since the days of Louisville Male High School product Winston Bennett, who played at UK from 1983-88. Tom Payne, an All-SEC center in 1971, was the only other black from Louisville to play for Kentucky, which has had problems in attracting black prep stars from the state's largest city. UK's racist image in the past had severely hurt the Wildcats' efforts to recruit African-American players from Louisville, Anderson's uncle explained.

"It's the Adolph Rupp stigma," Williams said. "It's the black and white issue. You know a long time ago Rupp supposedly made a statement that he would never use black athletes."

But Williams said Kentucky shouldn't be judged on what it has supposedly done in the past because people change, and added the black folks should look ahead and see what the future holds. For instance, Williams said, "You judge a man on his merits as you meet him. Coach Pitino was a good man. We respected coach Pitino. I don't know about coach Rupp. Derek wouldn't be playing for coach Rupp. So we couldn't judge Kentucky by coach Rupp.

"A lot of people hold stigmas and it's imbedded in some people. People plant seeds. It's planted in your mind and that's what people do, but I don't think that we try to look at life like that. We look at life as we treat people and as people treat us. I mean if you don't treat us good, then we move on. We don't keep bothering you. Kentucky treated us good and we reciprocated. I would recommend (UK) to any kid."

Because of Anderson's recent success at UK, Williams has seen the

*Derek Anderson, then a
junior, meets the press in
the dressing room after a
Wildcat victory at Rupp
Arena.*

Photo by Jamie H.Vaught

interest and acceptance of the Wildcat program gradually grow among the
Louisville black community. He also believes the racial barriers in the city
have broken down as well.

"I have had a lot of my friends send their children to Kentucky
now that Derek has gone there," Williams said. "I see the kids in the neighborhood, you know, in the west end who would never wear Kentucky
(apparel) now wear Kentucky because of Derek. I think he's had a very
positive influence on both sets of the community, the black and white,
because I think there was a division due to race. Derek took that away
because he's a nice individual and people on both sides like him. So it was
a positive plus for both of us."

 After redshirting during the 1994-95 campaign that saw
the 28-5 Wildcats end their promising season with a 13-point
setback to North Carolina in the NCAA Southeast Regional
finals, swingman Anderson found himself in the starting line-

up in his very first game as a Wildcat. Playing at shooting guard, Anderson pumped in four of six shots for 11 points before fouling out as No. 1 Kentucky raced to a 96-84 triumph over Maryland in the 1995 Hall of Fame Tipoff Classic in Springfield, Mass. He was on his way to an exciting injury-free season, starting 24 of the team's 36 games and averaging 9.4 points at mostly small forward, in Kentucky's memorable NCAA championship year.

Not surprisingly, Williams said UK's national title victory over Syracuse was the most enjoyable one that he has seen Anderson at Kentucky. He felt great especially when Anderson "hit the last two three-pointers. That was the moment." In UK's nine-point victory, Anderson played a crucial role as the junior had 11 points — including a three-point field goal which gave Kentucky a more comfortable 69-62 advantage with nearly four minutes left — and three steals.

Approximately seven months after capturing the 1996 NCAA championship, Anderson, who was then a senior, and sophomore Ron Mercer took the spotlight after the departures of four popular Wildcats — Tony Delk, Walter McCarty, Mark Pope and Antoine Walker. Big things were expected from the duo, popularly known later as the Air Pair. If Kentucky was going to make another Final Four journey, it had to have strong performances from them.

As expected, they did perform as Kentucky raced to a glittery 35-5 worksheet with their second straight trip to the national title game, losing to Arizona. Mercer played the entire season in becoming a first-team All-American and SEC's Player of the Year. But for Anderson, it was a different story. While he was on his way to stardom as perhaps the league's top player, he suffered a serious knee injury in mid-January, which practically ended his UK career. At the time of injury, he led the SEC in scoring with 18.6 points a game. Had Anderson stayed healthy, the story of UK's remarkable season might have been sweeter. The Wildcats might've won the school's seventh national title.

At first, it was believed Anderson had a bruised knee. But that wasn't so. It was bad news, meaning that he was likely out for the season. That meant Anderson probably had played his last game for the Wildcats. His once-promising NBA career was in doubt. Anderson's injury — which occurred in Kentucky's 77-53 home victory over Auburn — was front page news in Kentucky. The *Lexington Herald-Leader* even showed large illustrations of torn anterior cruciate ligament (ACL) in the knee. The personable Wildcat senior became a very hot topic of discussion in smoke-filled coffee and barber shops in the commonwealth. Everyone was alarmed about Kentucky's chances for the remaining season. Could the Wildcats repeat as NCAA champions? Most would say it was doubtful. And a very concerned Pitino compared the loss of Anderson to the team as if Wake Forest was losing its dominating 6-10 star, Tim Duncan, who has since moved on to NBA stardom.

Unlike some collegiate stars, Anderson's immediate family didn't purchase an insurance policy in case he had a career-ending injury, according to Williams. With Anderson out, was his supportive uncle feeling pretty low? Did Williams feel sorry for the youngster? "Not really," said Williams, who had seen his nephew play just about every UK home game. He sincerely believed there was a good reason for the injury to take place. "God tests us all," he explained. "I just thought that was a test of our faith. We put it in God's hand and like every season before Derek plays, I do my prayers and I put the season in God's hand. And whatever His will be. I mean I'm not to say what will happen to Derek. That's the way I look at it. I mean if He wants Derek to play, I want Derek to play. And that's the way I leave it."

Williams tries to look at life and basketball in proper perspective. "It's just a game," he said. "Derek has his health. He's accomplished so many great things. If he stopped (playing) tomorrow and he reflected back over his lifetime late in life, you know he's done a lot. I knew he accomplished a lot even with that (injury). And I love him for the person, not the athlete.

"The pro thing is a dream. Like I told him, it's the icing on the cake if it comes. There are so many kids whose game stops at just that last level. So, to me, it goes back to the degree. My biggest thing is his degree. I put that above the pros. (But) you know it's (NBA) a dream. It's a great thing. People look at the riches as a great thing. Don't get me wrong. I'm not gonna lie to you and say I don't (think it's wonderful). I take it as it comes."

 Not too long after his injury, Anderson made the front page again. This time around the publicity was not favorable. In one of the most embarrassing moments of his life, he got into trouble with the law in a highly-publicized case. He sup-

posedly had driven through a couple of red lights with a suspended license in the wee hours in a Louisville suburb. The police, as a result, arrested Anderson and placed him in a jail for two hours. The player was later released on his own recognizance.

While Anderson later pled guilty for charges on driving through the red lights and was fined $20 plus court costs, the court agreed to drop another charge in regard to suspended license because of an error by the state office beyond Anderson's control. The suspended license had resulted because of his failure to pay a speeding ticket in 1995. The ticket was actually paid, according to his uncle.

With Anderson admitting his mistake, Pitino questioned the incident's media-frenzy coverage, saying the injured guard had never done drugs or become drunk. The coach was upset about the unwanted publicity. Pitino also wondered why the officers had arrested the player for minor traffic violations.

Williams said the entire affair "was a learning experience. And God teaches you lessons in life. He (Anderson) didn't know how important he had become in the state of Kentucky. True, it was a trivial thing but it let him know that when you're out here in the media (spotlight) you're going to be news if you spit on the street and the wrong people are around. So it was a valuable lesson on one hand, but it was a lot of ridicule on the other hand. But we lived with it. I told him it was a bad news day."

 During the early part of his senior year when he was healthy, Anderson got to play in his hometown as the Cats battled Indiana at Freedom Hall in a December matchup. He loved another opportunity to beat his old Big Ten rival and coach Bobby Knight. For Anderson, it would be just like the old days when he was at Ohio State. It was a very special night.

"You know, he still has that Big Ten blood in him," said his uncle. "(He wanted) to beat Bobby Knight. Bobby Knight is an outstanding coach. Not many people beat Bobby Knight."

Before the largest crowd (20,074) to ever watch a Wildcat game in Louisville, Anderson turned in what was perhaps his most sensational performance of his collegiate career. He gunned in 30 points, tying his career-high, in sparking No. 6 Kentucky to a surprisingly easy 99-65 win over the eighth-ranked Hoosiers in a key showdown between two of the nation's top teams. In addition to Anderson's superb play, Kentucky also had a fine performance from 6-7 Mercer, who scored 26 points. The setback embar-rassed Knight, who suffered one of his worst losses ever at Indiana.

And the red-hot Anderson got to perform his famous act as a dancer after a nice play in front of his hometown crowd and the ESPN cam-eras. What did Williams think of Anderson's playful act? "It was appropri-ate," he smiled. "He was having a good game. He is one of the few play-ers who can probably say that he's beaten Bobby Knight three out of four times that he ever faced him (actually four out of six, including OSU's 1994 upset of Indiana when Anderson sat out because of an injury). It was a big game to him."

According to Williams, his nephew's little dance show was actual-ly for one of Anderson's ex-teammates. "He did that for Antoine Walker," added Williams. "He had seen Antoine do it."

 In January 1997, since Anderson hurt his knee, no one, including the doctors, had expected to see him play for the rest of the season. His college basketball career was over, they said. But Anderson — who later earned second team All-SEC honors despite missing the critical half of UK's season — defied the odds when his knee became strong enough to play in the NCAA tournament. Although he didn't log any minutes in the tourney, he did make two technical free throws in the Final Four, meaning his name will always be in the box score of Kentucky's national semifinal 78-69 victory over Minnesota. Anderson, a superb free throw shooter, got his chance in the second half when official Jim Burr hit Minnesota coach Clem Haskins, a Kentucky native, with a technical for unsportsmanlike conduct. The coach was angry over a charging call assessed against his squad.

"That was exciting for me," said Williams of his nephew's first appearance in nearly two and a half months. After the free throws, Anderson then returned to the Wildcat bench, flashing his famous smile.

During Kentucky's NCAA tournament run, there had been specu-lation that Pitino would insert Anderson in the lineup. With Kentucky 2-0 in NCAA tourney action, the doctors proclaimed Anderson's knee healthy. The guard was ready to play. But Pitino understandably refused to play Anderson, fearing another injury would end the charismatic youngster's promising NBA career. Anderson nevertheless supported Pitino's decision. Pitino "wanted to play him, but he just didn't want to take a chance," Williams explained.

Other than seeing Anderson shoot technical free throws, Williams admitted that he had hoped that Anderson would also get to see tournament action. "Sure I did," he said. "You know he's a competitor. I would be lying if I said I didn't want to see him to play, but I respected Rick. I mean we couldn't diminish him. We couldn't overshadow the coach in any way. It was his team. We wanted what was best for everybody and coach said, 'Well, it's best not to play.' So that's what was best."

 Unlike UK's national semifinal victory when Anderson made his dramatic appearance, there were no technical fouls called in the national championship game where Kentucky dropped to Arizona in overtime. That meant Anderson didn't shoot free throws. But that didn't matter. He wanted to see Kentucky win the Big Dance for the second straight year.

Like Anderson, Williams was very disappointed about the 84-79 setback to the Pac-10 team before 47,028 fans in Indianapolis. The loss hurt him. However, he didn't feel low or depressed as he knew Anderson's future was promising. He could hardly wait to see his nephew star again in the future. Anderson would have another chance to play on a championship team and it would be in the NBA.

"I felt disappointed for the kids," Williams said. "I would've loved to see him be one of the few people in America who'd ever been on a back-to-back NCAA championship (teams). It was a disappointment on one hand, but you're looking at his bright future and he was going to play again. He was headed for bigger and better things."

 Anderson's lifelong dream finally became a reality on the night of June 25, 1997 in Charlotte, N.C. The Cleveland Cavaliers had chosen him as the league's 13th selection overall — a lottery pick. With his immediate family and close friends on hand at the NBA Draft headquarters, a smiling Anderson got to shake hands with NBA commissioner David Stern and pose for pictures. It was a lifetime thrill.

He joined teammate Ron Mercer as one of NBA's 13 lottery picks. As the No. 6 pick, Mercer went to Boston. In the second round, the Houston Rockets selected former Wildcat Rodrick Rhodes, who had left UK after his junior season, as the No. 24 selection overall. San Antonio picked Tim Duncan of Wake Forest as the league's top choice.

Cleveland general manager and ex-NBA player Wayne Embry, who was named the NBA Executive of the Year by *The Sporting News* in 1998 for his bold moves in reviving the Cavaliers' franchise, said he attempts to look for players like Anderson who have good character and work ethics. Even with Anderson's questionable knees, Embry said the staff had the Kentucky star at No. 3 in a list of eligible players for the 1997 draft. Since Anderson was still available at No. 13 pick, Cleveland couldn't pass up a chance to pick the Wildcat standout.

Seeing Anderson in the NBA with a lucrative contract is "a dream come true," said Williams, who saw Cleveland and his nephew play many times in 1997-98. "To me, you know, that's what a lot of people don't understand about things — like when you watch a dream cultivate, mature and then actually become reality. It's like I tell people that dreams do come true. That's more exciting to me than where he goes because he was able to take a dream, work the dream and bring it out to reality. You know it's more than the magic. It is from a fantasy to reality."

Before the draft, Williams said he didn't have a preference on which NBA team Anderson would play for. "I wouldn't care if he went to the Sacramento Kings," he smiled. What about Boston, which had just hired Pitino away from UK? Williams commented that would be nice. "I respect Rick a lot," he said. "I like Rick a lot. I have the utmost (respect for him). I respected Dean (Smith) as a coach, but I respected Rick also. It was only Dean and Rick to me (as far as the greatest basketball coaches are concerned). It's just what they teach. It's their program. It's the mentality, you know, the work ethics.

"I think (Derek) has learned so much from Rick in the last couple of years (at UK) that you've seen the maturity. You know he's a kid who wants to get better and Rick is a perfectionist."

Several months earlier, many NBA observers had projected Anderson as a definite lottery pick. His knee injury in the Kentucky-Auburn game, however, changed the outlook. He wasn't a sure thing anymore. Some even thought his basketball career was gone. Many NBA scouts were skeptical about him because of his past injuries. They loved his potential as a shooting guard or small forward, but didn't want to risk spending millions of dollars on an injury-prone player.

As a result, Anderson — who received his bachelor's degree with a major in pharmacy — had to work out for several teams, including five teams with lottery picks, just to ease their concerns even though his knee was sound. The tryouts went well for the Kentucky guard and the NBA teams started to take him more seriously.

Williams said, "Before he went down, he was in the top four. So if you're in top four and they feel like you've recovered, then you really don't have to go back and do much more, but to show them that you recovered. They knew he could play."

 One of Anderson's highlights in his rookie season of 1997-98 came during the NBA All-Star Weekend festivities in New York City. He had been chosen to play in the Schick Rookie Game, joining the league's top rookies Ron Mercer (Boston), Keith Van Horn (New Jersey), Chauncey Billups (Boston), and Zydrunas Ilgauskas (Cleveland), among others.

However, Anderson didn't see action since he had suffered a partial tear in his knee several days earlier. He was disappointed as he had looked forward to playing in the Rookie Game. He flew to New York City anyway to take part in the festive activities and sat on the bench to cheer for his winning East squad. At the time of his mid-season injury, the part-time starter ranked No. 4 among the NBA rookies with a 12.0-point average.

With Anderson sitting out until the first week of March, missing a total of 15 games, the Cavaliers struggled. They lost nine out of 15 games. The team missed Anderson's instant offense, not to mention his enthusiasm and excitement on the floor. In other words, he was the spark plug of the team. But when the former Wildcat star returned to action, Cleveland found its winning touch, making the post-season playoffs. In a late-season matchup, Anderson — who had one day even worn a Wildcat football jersey with Tim Couch's No. 2 in a workout — pumped in a pro career-high 30 points, hitting 11 of 15 field goals, with a perfect 6 for 6 from the line, in an 105-93 setback to the Los Angeles Lakers. His performance wasn't enough to carry a small Cleveland team, which only had two players taller than 6-7 in the loss. The Cavaliers had three players, including 6-10 power forward Shawn Kemp, out of lineup. (The threesome were fined and suspended for one game by the league for participating in a brawl in the previous contest against Detroit. The suspension reportedly cost Kemp a one-game paycheck of nearly $100,000.)

Anderson also received a post-season honor. The Louisville product was one of the four Cavaliers selected to NBA's All-Rookie team, making the second team. First-year standouts Brevin Knight, Zydrunas Ilgauskas and Cedric Henderson received honors as Cleveland became the first NBA team in history to have four players chosen to the All-Rookie squad.

 Many Kentucky fans have wondered about Anderson's parents. What happened to his mom and dad? In the UK media guides, Anderson had always listed George and Glenda Williams as his parents.

Williams, however, didn't provide any clues. He didn't want to discuss circumstances surrounding Anderson and his parents that led to adoption by the Williams clan. "Well, we'd rather not talk about that," Williams said. "It is something we don't talk about."

It is something within the close-knit family, explained Williams, who added that he's from the mother's side.

"I've been with him ever since he was born," Williams said of Anderson. "You know I was with him alone before I got married or anything. I've raised both him and his brother. So I've got two boys to my credit." Williams also has a daughter, Margia, whom Anderson likes to refer to as his sister.

Anderson also has a daughter, DeAsia, whom he loves dearly. DeAsia — who was born when her father attended OSU — lives with her mother.

 Nicknamed "D.A." and "Lil' Smooth," Anderson is one of most likable guys around. He has a nice personality with a friendly smile. Williams is obviously pleased and he was asked if he had any part in Anderson's positive outlook. "Well, I told him today if I do I'm really thrilled because I love his personality," Williams said. "Like I told him, and I've always told him through life, I would rather see him be a better person than be a great athlete."

Anderson was probably the most easy-going player at UK, right along with his former teammate Cameron Mills. "I'm very easy going, very laid back, but I think Derek's got a great personality," said Mills. "He is always smiling. (He) is always in a good mood. We were always friends while he was here (at Kentucky)."

While at UK and Cleveland, Anderson has publicly talked about his faith in God in his numerous interviews with the media. For instance, he believes the knee blowouts he had at OSU and UK were a part of the plan to secure him a spot on the Cavaliers' roster. "I think God does things for a reason and He probably did this so I could end up in Cleveland," Anderson was quoted as saying in *Akron Beacon Journal* when he signed a three-year pact.

After interviewing his uncle, who is now in his mid-40s, it's easy to understand why Anderson shows deep respect for the Lord. Williams definitely has influence on the youngster.

Williams said he is a Baptist but he also respects all forms of religion. "I respect some of their practices and some of them I steal if I think it will help me be a better Christian and I use their faith, too," he said. "I'm not just stuck on one belief."

TUBBY AND HIS AMAZING CATS

What a difference a year makes!

In 1997, when Orlando "Tubby" Smith accepted the Kentucky post as the new head basketball coach, he was a rising superstar in the coaching profession. A former Rick Pitino assistant at UK, Smith had successful head coaching stints at Tulsa and Georgia where he guided both schools to the NCAA tourney's Sweet Sixteen appearances.

Since then Smith has become a very popular, nationally-known figure, leading his surprising Wildcats to the coveted NCAA crown in 1998. The national championship in hand meant more invitations for public appearances by the Kentucky coach — speeches, banquets, luncheons, fund-raisers and award ceremonies.

Smith said the public demand for his time has increased three-fold, or maybe more. Reluctantly, he has had to learn to say no. "My personality is one that is very open and inviting, and when that happens, it is hard to say no," said the coach in an exclusive interview for this book in mid-June 1998. "I have to learn to do that and I can do it in a polite way, say no. That is the toughest thing (to do) because there is not enough time in the day to fulfill all requests. (Ex-North Carolina coach) Dean Smith and other coaches who have been in this position, and even Rick Pitino, stated that is gonna be the toughest thing you have to deal with — the demands on your time."

With the help of veteran administrative assistant Marta McMackin in the UK Basketball Office, Smith is fortunate that he has someone who understands his high-profile position. McMackin, a native of Ohio, has worked in the Wildcat basketball program for many years, working for then-head coaches Joe B. Hall, Eddie Sutton and Pitino. Like Smith in 1998, Hall and Pitino won the national championship in 1978 and 1996, respectively.

"I've got great people around me — great secretary, administrative assistant in Marta McMackin because she has been through it with Joe B. Hall," Smith said. "She has been through it all. So she is very good about (handling the coach's schedule)."

Smith, who in 1973 launched his coaching career at Great Mills High School, his alma mater in Maryland, realizes that being the head coach at basketball tradition-rich Kentucky is a very public job which doesn't allow much room for privacy. Since winning the national title, he has become more well-known to the general public. Is that good or bad for him and his family?

"It's good in a lot of ways," Smith said. "Not that you're looking for it; I mean, it is just something that comes with the territory. It beats the alternative of not being known and people not wanting to know you. But there are the negatives that come with it. You don't have any privacy once you go out and dine. I've been very happy and pleased with the way people have respected me when I am out and about. They know that I'm gonna treat them with respect if they respect me and my privacy."

 Before coming to Kentucky, Smith was subject of several rumors linking him with other coaching vacancies during the 1997 NCAA's March Madness. But he wasn't very interested in leaving Athens, Georgia. He had plans to stay with the Georgia Bulldog program for many years. He had just guided Georgia to a two-year mark of 45-19 with a couple of trips to the NCAA tournament, including the Final 16 in 1996. His oldest son G.G. was a key player for Georgia. In addition, his younger son Saul was about to join the Bulldog squad as a non-scholarship freshman player. The future was bright for the Smith household. He was making good money. In early 1996, he reportedly agreed to a six-year deal worth about $3 million, which included his Converse shoe pact, after spending several months without a signed

Orlando "Tubby" Smith gestures as he talks with the media in May 1997 when UK officially announced the appointment of Smith as its new head basketball coach. UK president Dr. Charles T. Wethington Jr., sitting in his chair, listens.

Photo by Jamie H.Vaught

contract at Georgia. There was no reason for him to leave Georgia. He was content.

Kentucky athletic director C.M. Newton wasn't sure if Smith would leave Georgia for the Bluegrass after spending only two years at the Bulldog helm. After Rick Pitino informed Newton of his decision to leave UK for NBA's Boston Celtics, the Kentucky AD immediately went to work. He developed a short list of coaching candidates, with Smith on it.

"The only question I had was whether or not he wanted the job," Newton said in *Basketball Times*. "People talk about how tough it was to follow Adolph (Rupp) and there's no question that Joe Hall did a tremendous job. But following Rick is no picnic. I believe Tubby has the toughness and the understanding."

Newton also told the magazine the decision to hire Smith was a relatively easy one. "Really, it was sort of a no brainer. I thought there were maybe two or three people that could handle it, but he was always at the top of my list. I felt we needed someone who played the modern style of game, pressuring, running and shooting the threes. I wanted someone who was a good teacher and someone who had the toughness to handle the visibility of the job. Yet I also wanted someone who was different enough from Rick (personality wise) that he wouldn't constantly be compared to Rick. I thought all along that guy was Tubby."

Smith said he was in his office on the Georgia campus when Newton first contacted him shortly after Pitino revealed his farewell decision in a news conference at UK's Memorial Coliseum.

"Coach Newton called me about a half hour, maybe an hour later (after Pitino's press conference)," Smith commented. "He said 'Tubby, you probably just heard that Rick has resigned,' and he wanted to know if I would be interested in the job. That's when I first heard about it (the possibility of being the head coach at UK)."

It wasn't too long before Smith couldn't resist a golden opportunity to coach at Kentucky. But the Maryland native, who was 45 at the time, had to do some serious thinking about his up-and-coming career before making a move. "Kentucky is a great place. You've got all the resources, but I had a good job in Georgia," he said. "I had them going in the right direction. I knew that we were gonna be a strong program for years just like the Tulsa program. So I wasn't anxious to leave Georgia. I had just turned down Ohio State ... and you have to understand that I was getting up in age and had moved quite a bit so I wasn't really looking to move.

"From coach Newton I got the impression of having to follow in the footsteps of Rick Pitino and trying to (meet) the expectations that come with this job. So it wasn't one of those snap (decisions that) I'm coming. But (Kentucky) is a dream job as I have said before. What I mean is, you work so hard and when you get a better position, you had better make it your dream job or you're not gonna be successful. So coach (Newton) and I talked, and I came up and met with (UK president) Dr. Wethington and (UK senior associate AD) Larry Ivy. They convinced me this is a good place and that everything would go well. And I'm glad they did. I'm glad I came here, that's for sure."

Smith's son, G.G., was another concern. "I was concerned about him, my boy, because we had been together," said the father. "(It would be) the first time we had been apart and how he would react. I knew bringing both G.G. and Saul would be tough to do. It is tough enough on a coach to coach, much less have his son a part of the team. I knew coach (Eddie) Sutton had done it before and so it is always tough."

G.G. Smith, a starting point guard at Georgia, is the only member of Smith family who didn't come to Kentucky. Saul Smith said he wishes his older brother had transferred to UK so that they could play together for their father.

"I wish he would have come," Saul said in a 1997 interview which appeared in Middlesboro's *The Daily News*. "But it wasn't like I had a say in it because I was gonna support him whatever he did and I'm happy that he's happy with the decision that he made. Had he came to Kentucky, he probably would have had to sit out a year and that really was influential in his decision. He's made a home at UGA so I don't think that coming here (at Kentucky) was a good idea for him.

"I can't be selfish and want everything for myself and want him to be here for me. I think he needs to live his life and be one of the best guards in the Southeastern Conference."

Saul's mom, Donna, supported the family's decision to move to Lexington for the second time. "I think she (wanted Tubby to take the job at UK)," Saul said. "I think my mom was gonna support him in his decision. She really liked Lexington when we used to live here... I think she's happy." The elder Smith also said his wife encouraged him to take the UK job. The couple have another son, Brian, who is a teenager.

On taking the dream job at Kentucky, Smith told a large audience of electronic and print media when he was chosen for the Wildcat post, "Every program measures itself against the University of Kentucky. As an assistant coach under Rick, you worked so hard, you didn't think about much else. Those things come to your mind but I never dreamed I would be the head coach at the University of Kentucky. I never dreamed I would be a head coach at any Division I school. I wanted to be a high school coach and teacher because they were the people, other than my parents, who had the biggest influence on my life."

UK athletic director C.M. Newton (left) introduces Tubby Smith as the school's new basketball coach at a press conference held on the UK campus in 1997. UK president Dr. Charles Wethington and Smith's wife, Donna, look on.

Photo by Jamie H.Vaught

While endorsing UK's hiring of Smith, some sportswriters had thought Kentucky would go after a more established coach with a proven record.

Said *Atlanta Journal-Constitution* sportswriter Mark Schlabach, "I was somewhat surprised just based on the fact that he had been at Georgia for only two years. I thought that Kentucky may go after a more proven guy although coach Smith did have great success at Georgia. And of course, the thing that surprised me most was the short amount of time it took. I mean it was only a matter of hours before C.M. Newton had decided on Tubby Smith."

It was no surprise that Newton sought Smith, a highly-regarded coach who happened to be black, for the UK job. In the late 1960s and early 1970s, when he was the head coach at Alabama, Newton had the school's first black players on basketball scholarship.

"I'm not the least bit surprised Kentucky would hire an African-American coach," said *Cincinnati Enquirer's* Mike DeCourcy, who also writes a weekly column on college basketball for *The Sporting News*. "First, C.M. Newton was going to hire the best available coach and Tubby Smith was easily the most logical and best qualified candidate. Second, there have been black coaches all around the South in the past decade — Larry Finch (formerly of Memphis), Perry Clark at Tulane and even Rob Evans (formerly of Mississippi) — who were far more symbolic in regard to segregation than was UK as the result of the Texas Western game (in 1966).

"The media has a tendency to focus on what is easy: Kentucky played as an all-white team against an all-black team in the 1966 NCAA title game, and it was thus viewed as somehow more intractable than other schools in the region. Whether or not that was true never was a factor.

"I found it amazing that so many made such an issue of this. There's every reason for black Americans to feel proud of someone like Tubby Smith, but no reason for others to wonder whether his race will have a great impact on his tenure at Kentucky."

Unlike some Wildcat fans who initially took a wait-and-see attitude about the new mentor, the sportswriters, including those who regularly covered Smith's former team at Georgia, immediately gave a stamp of approval to Kentucky's decision to hire Smith. "I don't think they could have done any better," Anthony Dasher of *Athens Daily News* said in an interview.

Commented *Atlanta Journal-Constitution's* Schlabach, "I think Kentucky couldn't have done much better than him as far as a replacement for Rick Pitino. I'm sure the Kentucky people are gonna be real happy up there."

DeCourcy said, "The thing I love about Tubby Smith is that he consistently exceeds expectations. That is the most difficult thing to do in the college basketball business because everyone expects so much, but he has done it at Tulsa and even more so at Georgia.

"In this regard, Kentucky will be his most difficult challenge. The only direction would seem to be down, but Rick Pitino left room for improvement in terms of recruiting and there has been a lack of warmth about the program that I think Tubby can rectify. Kentucky basketball seemed more like a business under Pitino, even if he did remove a lot of the dealing. I think people will feel even more a part of UK with someone like Tubby Smith running the show."

ESPN's Dick Vitale liked Kentucky's decision, too. The sportscaster added the Wildcats had a tremendous hire in Smith, saying the new coach knows his X's and O's.

 Smith in his first season at UK has won over the demanding Wildcat fans with his down-to-earth demeanor and his excellent coaching as Kentucky captured its second national championship in three years. The coach indicated that he wanted to be judged by his on-the-court performance, not his race.

"It's more important that I am competent and be judged on the content of my character and not the color of my skin," he said in the press conference when he was named to the UK post. "I know that coach Newton hired me because of my competency as a head coach and that I can do the job and lead this program."

Smith later said in a 1997 interview with *Basketball Times*, "Kentucky basketball is bigger than anything else, race included. The issue here is whether or not you can coach. It won't be a question of whether I am black or white. That doesn't matter. The issue is whether I can coach. This is Kentucky and that is the issue."

Former Kentucky guard Cameron Mills said he still gets tired of people, including newspaper columnists, talking about the touchy issue of black and white. "When the article came out in the *Herald-Leader* (in 1997) that one lady had written, it upset me," Mills commented in the spring of 1998. "It probably upset a lot of people. When coach Smith announced he was coming, that lady wrote he shouldn't come because we are racist. (Smith) never made an issue (on black and white). He never made any comments about racism or never made any comments about how he was the first black (men's basketball) coach at the University of Kentucky. He just never did that.

"It was tiring because everyone was making such a big deal out of it and it really shouldn't have been a big deal. It should have been when we've gotten a new coach, but not when we've gotten our first black coach. I think they should let it (the issue) go. I mean he has obviously proven he can win and he has obviously proven he's a good coach."

Like Mills, Smith said he gets tired of hearing or reading about the racial issue. "You would think that we would be past that, but obviously we are not past that point," the coach told the author, "because that is what sells (the newspapers) and that is basically why they do it. It is controversial. It is a subject that there is always two sides. You see what I mean. And that is what the media is about. You know you've got to have two sides or it doesn't sell.

"I was the first black head coach here and there were the racial elements during the Rupp era. But that was everywhere and I said that all along. I didn't know why they singled out Kentucky. Nobody had black players up until the early '70s or late '60s. So I don't know what the racial (circumstances were) except there were things probably said or done that were a little more (controversial) over than, say, some schools."

 When Smith was playing college basketball in the late 1960s and the early 1970s, he wasn't a celebrity as his Kentucky players are today. At High Point College (now High Point University), located in North Carolina's Piedmont Triad Region of Greensboro, Winston-Salem and High Point, the 6-2 guard played under the shadows of Atlantic Coast Conference schools such as Duke, North Carolina, Wake Forest and North Carolina State. Dean Smith and Norm Sloan were coaching North Carolina and N.C. State, respectively. Those big-name schools weren't very far from High Point, just over an hour drive. They got all the ink. In Smith's junior year, the Tar Heels went to the 1972 NCAA Final Four.

During Smith's senior year, N.C. State got everybody's attention as it finished with a perfect 27-0 mark. But the Wolfpack couldn't play in the NCAA tournament because they were on probation. (The next season of 1973-74, the 30-1 Wolfpack, featuring David Thompson, Tom Burleson and Monte Towe, won the NCAA tournament, a rare feat by a non-UCLA team at the time.) High Point had local coverage, but that was it.

Smith remains a popular figure at High Point University, which has recently changed its NCAA classification from Division II to Division I and will compete in the Big South Conference in the fall of 1999. The 2,500-student university, affiliated with the United Methodist Church, is so proud of Smith that they had him on the cover of their alumni magazine in the summer of 1996 while he was still at Georgia.

"I try to make it back once a year," Smith said of his visits to High Point. "I'm on the Board of Visitors and I think they want to make me a trustee. You know I try to make contributions there, but it is so tough in this business as a coach to get back."

Smith, who was an All-State performer in the prep ranks, almost didn't come to the North Carolina school. He was set to go to Maryland, but the Terrapins had changed coaches, naming Lefty Driesell to the post. Driesell, who wanted to sign his own players, didn't really want Smith. As a result, the youngster went to High Point because he couldn't go to another ACC school due to a conference letter-of-intent he had inked with Maryland.

When Smith arrived at the North Carolina school in 1969, he was the only black among eight freshmen basketball players and became the college's second black roundball performer. Former ABA standout and current NBA assistant coach Gene Littles, who attended High Point from 1965 to '69, was the first African-American to play on the school's basketball team. According to a *New York Times* story by William C. Rhoden, former High Point administrator Bob Latta said the college didn't have many black players. He remarked that a good black athlete also had to be a good all-around citizen to be accepted on the campus.

According to Smith, only three black students were at High Point during his freshman year. "It was tough because there wouldn't be anybody to really relate to on campus," Smith recalled. The UK coach said the adjustment was made easier because the city folks of High Point embraced him. "I had access to the community and the city of High Point was very gracious. They really accepted me. They were very tolerant. They would let you come to their homes and so I could do and go to a lot of things. I could walk off campus because the campus is located right in the heart of High Point.

"(In addition) I got along pretty well with all the other white players and people who were part of the program. I never had a problem, but it was tough. I had a bunch of different people in my family, 17 different (brothers and sisters), so I got used to the differences being in a family of 17."

Like many college students at that time, Smith admitted that he almost looked like a hippie, sporting an Afro or long hair, and a Fu Manchu mustache. It was during the troubled days of anti-Vietnam War demonstrations, and the civil rights movement which was supported by several black groups, including the Black Panthers.

"It was a fad at the time," Smith said of his so-called 'radical' look. "Back then in the '60s or '70s, the Black Panthers were big. But I wasn't a violent person and their whole way of changing society was through vio-

Tubby Smith, shown here when he was coaching at Georgia against UK, didn't bring up the racial issue during the 1997-98 season, his first year at Kentucky, according to then-Wildcat senior Cameron Mills. Standing behind Smith is former aide and current Georgia mentor Ron Jirsa.

University of Kentucky Media Relations / Photo by David Coyle lence. A lot of black students at the time were very radical. I wasn't radical per se, that was just the (fashion) style back then. Growing up, those were some tough times because we saw JFK, Martin Luther King, Jr. and Bobby Kennedy being killed. So it was a real turmoil. Our country was really struggling with a lot of problems, riots and everything at that time."

 During Smith's four-year stay at High Point, the school's basketball program struggled to find stability in its coaching leadership. Smith had three different head coaches. One of them was J.D. Barnett, who would later become the head coach at Virginia Commonwealth and employ Smith as his assistant for six years in the early 1980s. It was Barnett who didn't like Smith's facial hair and long hair. The new High Point coach told the player to shave his Fu Manchu mustache and improve his appearance.

The coach's order upset Smith. "I tried to persuade him (to change his mind)," Smith said. "I tried to let him know it was a cultural (style). I told him (that) most Negro or black men have a mustache; this is part of our heritage or culture. But he didn't want to hear that. So he wanted me to do some research. He wanted me to write a paper. I did some (research), but that didn't matter.

"He wanted to make me (a leader). He said, 'Look if you are going to be a leader and going to be captain of the team, you've got to conform. If you do it, everybody is gonna do it.' And I wanted to be a leader on the team. I wanted to win. I wanted to be the captain. He gave me a day to think about it and I came back with no mustache. So that is part of the sacrifices that you have to make to be a team."

Smith wasn't a troublemaker. It wasn't his nature to stir trouble and he didn't have a chip on his shoulder. He was a product of his strict upbringing on a small farm in Maryland. An enthusiastic person, he had good moral values. He went on to finish his playing career as a captain and all-conference selection during his senior year, averaging 15 points (with a career high 32 points in one game), under the leadership of new mentor Jerry Steele, who is still the head coach today at High Point, approaching 600 career victories.

"I really enjoyed coaching him," Steele said in High Point's alumni magazine. "He was special. I knew he would be successful at whatever he did. That he chose to coach is good for basketball and good for the young men who play for him. We at High Point University can be proud that Tubby is part of us."

In 1973, Smith received his bachelor's degree in health and physical education, becoming the only one graduated on time among the eight
freshman roundball players who first came to High Point in 1969. And he
did it without taking a single class in the summer. While Smith, hurting
from a hand injury suffered in a late-season matchup, failed to make the
NBA roster, he later saw some of his collegiate rivals from Greensboro's
Guilford College succeed in the pro ranks in 1975. M.L. Carr, who would
later coach the Boston Celtics before Rick Pitino took over the helm, played
for the Spirits of St. Louis in the ABA for one year before going to the NBA,
and World Free signed with the Philadelphia 76ers.

Steele, who in 1987 became the youngest coach to be selected into
the NAIA Basketball Coaches Hall of Fame, commented that Smith had outstanding traits that helped the player achieve success later in life. Among
them were his work ethic and personality. "He got along with people —
faculty and students alike. He just seemed to like everybody, and everybody
liked him," Steele said. "He was a very hard worker — on the court and
off the court. You could see that he was determined to succeed, no matter
what it took. He always says he learned that from his parents, who are just
as extraordinary as he is."

Interestingly, Steele has a very close connection with CBS sportscaster Billy Packer, whom many UK fans dislike for his seemingly growing
bias toward the Atlantic Coast Conference. They both played college basketball together at Wake Forest under legendary Baptist preacher and head
coach Bones McKinney in the early 1960s. A very colorful personality,
McKinney died in 1997 at the age of 78.

Smith has an inspiring story about Steele, whom the Kentucky
coach said is part Indian who stands 6-foot-8 and weighs about 300
pounds. "I guess the best story was what Billy Packer told me about him
when both played together for Bones McKinney," Smith commented. "They
called him 'Chief.' He (Steele) was like the enforcer back in those days and
he would go in a game and he would just wipe people out. He was captain of the team and he tore his knee up, but they told about his courage.
Jerry Steele came off the bench with a torn-up knee to help them win the
(Atlantic Coast Conference) championship. They said that's the kind of
heart and kind of courage that he had.

"But coach Steele was always funny. He's always very comical. I
don't know if I should say things like this, but he would say, 'It's time to eat

glass!' I remember I got screened one time real hard and he said, 'You need to keep your blade up. I want you to castrate that guy the next time he puts a screen on you. I want you to hit him with that elbow and castrate.' He would always say funny things that I really enjoyed (hearing). I wish I had played for him longer. I only played for him for one year.

"Coach Steele has been my mentor. He has done just about every-thing ..... Obviously, he knows what he's talking about .... The way he han-dles himself makes you want to work hard for him. His philosophy about life is close to mine."

And it was Steele who introduced Smith at the New York Athletic Club in May of 1998 when the Wildcat coach was presented the Winged Foot Award, which is given annually to the coach of the national champi-ons. "I still stay very close with Jerry Steele," Smith said of his coach.

Prior to coming to High Point in 1972, Steele had served as the assistant coach and interim head coach of ABA's Carolina Cougars in the 1970-71 season. He was also set to be the Cougars' head coach for the 1971-72 campaign before becoming ill and ex-NBA star Tom Meschery took over the Carolina helm. Steele, however, stayed with the Cougars, working as an assistant to Meschery. Before his Cougar stint, Steele also coached at Guilford College for several years in the 1960s where he once had current Wake Forest coach Dave Odom on the playing roster.

While at High Point, Smith and his friends occasionally drove to Greensboro, which was a short drive from the campus, to see the Carolina Cougars play. Ex-High Point star Gene Littles, a 6-1 guard for Carolina, provided the tickets. "We went to a few games," said Smith, who was a big ABA fan. "I loved them (the Cougars). It was great." Back then, it should be noted that there were no Charlotte Hornets in the area. In 1988, the Hornets began playing in the NBA as an expansion franchise.

 As for Smith, High Point also provided another highlight in his life. During his senior year of 1972-73, he met a beau-tiful freshman cheerleader Donna Walls, a native of Virginia who would later become the school's first black homecoming queen. Smith said he had her attention when he proudly drove around the campus in his 1964 two-tone Impala.

Smith remembers their first date. "I took her to dinner where she worked, at Sir Pizza or something like that," he smiled. "We really didn't get to know each other until right after Christmas. In fact, the way we met, she needed a ride home to Richmond, Virginia, (which was on the way back to his home in Maryland) over the Christmas holidays. I gave her a ride and that was her way of getting to know me, I guess. I was BMOC, you know, Big Man on Campus, and she wanted to get to know me. So it worked. I'm glad we met and that we dated."

About three years later, they married during the Christmas holidays in 1975 when he was serving as the head coach at his high school, Great Mills, in Maryland. Before he began coaching, Smith had seriously considered a career in the U.S. Air Force as a pilot.

 Born on June 30, 1951, Smith grew up as the sixth of Guffrie and Parthenia Smith's 17 children on a tenant farm in a rural area near Scotland in southern Maryland. While helping his family with various chores, such as driving a tractor when he was seven, he was a typical kid who had favorite players, especially the ones who played for the NBA's Baltimore Bullets (now the Washington Wizards). He mentioned Oscar "Big O" Robertson of the old Cincinnati Royals, and Earl "The Pearl" Monroe, Wes Unseld and Gus Johnson, all of Baltimore.

Smith liked Robertson "because I was just impressed with him and because people called me the 'Big O' when I was in high school. I wouldn't be anything to compare to Oscar, though. You know Orlando is my real name so people would call me 'Big O.' I used to imitate Oscar Robertson and Earl Monroe."

Smith said his parents, who are in their mid-70s, have struggled lately for health reasons. They have problems getting around. So naturally they don't like to travel. As a result, they only saw two Kentucky games during Smith's first season as the head coach at UK. They attended the UCLA and Duke games during the NCAA tournament in St. Petersburg, Florida.

"My dad has had (heart) bypass surgery and my mom had a hip replacement back in November (of 1997)," said Smith. "So she couldn't get around. My mom also had one hip replaced about six or seven years ago. My dad just doesn't like to travel anymore."

But that doesn't mean they haven't seen their son coach at Rupp Arena. His parents did make a visit or two to Lexington earlier when Smith served as an assistant under Rick Pitino.

Smith's father, who received his GED while in the U.S. Army, has

Jeff Sheppard, a senior tri-captain who was a key figure in Kentucky's 1998 NCAA championship run, talks to the media after a Wildcat victory. For the 1997-98 season, he led the "Comeback Cats" in scoring with an average of nearly 14 points a game.

Photo by Jamie H.Vaught

worked in almost every job. He was a farmer; a barber; a construction worker; and a school bus driver. A Purple Heart recipient, the elder Smith was injured in World War II.

Tubby Smith, who is a Methodist, credits much of his success and attitude to his church-going parents who taught the values of respect and hard work.

Asked if his siblings tease him about his huge yearly salary of about $1.2 million in his current post, Smith replied, "No, not really. They don't say (anything). I try to do as much as I can to help out mom and dad, and help my sisters and brothers. They know that money is not going to change me and it isn't gonna change them. Because I have money, (that) is not going to make them any different or tease me any more. I think they are proud as I am of them that I'm successful and that I do have the opportunities to be visible and be in a leadership position. I'm always proud to mention them and give a lot of credit to what they have done to help me be who I am. So I'm trying to give back as much as possible."

Smith, by the way, is the only person among his 17 brothers and sisters in coaching.

 While Smith is in hefty demand for speaking engagements and public appearances, many sports journalists said the Wildcat mentor is one of the more accessible "big-time" college basketball coaches you will find anywhere in the nation.

The coach will try to accommodate media's endless requests for interviews and photo sessions. Even though he earns big money for coaching, Smith's cooperation and genuine attitude should be viewed as remarkable. Those positive traits aren't found in every coach. It's difficult to find a sportswriter or anyone else, for that matter, who will speak negatively about the Kentucky coach.

Mark Schlabach of the *Atlanta Journal-Constitution* said, "I felt that coach Smith and I had a great relationship in Georgia. He was always accessible. His practices were always open, or 99 percent of the time they were open. He was always prompt in returning your phone calls and really never tried to cover anything up. He was a great guy to work with when he was a coach at Georgia.

"I guess the one thing that I remember the most is him going to pickup games with the writers covering him. He did it out in Albuquerque in the first NCAA tournament (in 1996). He obviously was a great basketball player and it is just rare that a coach would get involved in a pickup game with journalists, I guess.

"I remember when he first got to Georgia the thing I was really impressed with was he just hit the sidewalks, pounding the pavement and bang on every fraternity and sorority house, introducing himself to all the students. (He was) just trying to spark up some interest in the basketball program because it had gotten to where it was pretty dormant during the last few years. Tubby really went out of his way to get to the student groups and also to get involved in the community and just get the awareness of the program back up."

Sports columnist Jemal Horton, of the *Macon Telegraph*, echoes similar sentiments about Smith. He agrees that Smith is very cooperative. "He was very accessible, but I believe that Tubby kind of felt like the media was a necessary evil," said Horton. "I didn't feel like he was very comfortable sharing, opening himself and his life and his family to the media. But he was always very cordial and very cooperative. He did answer every question. I still think that he was very, very uncomfortable with, I guess, his fame. I think he did come to realize that it kind of came with being a very successful person and basketball coach."

Horton likes to describe Smith in the mode of Dr. Jekyll and Mr. Hyde. "Before the game (he was a) very calm, very subdued and very cordial man," he said, "and then as soon as the tip-off, it was a totally different Tubby. It was like I couldn't recognize him. I mean the eyes were bulging out of his head like Uncle Fester from the Addams Family (TV series) and the stomping and everything.

"I mean he is a very intimidating man because when you can hear a man stomp with 15,000 people (watching or yelling), he's stomping pretty hard. But then right after the game it was back to the very low key, subdued Tubby. That was the thing I remember most, how he could turn that light off and on, you know, in a matter of seconds."

Atlanta Journal-Constitution sports columnist Mark Bradley had a good working relationship with Smith at Georgia. "I had no problems with him," said Bradley, who is from Kentucky. "My impression was that he was one of the best coaches in the country. I thought he did a wonderful job at Georgia."

Mike DeCourcy of *The Sporting News* commented that Smith in his first season has already changed the once-intimidating atmosphere of UK's basketball program by making it more fan-friendly and personable. The Kentucky coach is also looked at favorably in comparison with some of his peers. "Tubby Smith has successfully demystified the position of UK head coach," DeCourcy explained. "There was always an imposing atmosphere around Rick Pitino that I think he wanted to exist to keep distractions to a minimum. It's something (former North Carolina coach) Dean Smith used to his advantage and that (Indiana's) Bob Knight has perfected.

"Tubby seems to be more like the other college coaches — guys like Gene Keady (of Purdue), Tom Izzo (Michigan State), Fran Fraschilla (who left St. John's after the 1997-98 season) — except that he happens to have the advantage of Kentucky tradition behind him when he recruits.

"The most difficult coach to reach is John Thompson (of Georgetown), and he likely will be for as long as he coaches. I remember one time when I was advancing a Pitt-Georgetown game (for a pre-game story), the closest I could get to him was having the Georgetown SID (sports information director) play a tape for me of questions he had asked regarding the game and the Hoyas' status at the time. When I got to D.C.

for the game, I noticed the *Washington Post* had used those same quotes. Thompson didn't even have time for them. Nice to know, at least, that he didn't play favorites."

While Smith and Pitino are both fiercely competitive in their own way, comparing them is almost like night and day. It doesn't take a genius to point out their contrasting styles in coaching and fanfare. They both look at things differently.

"(They're) different in their approach, different in their style," said sportscaster Tom Hammond. "Tubby Smith is a little more involved with his players. He is not up here on a pedestal — unreachable somewhere. He is the guy that you can go in and ask a question to at any time. I think he is more accessible to his players.

"Pitino was a hard-driving task master and Tubby Smith is demanding, too. But I don't think anyone is quite as demanding as Rick Pitino. Rick Pitino could also dress a player down in the best Rupp fashion. But I do think that everyone, players included, thought he did have their best interest at heart, as harsh as he could be at times on a player. I don't think there is any question that Tubby Smith has their best interest at heart. He shows that, I think, in every way he operates. So they are different in that respect.

"I think coach Pitino was what we call a control freak. He wanted to control everything about Kentucky basketball (the media, the ticket distribution, etc.) and he was good at it. I don't think Tubby Smith is quite that demanding of control. He is more of a delegator than Rick Pitino. Coach Pitino used to wear a microphone in practice so that the players could hear him on the speakers. That just doesn't seem like Tubby Smith's style.

"(They're) different in style. Tubby Smith is more down home than Rick Pitino. There is not that Eastern flash, that show business glitz and glamour."

After playing for Pitino for three years at Kentucky, then-Wildcat player Allen Edwards found Smith to be quite different as far as coaching styles are concerned. How different? The language is probably the biggest difference, Edwards said during his senior year of 1997-98 when he served as the team's tri-captain. "I think coach Smith has a more laid-back approach of coaching us," said the 6-5 swingman from Miami, Fla. "Coach P is just all out hyper, a hyper-drill sergeant type." Unlike Smith, Pitino is known to speak in R-rated language in practices or games.

However, Edwards pointed out that Smith can be brutal or emotional sometimes. "He gets rough. He gets excited. He gets angry. But he has a more laid-back approach to it." Edwards is also impressed with the fact that Smith is "like a father to all the players."

 One of Smith's closest friends, George Felton, has known the Wildcat coach for two decades. They met in the late 1970s when Felton served as an assistant at East Carolina and Smith was the head coach and teacher at Hoke County High School in Raeford, N.C. Felton, the current Wildcat assistant who arrived at UK in 1997 shortly after Smith was hired, said the Kentucky coach is "a man of principles" in Middlesboro's *The Daily News*. "I tried to recruit one of his players. The young man went to N.C. State, but from that point in time I was always impressed with the person, Tubby Smith. He is a person who I would say is people-oriented. He loves people and his personality is genuine. He always looks to help others."

As many UK fans are aware, Felton and Smith have a rather unusual working relationship which has survived through awkward moments sometimes. The former head coach of South Carolina for five years, Felton had Smith on his Gamecock coaching staff, and now he is working for Smith, his current boss. Felton, who came to Kentucky from Oregon State where he was an assistant, said that he has no qualms about working with Smith in a reverse capacity.

The situation is not awkward because "we've had a great relationship for a very long time and I look at coach Smith as a friend," explained Felton, a native of the Bronx in New York. "In our profession, I think it's really important that you have people that you can lean on and that you can communicate with. We've certainly been able to do that for a long period of time. I probably know the assistant role better than I did as the head coach."

Besides Felton, Smith's other top assistants on the Kentucky coaching staff include Shawn Finney and Mike Sutton, both of whom joined Smith in 1997 from Georgia.

Brooks Downing, the man who generates the publicity machine for the UK roundball program, is also impressed with Smith's wholesome manner. "His personality is an open door personality," said the UK publicist. "He is the kind of guy who will be friends to everyone. He doesn't have enemies and I think that really transcends over to the players as well because it gives them a whole different perspective of people in that type position with all that pressure on them and all the attention on them.

"(Smith) is in such a fish bowl environment with the entire state of Kentucky and fans all across the country watching every move that he makes and yet he is able to maintain that wholesomeness about himself. I think that is the biggest attribute that he carries other than his coaching skills."

Downing will never forget the day when UK coach pulled a prank on him. It all began when he earlier had asked Smith if he would like to go to the 1997 World Series for Game 5 in Cleveland since he had tickets. The coach said he couldn't go so Bill Keightley, UK's long-time equipment manager for the basketball team, went with Downing.

About 30 minutes or so before he was set to leave his Memorial Coliseum office, Downing received a call. It was the coach on the line, wanting Downing to come upstairs in his office.

"Hey, Brooks, we've got something terrible wrong here. I've gotta get to the bottom of it and it's going to take me a while. When are you leaving?" Smith asked.

"Well, I'm getting ready to leave now," said Downing, who was beginning to feel nervous about the situation.

"I'm gonna need you to stick around and do a (press) release probably later this afternoon," commented Smith, adding that 6-10, 240-pound center Jamaal Magloire had gotten in trouble.

"Coach, are you serious?"

"I know you've got the World Series tickets. I know all that is going on, but I need you to stay."

"Oh man. How about Tony Neely (who primarily handles publicity for the football squad)? Tony can take care of it," Downing told the coach.

"No, I'd rather have you," said the coach.

"All right."

An infuriated Downing went back downstairs, heading to his

sports information office. He was very upset and felt like crying. It appeared that he would miss the World Series. A few moments later, he received word that the coach wanted him back again in the office. As Downing approached Smith's office, he noticed that senior guard Cameron Mills was having discussions with the coach with the door closed. Downing nervously waited for 15 minutes, looking at his watch every minute or so, still hoping to take off for the fall classic if he quickly got his last-minute work done. But things weren't looking very promising for Downing.

Then Smith called the publicist to his office. He shut the door and sat down.

Smith looked at Downing and said smiling, "I got you."

"Oh, are you kidding me?" Downing said.

Then they burst out laughing and the media relations guy hurried on his way to the airport. It was a close call. "So he teases me a little bit, too," said Downing.

 Not long before Smith made his successful Wildcat head coaching debut with a lopsided 88-49 victory over a Kyle Macy-coached Morehead State squad, one Georgia sportswriter wrote a blistering column about the new Kentucky mentor. Terence Moore predicted in the *Atlanta Journal-Constitution* that Smith would be sorry for leaving the Georgia Bulldogs. He explained that Smith would have a deadly job in following Rick Pitino's footsteps because, for one reason, he would have to deal with demanding Wildcat fans, who are known to be difficult to please.

Moore's predictions didn't pan out. The Wildcats, however, still had their share of critics. In mid-February, some grumbling fans expressed unhappiness with the team's performance, even when Kentucky still ranked in the Top 10. They felt Kentucky should be playing much better basketball. They certainly didn't like seeing Kentucky lose on its home floor and it happened three times, dropping to Louisville, Florida and Mississippi.

In UK's 79-76 upset loss to a weak Louisville team during the holidays, which dropped Kentucky's record to 10-2 on the season, the Wildcats simply weren't prepared and didn't hustle enough to win. "U of L outhustled us today," explained a disappointed Smith shortly after the loss. "That was evident throughout the game. Proof of that was at the end of the game when (Louisville's Cameron) Murray forced the shot over

(Wayne) Turner, and U of L got the long rebound by hustle."

"(Louisville) had a better game plan today. At times, U of L outworked us, U of L's defense was excellent, they switched from man-to-man to zone and we didn't adjust well to that today. That is a sign that we were not mentally focused." As a result, the Wildcats shot only 37.5 percent of their field goals. Louisville, which later finished its dismal season with a 12-20 mark, made 50.9 percent of its shots. The nationally-televised setback ranks as one of UK's biggest upset losses in its storied basketball history. That was the beginning of the fans' grumbling and the grumbles naturally grew with the other two Rupp Arena losses.

The loss to Louisville "was our worst game of the year," Smith later said in the summer of 1998. "That is not to take anything away from Louisville because they played pretty well. But you know as a coach you've got to know your team. You've got to know when they are ready and how to get them ready. (When) you look at the Louisville-Kentucky series, you know they don't need any more rah, rah. You don't have to pump them up anymore for this game because it's as good (as the rivalry gets).

"But in actuality I had to pump them up. (Before) I thought I would have to tone them down so they didn't get too high, which was just the opposite. We were like 10-1 going into the game. I think we were a little bit overconfident, not cocky, thinking we were better than we were at the time. I think that had a big influence on it."

In the aftermath of Kentucky's loss to U of L, Smith decided to institute a new policy for the team: No facial hair would be allowed. The coach got the idea from his old college days when he was forced to shave his mustache.

"It seemed like we were losing some of our discipline and some of our self-discipline," Smith explained. "Guys were starting to wear beards this way and mustaches that way and just looked raggedly. So I just felt like we needed more uniformity and more conformity. I just said it at the end of the game to get their attention. It was like an after thought. I just said, 'I want all the facial hair cut off. You guys look like a bunch of bums, hobos with your facial hair growing one way. I want it all off and that's (for) everybody. If you don't have it off tomorrow, don't come back.' "

While the affected players expressed some displeasure with the new policy, Smith's disciplinary measure worked. The Wildcats won 12 of their next 13 games. "I could see that the guys had refocused and that the loss (to Louisville) was behind us," Smith said.

Eight days after Kentucky suffered a heartbreaking 73-64 loss to a fine Ole Miss club on Valentine's Day at home, the Wildcats squared off with Georgia at Rupp Arena in the second father-son matchup of Tubby Smith versus G.G. Smith.

While the Bulldogs were in town, the elder Smith got to see his former boss at Georgia, athletic director Vince Dooley, who also brought along Dr. Michael Adams, Georgia's recently-named president with Bluegrass connections. (A former senior aide to then-U.S. Senator Howard Baker and then-Gov. Lamar Alexander, both of Tennessee, Dr. Adams lived in Danville where he served as president at Centre College from 1988 to '97.)

And the Georgia contest would mark the last home game for three Wildcat seniors — Jeff Sheppard, Allen Edwards and Cameron Mills. It was a very special Sunday. On this festive Senior Day, UK had to overcome a slow start before defeating the Bulldogs for the second time in the season with an 85-74 triumph. The win gave the Wildcats "the confidence and mental toughness that we can come back from a deficit," Tubby Smith said. "We haven't played well at home, and today I felt the same intensity."

Smith also praised UK seniors for the team's success. "We were happy the seniors could go out with a win.....Their leadership has been the reason why we have been able to get 24 wins," he said. "They're the link between some great teams here. The years Cameron, Allen and Jeff have been here have been some of the winningest years at UK. They've had the experience and maturity both on and off the court."

Smith felt bad after the game because his oldest son had lost the contest. On facing G.G., a 5-11 junior who poured in 19 points for the Bulldogs, the elder Smith said, "When you are competing, it doesn't matter who you are playing. I'm trying to get our players to reach their full potential. But it is kind of awkward. You want to see him do well, but not too well." The younger Smith was later named a third-team All-SEC selection at the end of the season.

Kentucky never looked back, winning 11 more games as it stunned the college basketball world with their inspiring comebacks in the NCAA tournament, capturing the 1998 national crown with a phenomenal 35-4 mark. "We work really hard and we know not to give up," said 6-6 forward Heshimu Evans of Bronx, N.Y. "I mean we have been in situations where we have had to come back, we are a fighting team, the Comeback Cats."

The campaign had a couple of turning points, according to Cameron Mills. "After the Ole Miss game, we started having 6 a.m. practices and that continued the rest of the year," he said. "We started winning and there was no reason to change anything. We wanted to keep things basically the same as long as you're winning the ballgame."

But the squad didn't embrace the idea of waking up very early for morning workouts. "We didn't like it," Mills admitted. "Obviously, no one likes getting up that early. Getting up was the worse part. Once you're over here in the coliseum, you've got your practice jersey on, you're stretching and starting to get loose and warm, you don't feel tired at that. You know it could have been three in the afternoon. (But in the morning) you get the blood flowing and you feel good. So once we're over here and practicing, it was no big deal because practices weren't really hard. They weren't excruciating. They weren't long. But they basically just kind of served to get us focused on what we were doing. So we didn't like it, but at the same time it was worth it so we did like it.

"When we lost the game to Ole Miss, we started to really gel together as a team. You know it doesn't matter how much talent you have on a team, it matters what kind of team you have. You look back at the Fab Five at Michigan — they had so much talent, I don't think they ever really played well together as a team — they never won a national championship.....We didn't necessarily have the talent to win a national championship, but we played well together on and off the court, which is why we won."

Another turning point in UK's improbable national title success was the untimely death of Allen Edwards' mother at the end of the regular season which made the team closer. His mom, Laura Mae Edwards, died of cancer. "When Allen's mother died, I think that was something that brought us closer together as a team," Mills said.

Coach Tubby Smith said 1997-98 was "a smooth year." He added, "We really have not had many ups and downs. We try to stay very focused and positive all year long. At times we weren't playing as well as we thought we should and others thought we should, but we were pretty consistent in our effort. What you want to do is reach your potential and give some effort every time."

While winning the NCAA title is the goal of every coach, Smith admits that he is surprised that his team went that far. Kentucky's national title came about because of the strong leadership exhibited by senior tri-captains Mills, Edwards and Jeff Sheppard, according to the coach.

"The leadership that we had is the best leadership that I have ever been around in my 25 years plus as coaching and playing," said Smith, who was named the National Coach of the Year by *Basketball Weekly*. "I've never seen a group of young men bond as well as this team. They really became a family led by Jeff Sheppard, Allen Edwards and Cameron Mills. Those three young men, I've really got to give them most of the credit.

"I'm sure there were times when (the players) were squawking and I'm sure there were a lot of negative things said at times. Guys concerned about playing time. But they all knew and understood their roles. I think they (the seniors) were able to help guys understand why we were doing things because they had been through so much.

"Look at the adversity that each one of these kids went through. Allen Edwards came here as a highly-recruited player and didn't really get a chance to start. Then his mom got sick and passed away during the year. Cameron Mills had to walk on. He had to beg to come to school here. And look what he did now. Jeff Sheppard came here as a highly-recruited player and only averaged 13 minutes a game (as a junior). He has had to sit behind Tony Delk for three years. Also he had to sit behind Ron Mercer and Derek Anderson for a year. And then he redshirted because they were back again. He became the MVP in the Final Four. That's a remarkable (feat)."

Not long after the Wildcats made the cover of *Sports Illustrated* three times in four weeks during their successful NCAA tournament run (in addition to the magazine's special commemorative issue on UK's national title season), Kentucky's hoops program took a public relations beating. Two then-freshman players — 19-year-old Ryan Hogan and 20-year-old Myron Anthony — both got in trouble with the law in two separate incidents. Hogan was arrested for driving under the influence, while Anthony belatedly confessed that he was the one entangled in a hit-and-run accident, which involved a borrowed automobile belonging to teammate Wayne Turner. Earlier, it was thought Turner had gotten himself embroiled in the hit-and-run episode, which occurred in September 1997. The controversy attracted national attention, including a story in *Sports Illustrated* on Turner before Anthony came forward.

In mid-June, 6-10 center Jamaal Magloire, 20, also made the news when two of his traveling companions in a Jeep were arrested by the police in Jefferson County for possession of illegal drugs. The police also searched Magloire, but found no drugs on him. The player was not charged.

Coach Smith said he was very upset and disappointed with them, adding that these off-the-court troubles took away some of UK's championship glory. It was a poor judgment on their part, creating unnecessary distractions for the program, according to the coach. Later Smith commented on Lexington's WVLK Radio that the affected players will be disciplined and suspended from some games in the 1998-99 season.

The Wildcats also made the news in the spring when 6-10 junior center Nazr Mohammed, the team's second-leading scorer and top rebounder, announced his decision to enter the 1998 NBA draft. It was a mild surprise as most observers had believed that Mohammed, once labeled as "project," needed another year in college before reaching his full potential. After changing his mind "four or five times," Mohammed said he finally made the difficult decision.

"I was caught between deciding to return to the University of Kentucky and trying to win a third national championship during my tenure, or to declare myself eligible for the NBA draft, which would allow for a better life for my close friends, family and myself," Mohammed said. "After discussing my decision with my father and coach Smith, I have decided that it is in my best interest to declare myself eligible for the NBA Draft." At that time Mohammed also left open a slight possibility that he might change his mind and return to school since he still hadn't hired an agent.

Responding to NBA's scouting director Marty Blake's comments that Mohammed isn't ready for pros, the Chicago native said, "A lot of people said I wasn't ready for Kentucky basketball. I think I came here and did a good job. The university has done a lot for me, and in turn I think I have done a lot for the university."

Mohammed's coach was obviously disappointed, but respected the player's decision. "I know this has been a tough decision for Nazr," Smith said. "Certainly I believe that Nazr should stay, but that is just my opinion. He's got to make his own decision. It's like in recruiting. No one can tell him where to go to school. This is the same type of situation. We talked about that. Everybody knows what is best for him, but only Nazr, in his heart and mind, can come to a decision."

On Mohammed's turning pro, Cameron Mills said, "I didn't give him any advice at all. We talked a little bit about it. Actually all that we talked about was that he was telling me what he was gonna do. We didn't talk about what he should do. He didn't come to me for advice at all and I didn't offer any. It was his decision."

Projected by some scouts as a probable lottery pick in the NBA Draft, a disappointed Mohammed didn't go as high as he had expected. The former Wildcat was chosen as the league's 29th pick overall in the first round by the Utah Jazz. Less than an hour after the selection, Utah sent Mohammed to Philadelphia for a future first-round pick. His teammate, Jeff Sheppard, meanwhile, wasn't picked in the draft.

One of Smith's 1998 summer highlights came in early June when he and his assistant coaches traveled to South America to participate in a basketball clinic as instructors. They were the only U.S. coaches at the clinic. The trip was planned long before the Wildcats had won their national title in March.

"They invited us a way back," Smith said of the clinic which was held in Santiago in Chile. "My staff went down a couple of days early and I went down (later) for three days. They brought in people and coaches from all over Chile. They had about six (club) teams (locally). They had a team from Richmond, Virginia. A team we played, Court Authority (in a 1997 pre-season exhibition game), was there. So they flew a bunch of teams in. It was like a tournament there and then they brought in a team from Spain and Yugoslavia. All these teams were probably getting ready for the World Games.

"They really took care of us. It was a great experience and it was the first time I've used translators. They have somebody up in the booth talking when you talk and it was translated in Spanish to them. It was a good clinic."

It is known that former UK coach Joe B. Hall once kept a "hate file," which was comprised of letters from angry fans, criticizing his squad or his coaching style. Unlike Adolph Rupp, who apparently let his secretary screen his letters, Hall said he read the letters mainly because he wanted to develop

Kentucky basketball coach Tubby Smith

Photo by Rogers Photography

thick skin so he could handle criticism.

What about coach Tubby Smith? Does he keep a hate file?

"We keep a file," commented Smith. "We haven't gotten much hate mail at all, but I mean there is not much to hate. It is not like we didn't win the national championship, and things went well for us this past season. I've been very fortunate. We didn't have many problems at all. We had a few at the end of year, disciplinary problems, and problems with some of the players.

"(Administrative assistant) Marta McMackin does a good job. She screens a lot of them (letters). She would say that I don't need to read them anyway. I'm sure Marta keeps them around and there are some. But I've always used it from the positive standpoint whenever someone criticizes. I can take the criticism. I've been in it long enough and it is no big deal with me."

However, Smith said he gets emotional and upset when the fans criticize the young players who actually aren't far removed from high school. "What concerns me is when people write, expressing their (feelings) that maybe one of the players did something wrong," said the coach. "They're seeing these big players in the media and they think the players gotta have millions of dollars. Most of the kids come from places where they don't have a penny. You know everybody thinks that somebody has gotten more than they have, which is sad. That is the way our society is. These athletes are looked at because they are big and strong. Most of them are 17-,18-, 19-, or 20-year-old kids. They really have not matured as adults yet. So that angers me more than anything else. The rest of them (criticism) I could care less about."

College basketball has several difficult issues to deal with, according to Smith. Gambling and the influx of underclassmen leaving for pro ranks are some of the primary concerns that Smith has.

"It is not just an athletic problem, it is a whole societal problem," Smith said of gambling. "The other thing I think we've got to deal with is the players leaving early. There are only a handful of them good enough to leave early. I know the other thing is keeping basketball being the best sport there is. We've got to be careful that we don't dilute the product because we saturate the people and the market with basketball. The media has a tendency to show so many games and see so many games. Because attendance in some of the college programs is dropping, we have to be careful.

"We need to continue to keep the proper image, and we tell people that we have a great product and that we are teaching the values and the character that we build in our athletes. (This) is what the alumni, fans, or paying customers want to see. So we teach those values that you're taught maybe in church or home — teamwork, cooperation, sacrifice, discipline, you name it.

"That is what the NCAA tournament did this year (1998) and I thought that is what our team did this year. I think people went back to just basics. You know what I mean? It's a team game and not just individuals out there trying to market themselves to get to the NBA or get something more. That (concept) is what I thought it brought back this year. You had four teams (in the Final Four) — Utah, Stanford, North Carolina and Kentucky — that reflect what I consider is good about college sports and college basketball."

 Florida assistant coach John Pelphrey, who played at UK when Tubby Smith was an assistant, said he wasn't surprised with the harsh criticisms placed on Smith and UK during the middle of the season especially after they dropped three home games.

"I think that just gives you an idea where the (UK) program is at, and certainly our fans at the University of Kentucky have high expectation levels," said the former Wildcat. "I think if you ask anybody in the basketball world who has a good feel for basketball would have to admit that he (Smith) is doing a great, great job with the group of players who were basically raised to play a certain thing (style under Pitino). He has brought in his own style of play and hasn't missed a beat. He has only lost four games and has played an unbelievable season."

Ironically, Pelphrey, one of Kentucky's four Unforgettables in 1991-92, made his comments just before the regular season had concluded, saying the Wildcats were unbelievable. You couldn't help wondering what would have been his description after Kentucky amazingly won the whole thing in San Antonio, beating the Utah Utes 78-69 in the finals? One thing for sure, he would be hard pressed to find another word better than unbelievable. As UK's faithful fans will attest, Tubby Smith and his Comeback Cats will always be a part of Kentucky's storied basketball heritage.

Forever.

Cats up Close

Mail to:
McClanahan Publishing House, Inc.
P. O. Box 100
Kuttawa, KY 42055

For Orders call TOLL FREE
1-800-544-6959
Visa & MasterCard accepted

Please send me _____ copies of

Cats up Close

@ 16.95 each_____

Postage & handling   4.00

Kentucky residents add 6% sales tax @ 1.02 each_____

Total enclosed   _____

Make check payable to McClanahan Publishing House

Ship to:
NAME _____

ADDRESS

_____

CITY _____ STATE _____

ZIP _____